D0849675

Ritual Cosmos

RITUAL
COSMOS

The Sanctification of Life
in African Religions

EVAN M. ZUESSE

 Ohio University Press: Athens, Ohio

© 1979 by Evan M. Zuesse
Printed in the United States of America
Library of Congress Cataloging in Publication Data

Zuesse, Evan M
    Ritual cosmos.

    Bibliography: p.
    1. Africa—Religion. 2. Ritual. 3. Occult sciences—Africa. I. Title.
BL2400.Z83   299′.6   79-13454
ISBN 0-8214-0398-2

To Ingrid

The fruit-bearing tree is lovelier and more perfect than that without fruit, and the living stream that fructifies and is in constant motion is incomparably more beautiful than standing, even though crystal-pure, water.

Judah Abravanel, *Vikkuach Al Ha-Ahavah*

TABLE OF CONTENTS

PART THREE
THE STRUCTURES OF RITUAL SYMBOLISM

PART FOUR
RITUAL ENCOUNTERS OF SELF AND OTHER

Preface

This study is an attempt to bring together the two disciplines that are most concerned with the investigation of African religions: anthropology and religious studies. There has been a tendency on the part of each discipline to go its own way. Perhaps this is justifiable in some contexts, but each has a great deal to contribute to the other. Many of the basic theoretical approaches in religious studies are still determined by Christian theology, and are essentially irrelevant for a study of African religions. The rich data and insights of anthropology help correct this theoretical provincialism. Yet anthropological studies are still very uncomfortable with the problem of spiritual meaning, while religious studies have developed a subtle and profound method of articulating such meaning, the phenomenology of religion. Actually the phenomenology of religion is not just one method but several. One approach commonly called "phenomenological" is comparative in orientation: symbolisms of the Cosmic Tree, or initiation rites, for example, might be examined across various religions to discover what underlying common meaning all varieties may be said to possess. Another approach, the one stressed here, is concerned with discovering how the various aspects of a *particular* religion "hang together" and generate as a whole a specific kind of spirituality. We may call this a quest for the "existential" meaning of a particular religion. Yet the two methods cannot be absolutely separated, for as we move from one religion to another, particularly when these are historically related or part of the same geographical area, we cannot avoid recognizing common symbolisms and rites, and especially common underlying attitudes. After devoting many years to studying African religions, we even come to sense a deep orientation uniting almost all of them, however difficult this may be to delineate. Certainly this basic focus of African religions is very different from traditional Christian orientations, and it has as a result a great deal to teach us of spiritual possibilities we may have ignored, and may even teach us to understand ourselves differently.

This study begins, therefore, with a preliminary attempt to articulate just what this basic spiritual attitude so characteristic of African religions might be. It then proceeds to detailed discussions of a number of specific religions, keeping for the most part to central Africa; Zaire (formerly the Belgian Congo) and its neighbor to the south, Zambia (formerly Northern Rhodesia), are the chief regions described. In the course of entering into the universes of the Mbuti Pygmy hunters of Zaire, the hunting and farming cultures of the Lele and the Lega of Zaire, and the predominantly farming and pastoral world of the Ila and related peoples of Zambia, we discover the spiritual meaning of religious taboos, of sacrifice, of sex roles and age groups, and so on. We will see that the increasing complexity of the societies and religions conveys not a sense of radical change, but rather of gradual transformation and evolution of basically similar spiritual assumptions. These are spiritual universes held together by certain very deep ritual symbolisms and practices. To understand them, we must understand the hidden logic of ritual itself. A great deal of this study is devoted to this topic, and in the final part of our investigation, enters explicitly into an analysis of ritual symbolism. Taking examples primarily from west African societies (to impart something of the extraordinary variety of African religions), it analyses such essential forms of cult as possession trance, initiation, divination, millenary movements and witchcraft.

The task is complex and difficult, for despite the common elements in African religions there are many remarkable differences and variations, and the level at which we approach this topic, in terms of the meaning of ritual action, is a particularly profound one. Nevertheless, it is a main goal of this study to understand some of the main forms of ritual *per se*. If, by its conclusion, the reader will have a better understanding of the structure and meaning of ritual, and a deeper appreciation for the spiritual depth of African religions, the author will be amply rewarded.

Obviously this entire essay in the phenomenology of African religions would have been impossible without the brilliant work in anthropology of such scholars as Victor W. Turner, Mary Douglas, the unfortunately neglected Hans Schärer, and many others, or without the penetrating studies of phenomenology by Edmund Husserl, Maurice Merleau-Ponty, and especially Mircea Eliade and Charles H. Long, under whom I was privileged to study at the University of Chicago Divinity School. To the acute criticisms and comments of J. David Sapir, who as reader for Ohio University Press went patiently through various drafts of this book, I owe much of whatever coherence and effectiveness it possesses. I need hardly say that with such mentors, deficiencies in the work are the result only of my own inability to attain the standards set by them.

E.M.Z.
Cleveland, Ohio

Introduction

Introduction:
The Fundamental Orientation
of African Religions

It is often the simplest realities which are the most profound and complex. This is certainly true in religious matters, at any rate, where we find the most pretentious theologies and metaphysical or mythical flights unable to exhaust the meaning of the least imposing everyday ritual gestures. Perhaps this is why we like to ignore the origin of our religious wonder in humble ritual encounter, and instead to praise trance states, imposing myths and theories, and all out-of-the-ordinary spiritual revelations. So often we suppose that *real* religion is not or *should* not be concerned with such mundane matters as human and natural fertility, or social harmony, such as most ritual (and especially African ritual) aims for; instead, we insist, true spirituality concerns personal salvation from the banal structures of everyday life.

What, then, are we to do with African religions? For here we find the most explicit emphasis on everyday, normal life and its concerns. Nowhere do we discover the laudation of personal salvation so characteristic of Christian theologies. In these religions the focus of all aspiration, of genuinely religious intensity, is on the transcendental significance of everyday life. All energies are directed to the ritual sustenance of the normal order—"normal" in two senses, as imbedded in norms going back to the beginning of time, and as usual and commonplace reality. Life itself, without fevered mystical intoxications, is both transcendental and actual, both sacred and ordinary. This is much more mysterious and complex than our own theologies, and so we end up simplifying and misunderstanding it.

Real religion, says Rudolf Otto, the leading theoretician of the academic study of religion, consists of the ecstatic encounter with the Wholly Other.[1] When the utterly transcendental "Holy" is experienced, the worshipper is overwhelmed with trembling awe and involuntary fascination. He is often ecstatically beyond time and space, and is unconscious of all else. The "savage" cannot interpret such terrific experiences correctly, but rather interprets the Wholly Other as demonic ghosts or witchcraft, developing propitiatory or magical rites to contain or apply the sacred. (Only Christianity, Otto shamelessly insists, and in Christianity only Lutheran thought, understands the Holy correctly; Luther is therefore the perfect distillation of the primeval savage gibbering at ghosts.)

Such attitudes do not really take us very far in understanding African religions, however modernized or toned down in the reformulation they may be. We need an entirely different approach to the holy, and to the ritual path of life, to appreciate what the positive spiritual significance might be of seasonal rites to make the crops abundant, menstrual taboos, or medicines hidden in the roof thatch to ward off witchcraft.

One thing, at least, is of value in Otto's approach to religion: his explicit programmatic aim of describing the actual experience of religion, his insistence that religion centers on transcendental *meaning,* not any other thing (such as psychology, sociology, or even logic). The core of religion is the experience of and aspiration after the holy; this is the real point of all cults. In a more imposing terminology, Otto initiated in religious studies the phenomenological approach, which is interested in the structures and implicit goals of awareness. These implicit goals, the tacit aim of every movement and moment of consciousness, are called "intentionalities." The motive power behind all *religious* behavior is the yearning for and experience of transcendental meaning; we may call this a transcendental intentionality.

Otto may have overemphasized the unusual, extreme or anomalous expressions of this intentionality; we would be more hopeful of finding a more positive evaluation of everyday social life and its role in religion within the discipline of anthropology. After all, did not Emile Durkheim, the contemporary of Otto and the founder of social anthropology, insist that religion does not at all concern the extraordinary or the exceptional, but rather is dedicated to the preservation of the normal round of things?[2]

Yet current anthropological research into African religions disappoints our expectations, both on the part of those anthropologists who are not bashful about calling all religious explanations of cult, and all religious intentionalities as such, sheer "nonsense,"[3] and on the part of those anthropologists who grant importance to religious factors and seek to take account of them when explaining African realities. The first group comprises those who have rebelled against Western religious ideas in general and avoid the topic of religion or seek to explain it away as being *really* a form of sociology, or psychology, or false logic, or even misapplied science. The second very much smaller group, in searching for categories to use in describing the indubitably religious behavior they see, have only the aforesaid Western theological categories and ideas to fall back on, and so their descriptions are inevitably distorted even despite their frequent brilliance and insight. For example, E.E. Evans-Pritchard, the author of such classic studies of particular African religions as *Nuer Religion* (Oxford: Clarendon Press, 1956) and *Witchcraft, Oracles and Magic among the Azande* (Oxford: Clarendon Press, 1937), unfortunately bases the entire former work on Otto's definition of the Holy (his genius here being devoted to showing the profundity of the Nuer view of the *mysterium tremendum et fascinans*—Otto's terminology for the 'terrifying' and 'fascinating' sacred reality), while the latter work accepts a distinction between spiritual religion and merely everyday pragmatic magic, classifying the greater part of Zande life in the latter category. What if everyday pragmatic "magic" were really religious, however?

The inadequacy of traditional Western categories can be best shown through an example, the institution of bwami, an initiatic cult of the Lega, a Bantu farming culture of eastern Zaire. The Lega are a numerous people, scattered over a vast area of the Congo forest in small villages, each of which is situated on the occasional ridges that jut above the dense forest cover like islands in a green sea. Since they lack centralized kingship, the villagers would be utterly isolated from each other were it not for bwami: it is their "king" *(bwami* means "king"). People gather for its celebrations from entire regions. Bwami is entirely apart from general village society; its elders, exemplars of calm poise, abstain from the fierce local village politics. Village chiefs and even the regional priests of the Earth *(nenekisi)* do not necessarily attain high initiatic rank in the society; it stands for a more universal truth.[4]

How does bwami accomplish all this? Simply through the teaching of proverbs. Candidates are taught hundreds of proverbs at each grade of initiation (there may be seven or more grades, each with lesser steps within it); by the higher ranks, a member will have memorized thousands of aphorisms. There is nothing very special about these sayings, taken one by one; they resemble the folk wisdom that is so widely diffused in Africa, invoking characteristics of common utensils, plants, and especially animals of the forest to make witty moral points. Daniel Biebuyck, who was initiated into the cult, confesses that he was confused at first by the seeming disorder in which the proverbs were presented. No obvious logic unified the order of proverbs, and they varied from region to region even within the same grade of bwami. But as he went through the entire experience of the initiation, which even at the lowest level consisted of over three hundred proverbs, he came to understand that the Lega

> tend to emphasize and visualize the totality of events in a sequence, the totality of sequences in a rite, and the totality of rites in an initiation, rather than each individual happening or component . . . It is the total impact that matters.[5]

Each proverb is taught as an aesthetic whole; it is sung, and dramatized as a story which is danced out before the initiate. Carvings may be made and presented to the novice which represent the point of the saying. After the initiation, the initiate will be expected to review repeatedly all that he has been taught, until it is completely mastered. He may spend so much time on them that other activities become secondary. All gathering of wealth and cultivation of patrons and friends may be done with the hope of future nomination to higher grades. Initiates who are skillful in song or dance, or in tutoring others, will be much in demand at other initiations, and the friends and clients gained in such activities will help in the organization and finance of later initiations for oneself. Such total concentration transforms the way the initiate looks at the world. The "total impact" of the proverbs comes to control the way all things are perceived, and the way events are reacted to. Outwardly unimportant things of everyday life become emblematic of the truths which are so much more the center of attention. A chance word in the course of conversation, an unreliable neighbor or a dog chasing a chicken, will evoke spontaneously in the initiate's mind the appropriate saying which reveals the eternal reality in the midst of passing change. Where others only see unconnected banalities, or relate things only to their own personal interests, the initiate perceives a universal structure. The very way events are perceived relegates merely personal reactions to a secondary place. An annoying incident may take place, for example, which involves an acquaintance who is known as a braggart; the initiate may recall the song-proverb he learned which likened the *non-initiate* to a shoulder-bag: "It has a mouth but no heart." Such people are unreliable. Bwami alone is what provides solidity and dependability to a person. In this response, the initiate ends up affirming bwami again, taking his neighbor as the now entirely subordinate cue. In the same way, shoulder-bags (a common article of dress among the Lega) are elevated into a universal meaning. They are visible archetypes, symbols of eternal wisdom, the sight of which contains mysteries known only to the sages.

Due both to this transformative logic at the heart of bwami symbols, and to the explicit moralism taught in the proverbs, as the initiate rises higher in the cult and is absorbed further in its wisdom, he inevitably comes to embody in himself the restraint and imperturbability the proverbs praise. He ceases to take things personally. In fact, lustful, ambitious or crude people never get nominated for the higher levels; only the person who has been able to work together with many others tactfully and unpretentiously, shouldering the varied responsibilities connected with bwami celebrations and helping others rise in the society, will be nominated and aided in turn. The proverbs mock the coarse and the self-centered. The true initiate is said to move lightly through life's turmoil, like a bird floating in the sky. He lives for bwami.

The example of the shoulder-bag suggests a good deal about the way bwami ritualizes the whole of life. There are a number of ways in which a shoulder-bag can be seen. One may simply observe it on a sensory level, as a physical object or human artifact. One may regard it in terms of its personal use and social importance, as a way of carrying one's things, or, as a result of its ornamentation, as an index of one's social prestige and wealth. Or, one may see it as bwami teaches one to, as a symbol of cosmic truth. All of these levels may be present, but bwami puts the transcendental and cosmic level first, thus transforming perception itself. As we shall see from later discussions of ritual, this process of transmutation of awareness from a literal or personal, or even social mode, to a symbolic and transcendental one, lies at the heart of all ritual action.

But what is the nature of the transcendental reality bwami serves? Clearly, it is not Wholly Other. Bwami does not insist on personal salvation, or emphasize ecstatic states. It requires no sacrificial rites nor even prayers. It does not even center on personal deity, although it is important to add that Lega believe bwami aids Kingunga (God) and Kalaga (the culture-hero; in some areas also the name of God) against Kaginga (evil, chaos).[6] So true is this, that a village suffering from dissension, disease, poor hunting or sterility can be cured merely by enacting bwami proverbs in it. The ashes of leaves burned in the rites have medicinal powers. Witchcraft cannot resist bwami; if a witch is discovered, mere induction into bwami will cancel out the evil-doer's power.

Bwami is a sterling example of a fundamental type of spirituality very widespread in African religions, the religion of structure. Rudolf Otto well describes a type of spirituality in which the transcendental intentionality centers on power or being outside of structure; salvation is a natural longing for those that experience such unworldly transcendence. But the religious intentionality centered on holy structure seeks to actualize this structure in all aspects of experience; its goal is the active sanctification of life, not escape from it as "illusory," "evil" or "sinful." Religions of salvation have a low estimation of all that is relative, due to their longing for what is absolute, immutable, *finally* real. Religions of structure find fulfillment precisely in the norms and eternal relationships which structure all process and change in this world. The first revels in abnormal, anomalous and extreme states because they betoken the exceptional break-through into unworldly eternity; the second rejoices in the sanctification of everyday life, and finds eternity in the midst of change. Most religions, we must admit, mingle the two types of spiritual intentionality, although the emphasis differs sharply from religion to religion and even from group to group and age to age within the same religion. Christianity, for example, has historically heavily emphasized salvation and denigrated the things of this world, including the "Law" which orders them, but in the last two centuries a more structural and this-worldly attitude has begun to develop. Judaism, on the other hand, evenly balances the two intentionalities, although salvational ideas often dominated the Middle Ages and structural ideas the Biblical period. African religions heavily stress the structural intentionality, as we have seen. To understand them well therefore reveals a fundamental type of spirituality that is recognized to greater or lesser degree in all religions. The study of African religions has an importance even beyond its own intrinsic great significance.

Religions of structure must necessarily be more complex than religions of salvation, since as we noted at the start, the integration of the simple things of everyday life is far more complex and profound than any artificial narrowing of the spirit to exceptional experiences. The personal egoistic sphere, the social sphere, and the transcendental cosmic one must all be brought together. Religions of structure generally do this through ritual, and through the ritual type of instruction which emphasizes the concrete and transforms it into a symbol. Bwami instruction in proverbs offers a very good instance of this concretized, "ritual" type of instruction. The Lega custom of embodying proverbs in carvings, which are accumulated by the initiate, only deepens this emphasis. The entire purpose of the religion is not to remove the cult member from the experiential world of multiplicity (as instruction in elaborate theologies and intricate logical, mythical chains of thought would tend to do), but to anchor the cult member *in* this world, at the same time as the instruction renders this world of multiplicity transparent to eternal meaning. A different mode of concentration is evoked by such a thorough-going religion of structure: to grasp transcendental truths, one must learn to enact the world differently. One must see every *thing* as *symbol*. It takes constant repetition and dramatization to achieve this ritual vision of life. Religions of salvation, on the other hand, inculcate a type of concentration which systematically removes attention from sensory experience, and focuses it on the internal processes of subjective thought and awareness. The outside world and physical drama as such as only experienced as a distraction in this more abstract form of meditation. Ritual is therefore demoted from a central to a peripheral role; it ceases to enter the whole of life but is instead secluded in rare times and special, non-ordinary places.

Since the content of religions of structure is discovered in the entire world of events, it is more difficult than in religions of salvation to delineate the specific guiding categories and the specific vision of the real that dominates spiritual life. These are more diffused religions, with every aspect of activity involved in tacit or explicit ritual. Personal goals and social norms are sanctified along with transcendental aspirations, not by accident but because such integration is precisely the content of transcendental aspiration.

This poses a problem of method. How can we discover the specific form of religious intentionality, the actual structure *per se,* that a given religion contains? Biebuyck tells us that bwami proverbs conveyed a "total impact," in which each proverb is really important only insofar as it implies the whole world of bwami values. We provided an instance in the case of the "shoulder-bag" braggart, who is understood archetypally only to the degree that he comes to be subordinated to the entire bwami structure of values. Each proverb, in effect, asserts the tacit existence of all others. In such a maze, we can begin to distinguish order by looking first to the *spatial implications* of ritual symbolisms. In "spatial" we can include also "we-they" distinctions (marking what some phenomenologists have described as the "social spaces" of the "life-world"). Such distinctions provide a fundamental ordering principle for all orientation in the world, which is to say all meaning. Ritual itself is concerned first of all with ordering bodily movements in space, and clearly the body is the foundation for all awareness. But ritual not only provides for classifications of bodily, social and especially cosmic space, it also seeks to interrelate these spheres in a harmonious and fruitful manner, so as to transform and renew the universe. We must therefore seek the method a given religion uses to regenerate the world. As we shall find, these transformations are often modelled on symbolisms derived from direct social and above all bodily experience, with integration, for example, often symbolized by sexual motifs.

The entire work before us in future chapters may be said to be an exploration of these methodological remarks, but perhaps some preliminary application to the Lega cult of bwami will serve to show their usefulness. Without more of the proverbs, we are greatly hampered in our interpretation, but a few remarks can be made.

Many of the proverbs affirm the centrality of bwami itself in the world. It is the focus of the universe, the central fact: "The middle pole sustains the forest hut; when the pole is removed, the hut collapses."[7] The implication would seem to be that without bwami, all culture as such would disintegrate, and the wilderness would invade the village which exists in the center of things. Another proverb also stresses the mystical centrality of bwami by comparing it to a cosmic tree: "Bwami: the lukundu tree has made its buttresses and aerial roots reach far."[8] Yet another makes a provocative comparison with the heavenly moon, serenely ruling over everything, equidistant and transcendent over all social groups as well: "Bwami, the crescent of the moon, every clan is seen from it."[9] In the important summary offered by another proverb, "The words of the land are things that tie together, things that transform [like the clouds], things that are high [like the sky]."[10]

The nature of bwami's centrality must be defined with care. The proverbs suggest both a continuity with the natural universe, and a distinct discontinuity. Ironically, the dialectics of this relationship come out precisely through the constant use of animal and forest imagery in the proverbs, imagery which to the careless observer might indicate a sense of boundless communion with nature. But the very use of animal metaphors underlines the difference between man and beast, culture and nature. Each proverb is concrete and fragmentary; each animal has as its innermost significance a single moral point. Only in man are all the meanings unified. One proverb affirms the virtue of conviviality and social attachments by comparing bwami initiates to "nesting pigs that herd together." Another speaks allusively of bwami as the leopard who royally distributes justice and cannot be gainsaid, while a third evokes "the little spear with the sharp blade" that Lega men carry, implicitly referring to bwami members who never act overbearing, but are dangerous if roused. No one animal species or thing transcends a fragmentary type; only in man when fully wise are all the attributes that are scattered through the universe drawn together into a centered life and given an order and unity. The fully conscious person preserves thus the integrity of the universe. Bwami "ties together" the divine order and reveals the purpose for which all was created. The proverbs locate the meaning of every species and object, disclosing for the initiate a cosmos which radiates symbolically away from him in all directions, falling into mere fragmentary happenstance at the periphery. Bwami, in short, is the ideal and necessary form of the universe, the underlying harmony of all things, the transcendental form of nature.

We might be tempted to say that bwami is built on a kind of neo-Platonic view that society rises out of nature and is continuous with it. Yet as we have seen, bwami is not to be identified with Lega society. The proverbs mark out other boundaries within the village itself, in particular those between initiate and non-initiate. Many proverbs describe with relish the animality or mere natural crudeness of non-initiates. Impulsive people, for example, are (like) zogozogo monkeys; yes-men are like the "cut tree that still shakes its leaves while its roots are rotten." A non-initiate is a raffia walking-stick: when leaned on, it breaks. He is lustful, as are dogs. And so on. The negative attributes of natural objects are located in the human sphere in non-initiates; they are reduced to stereotypes, unlike the fully developed, harmoniously realized humanity of the high initiate. The bwami member learns how to select the positive and harmonious aspects of the cosmic order and bring them together in himself; those who do not participate in this renewal of the world at the center of things belong instead on the periphery, symbolically on the boundary or actually in the forest wilderness like non-Lega peoples.

These comments begin to uncover the spatial and spiritual universe of bwami proverbs. With more of them to work from, we could better understand the village-forest distinction and go on to define the even more intimate boundaries and interrelations between male and female, children and adults, Lega and non-Lega, man and spirits, etc. As we shall see in relation to other African religions, such matters are often of deepest spiritual significance.

There is a sub-discipline of anthropology that might appear to analyze precisely the same material that we have touched on here, and even its name seems promising: structural anthropology. It is concerned with the structures of thought, the hidden logic, that determines the choice of this item or that for a myth or ritual. In analyzing the Lega, attention would be paid to the correlations specified in bwami proverbs between specific items, and very much might be revealed in this way of Lega assumptions. Scaley anteaters, a major focus of bwami celebrations, might be shown to be related to water-snakes, for example, as initiated Lega men are to pregnant women, or filed teeth might be found to signify the logical antithesis of gluttonous table manners. Complex links between the seasons, parts of the body, myths, and ritual items might be discovered, as has been done in a study of another Zaire culture not far from the Lega, the Luba.

Luc de Heusch, in *Le roi ivre, ou l'origine de l'etat; mythes et rites Bantous* (Paris: Gallimard, 1972), decided to employ structuralist methods to answer a question disturbing him: we know a good deal of the everyday folk culture of the Luba, but nothing of the esoteric wisdom taught initiates, which is the real heart of their culture. If, however, we could discover the implicit logic linking things together even on the folk level, we would find the mythic world view which would necessarily be at the basis of what was disclosed explicitly on the esoteric level. Initiatic wisdom, in short, must consist of a higher order integration of what is present already to the uninitiated; this is why it carries conviction when it is revealed. So de Heusch pulls together all he can find out about folk customs and myths, and also makes full use of other central African religious material, particularly from cultures related to the Luba. The result is an extremely ingenious and imposing mythical system. Even minor practices celebrated at the various seasonal rites are shown to fit into a grand myth of the universe. An innate logic is supposedly revealed, obeying laws that are universal to all thought but operating with Luba materials.

But a number of doubts arise. Were the Luba as rigidly logical as de Heusch? Does in fact their initiatic wisdom have to consist of only one possible synthesis? Even beyond this, is the purpose of initiation, the content of wisdom, really only the instruction in the correlation of many things, or is it not rather the possession of an inner poise, a stance toward the world and a way of entry into its workings? In terms of awareness, religion is not really a matter of the specific data of consciousness, so much as it is a matter of the value given them. Two scientists, for example, might know precisely the same information about atomic structure, but for one that structure might be awe-inspiring and part of a mystery to which one submits with reverence, and for the other the same data might be boring, or merely a matter for professional experiments. ("Religious" symbols can evoke the same variety of response.) What makes the same cognitive content religious for one, and not for another, is the presence or absence of the transcendental intentionalities finding in that content primordial formlessness or sacred, ultimate form. Only when these realities are seen in things do we have genuine religion, orienting life and thought, providing a *focus* for existence. The Lega share with the Luba very many of the same folk customs and myths, but as we have seen, their initiatic wisdom is not of a mythic nature at all. It is a training in a way of beholding the world and acting in it, a spiritual focus. Non-initiates may (and do) *know* many of the bwami proverbs, but they may not "possess" them (or repeat their songs and dramatizations). The proverbs have not entered into the non-initiate through constant ritual repetition and enactment. They do not present a universe to the non-initiate as they do for the initiate. Each proverb really signifies a vaster meaning to the initiate, beyond the specific content: a transcendental normative order which lies just beneath the surface of life and shapes everything in it.

Our brief look at the bwami has given us a useful preliminary insight into the basic assumptions of African religions, and has demonstrated as well that "ritual" encompasses more than the circumscribed ceremonial we tend to associate with it. The use of proverbs not only ritualizes language, but even perception and awareness itself. This deeper level of ritual influence is, if possible, yet more evident in the next people we now turn to, the Mbuti Pygmies of eastern Zaire, forest hunters who dwell in bands in the same endless wilderness the Lega villages overlook.

NOTES TO THE INTRODUCTION

1. Rudolf Otto, *The Idea of the Holy,* trans. J.W. Harvey (Baltimore: Penguin, 1959), first published in 1917 as *Das Heilige,* but still determinative of most approaches in the discipline of Religious Studies; the current *Encyclopaedia Britannica* articles on religion base themselves on Otto, for example: see *Religious Studies Review,* II, no. 1 (January 1976): 1-11. Since he was a Lutheran minister, it is hardly surprising to find that his theories conform entirely to Lutheran theological axioms and prejudices.

2. Emile Durkheim, *The Elementary Forms of the Religious Life,* trans. J. Swain (New York: Collier Books, 1961), p. 4; first published in 1912.

3. See Claude Lévi-Strauss, *The Savage Mind* (Chicago: University of Chicago Press, 1966), pp. 227f.

4. This and the following paragraphs are primarily based on Daniel Biebuyck, *Lega Culture* (Berkeley: University of California Press, 1973). Biebuyck was himself a bwami initiate.

5. Ibid., p. 125.

6. Ibid., p. 69; also see Barnabé Mulyumba, "La croyance religieuse des Lega traditionnels," *Études Congolaises*, 11, no. 3 (Juillet-Sept. 1968): 3 et passim.

7. Biebuyck, *Lega Culture*, p. 127.

8. Ibid., p. 126.

9. Ibid.

10. Ibid., p. 141; parenthetical remarks in text.

PART ONE:

FORMS OF HUNTING RELIGION AND RITUAL

Chapter 1

Religion and Ritual
among the Pygmies

In a survey of ritual structures in the history of African religions, the
Pygmies provide at once the most logical and the least propitious starting
place. At one time, during the Paleolithic epoch that witnessed the
flourishing of cave art in southwestern Europe, what may have been the
ancestors of the Pygmies and the ancestors of the Kalahari Bushmen
apparently divided almost the entire African continent between them. The
Paleolithic-Negritic peoples of short stature and Pygmylike culture
occupied the forested areas (much wider in extent then than now), while the
archaic Bushmanlike cultures spread through the savannas that bordered
the forests down through east Africa into the central and southern regions.[1]
Some have asserted that the Pygmy peoples were related to the early Negro
peoples, while others insist on their physical and cultural similarities to the
Pygmies of Malaysia, the Philippines, Indonesia, and elsewhere, which
would suggest that they are branches of an extremely archaic, distinct, and
non-Negroid people. We need not make a decision between these theories
here, but it is evident in any case that there is a considerable continuity
between the cultures of certain Negro communities and that of the
technologically less sophisticated Pygmies, and this will offer us the basis
for a useful discussion of similarities and differences between the religions
of hunting-and-gathering bands and the agrarian societies of central
Africa.

At the same time, however, many factors of Pygmy culture remain
enigmatic. Edward Tylor insisted all the way back in 1871 that those
Western theorists who have eagerly sought to find a people utterly without
religion have invariably relied on inaccurate or incomplete information.[2]
The religious quest is a universal human characteristic and touches at the
root of what it means to be human. Yet one culture may pursue this quest
with less intensity than another, and recent research into the Pygmies has
painted such a nonritualistic culture that they have been called
"secularist," and grouped with our own Western culture, in a brilliant
study of fundamental religious typologies by Mary Douglas.[3] Since our

study is of ritual behavior, the Pygmies would hardly seem to present a promising beginning.

Yet, ironically, it is possible to argue that the Pygmies exceed Brahmanic priests, or the Hopi and Zuni Pueblo Indians, in the extent of their ritual life; and that rather than being like secular Westerners they represent the opposite possibility—a people so given over to religious and ritual celebration they know nothing of what we call the "profane." Their daily life is itself profoundly ritualized, so that there is nothing unaffected by ritual gesture. It is this sense of difference from our own culture that endows the study of the Pygmies with such a fascination for us.

To argue against Douglas, however, we will need to support our analysis with a close examination of Pygmy culture. As we have seen from our earlier examination of ritual phenomenology, cultic actions structure spatial and temporal boundaries and realms, among other categories. We begin our investigation on this most fundamental level.

THE SPATIAL CONTEXT OF EPULU MBUTI LIFE

There are two major accounts of Mbuti Pygmy culture and religion, and each reflects a different methodological and theoretical orientation in modern ethnology. Father Paul Schebesta's detailed monographs surveying a wide number of Pygmy bands reflect the Austrian cultural-historical school founded by Father Wilhelm Schmidt; here, the Pygmies suggest humanity's first religion. The more recent investigations of Colin Turnbull exemplify the functionalist orientation of English social anthropology, and in accordance with the principles of this approach eschew extensive cultural surveys or historical and philological reconstructions in favor of focused field research on one band. Turnbull's careful (although somewhat sentimental) study of the Epulu band therefore complements nicely Schebesta's wide-ranging survey; the two researchers also correct each other in their conclusions, and we shall refer to both throughout our discussion of the Epulu.[4]

In the accounts of both of these authorities, the fundamental reality to the Mbuti is the forest itself, the "place" of the universe. Their entire life is passed within its green and shifting light, surrounded by its vibrancy. Around them dwell the spirits of the forest, the benevolent and malevolent dead, and even troll-like monsters, but all of this manifests the unceasing activity of deity. "*Ndura nde Kalisia, ndura nde Mungu*," say the Epulu: the forest *is* Godhead, is the Creator Himself.[5] Man dwells in the midst of divine fullness. Its presence is even felt within, in the *pepo*, the soul as life-force. Pepo animates all moving, living beings, even the forest itself as the breeze; the human pepo participates in and condenses all this, drawing from "not just the trees or streams, or the sky or the soil, but from the totality, down to the last grain of sand."[6] In another sense, this force is represented in the *keti*, disembodied human and animal spirits, in a vague way including the dead, who carry on their activities in a shadow world coinciding with our own. They also hunt and dance, and it is possible for a Mbuti to hunt together with them; then the mirror images coincide exactly and it is a "strong" hunt, producing much game. But such heightened states are dangerous and fatiguing and so are only sought at times of particularly poor hunting. Raising the underlying spiritual participation to full ecstatic consciousness in this way is avoided under most circumstances as disruptive to human life. "Ideally the Mbuti and the keti should follow each other closely, but always remain just slightly apart."[7] The keti, and the spiritual intensity they communicate, are like dangerous fire, cold fire, one may say: according to Schebesta, the keti are kindred to fire and are like flames, but they dwell in cold, dark, and wet regions, like the faeries, ancestral dead, and demons of pre-Christian Europe, and the dead of India, China, and Japan.[8]

Yet despite this profound spatial immanence of divinity, there is also a transcendent aspect. One may see this not only in the terrific and frightening face of the forest in storm and lightening, when it appears as stern judge over mankind,[9] but even more in a celestial mode of the supreme being, beyond the forest realm. According to Paul Schebesta, one can discover in Pygmy religion a tripartite or three-leveled conception of the supreme being (not distinguished as such by the Pygmies, but implied everywhere among them). There is the heavenly high god, apparent above all in the moon and rainbow ("rainbow serpent"), and the center of the mythology; the earthly form, ruling the daily life of the Pygmies from the forest; and the underworld, chthonic aspect, lord of the realm of the dead and possessed of a demonic side.[10] The transcendent divinity is brought into relation to the actualities of Pygmy life through the forest aspect, so this is the most stressed mode of the divine, while according to Schebesta the underworldly realm is far more real and significant to the Bantu cultures of the forest than it is to the cheerful Mbuti.[11]

In any case, it is evident that the Pygmies perceive a distant realm of being beyond the divine "place" of the forest, above and overseeing this expanse, and the ultimate arbiter of all that occurs below. In the ordinary view, however, these realms flow together into the plenitude of existence that the forest provides. It is only on extraordinary occasions, like those of death and disease, or even in terrific thunderstorms, that what is far away comes near while preserving all its spiritual remoteness. This unwonted intrusion of the inhuman, almost demonic divine, man cannot endure. Following a death, the band abandons the campsite. It is not the dead so much as the alienness of the mode in which divinity is present that they flee.[12] And the most important ceremony of the Epulu, the *molimo*, is conducted in response to the spatial-spiritual confusion that death, illness, or poor hunting signals. As we shall see, the molimo seeks to return the remote aspect of divinity to its proper place, restoring the benign intimacy with God that permits mankind to exist. Thus, both in the case of the keti and in regard to the breakthrough of spatial-spiritual remoteness into the human sphere, a too-extreme submersion of humanity in the divine cannot be borne. Human culture and consciousness need a space for themselves in which to develop. The inner dialectic that this generates, so contrary to a thesis of primitive mystical participation in nature, shall draw our attention throughout our discussion.

The Epulu rites that accompany birth and the unfolding life cycle outline graphically a process that begins with an infantile communion with divinity and ends with a consciousness in maturity of distinct individual personality. Already at birth, the infants are bathed daily in the juices of special vines, "to make them strong"; a vine bracelet tied on the infants' wrists or around their waists invigorate them by giving them the protection and strength of the forest. The best place for coitus and conception is in the forest; the forest is able to aid in difficult births. And, at the first sign of sickness, both children and adults undergo scarifications during which ashes from forest herbs are rubbed into the cuts. When the skin grows back the forest life is captured in the body, assuring healing and good fortune. While the baby is still crawling (and so partakes strongly of the animal condition), the parents may not eat meat from the hunt. The killing of the hunt makes a break in the man-forest unity, and though the father may help in the hunt for the sake of the band, he may not eat of the kill.[13]

Physical maturity increases the discontinuity of the relationship with the forest and with divinity. Man learns that he is bound to the forest but is not identical with it, and the nature of the relationship receives a number of symbolic expressions, among them the erotic. For the Mbuti, sexual love is based on participation within difference. One of the most significant divine presences is the moon, and the Epulu along with other Pygmies regard it as linked both with the supreme being and with menstruation and fertility. "Mother moon, mother, mother, hear us mother, come," they sing in the course of the molimo, and Turnbull tells of young men performing erotic dances to the forest in the moonlight.[14]

When the Mbuti seek to abstract from their lives the essential elements that prevail now, and must have been present in the beginning, we find emphasized again the generative forest and also the theme of alienation. In many of the creation myths collected by Schebesta it is said that in the beginning, perhaps growing out of a primal stone, there existed the Ti'i or

Tahu tree, first tree and origin of all later vegetative life. That actually all life springs from this cosmic tree is the import of some myths. According to one such, recited by the Kai-Kou band, in the beginning there was a great tree in whose branches roamed the ancestor of all animals, a goat. Also slipping about through the branches and overseeing everything was the little chameleon, emissary of the supreme being, who would eventually name and assign the functions of the various animals. Now it happened that in the primordial silence of the beginnings, the chameleon heard a knocking coming from within the tree. Intrigued, he split open a crack in the trunk, and water gushed out like amniotic fluid. Then forward emerged the first man, Mupe or Magidi, and the first woman, Matu or Otu ("blood," especially menstrual).[15] One variant on this myth that is astonishingly like the Genesis myth relates that a serpent tempted the first woman to taste of the fruit of the Tahu tree, though this had been explicitly prohibited by God; her husband joined her in this disobedience, and both were driven out of the presence of the supreme being into a world of culture, work, and suffering.[16] But even if this myth reflects an ancient Jewish or Moslem or a more recent Christian influence—which is probable despite Schebesta's objection—it still agrees with the Mbuti conception of the forest as the source of reality and the locus of the human condition, from which mankind must (always through a theft or other improper, aggressive act) wrest its self-consciousness. Many stories of unquestionably indigenous provenance tell how in the very beginning mankind stole fire, food, or even the mystery of sexuality itself from the supreme being or a forest representative, or even from the monkeys, those intermediary beings between humanity and the primordial wild.

One of the most significant of these stories, repeated in numerous versions from band to band among the Mbuti, concerns Matu, the mother of Tore, master of animals. Tore, who is also a form of the supreme being according to some accounts, is portrayed swinging from tree to tree through the forest, playing like the monkeys in his domain. His great treasure, fire, he leaves under the watch of his mother. She, however, is too old and frail to remain alert for long, and, warmed and soothed by the fire, she falls asleep. This is the chance that the heroic Pygmy ancestor peering from the bushes is waiting for. He leaps out and runs off with a flaming brand to his family shivering in the cold, wet forest depths. Feeling the sudden chill, Matu awakens and screams for Tore. Tore swoops through the forest to the thief and snatches back the fire. This happens several times (the Mbuti narrator acting out the whole drama), until at last the ancestral hero gets too great a head start on Tore; the deity can only stand and watch the disappearing figure of the robber and wail out disconsolately, "Here is an equal to me! Doru, we both come from the same mother! If you had only asked, I would have given it to you!" The gratuitous crime had even worse consequences; when Tore returned to his cold hearth, he found his mother chilled to death. At that, he cursed mankind to die as well; Matu, associated now with the moon, from the Other Side now became Mother of the Dead, who appears occasionally roaming in the night forest or luring hunters astray in the distant reaches of the forest, kidnapping small children or plaguing mankind.[17]

This haunting, profound myth illuminates much in the Mbuti universe. Through violent, gratuitous but irrevocable acts man establishes the separation of distinct realms out of the primal unity. The withdrawal of the divine to the distance or the above, creates near and far, above and below, day and night, hot and cold, life and death, the human (cultural) and the transcendent. Yet the divine is still present, the forest is still good, and in the new order generated by the first theft there is a benevolent and sustaining divine presence, through whose grace mankind is permitted to persist. The myth also stimulates questions. Already in our brief survey of myths we have encountered puzzling continuities. Can the "Mother Moon" the Epulu youths sing their love songs to be the same reality that the night-hag Matu, Mother of the Dead, represents? Why indeed is her name *Matu*, which signifies genital blood, especially menstrual, and what is the point of the association with fire? To this we must add that the Mbuti consider this myth to reveal the theft of sexuality from the divine, yet the theft also brought death.

It is not much relief from these paradoxes and confusions to learn that not all Mbuti recite just these myths; in fact, there are endless variations of these and other myths told from band to band and even person to person within the same band. Names of principal figures may differ, or one band member may deny the existence of a myth another member narrates. The Epulu that Turnbull lived among may have been affected by their proximity to a main road and to European and Bantu settlements, and apparently had none of the myths we have presented, or they may have decided not to share them with the anthropologist. Yet even the Epulu, as we shall see, know of a mythic theft of fire (Turnbull tells us this but does not give the myth itself—his own interests ran in other directions), and they associate with fire sexuality, women, and the creation of culture. There is, apparently, something for the Pygmies in the nature of fire as such that also implies violence, spiritual discontinuity, and death. We shall find these interconnecting themes everywhere in Mbuti religion. They seem to resolve themselves into the fundamental theme of transformation. Fire, sexuality, death, theft, and the creation of culture itself all act to bridge boundaries between spheres. They are all liminal and generative, and their symbolisms would be likely to recur at times or places of transition.

Within the grand space of the forest, there are other boundaries that determine the movements and shape the ritual of the Mbuti. Each band possesses corporately a territory sufficient to supply it with game for the full round of the year. The band moves about from place to place within this territory, which for the Epulu band was thirty miles wide and sixty miles deep. When animals are hunted out of one area, the band shifts to another, remaining always within its territory. Game is plentiful, and there is little need to raid other territories. Both Turnbull and Schebesta impress upon us, in fact, that the Pygmies are a people of peace. Yet the idyllic picture both authorities paint (and even suggest was typical of the earliest hunters or small hunting-and-gathering bands) is jarred by the account by a journalist (admittedly no expert) who stayed in the Epulu area for an extended time. He reported that the Pygmies zestfully recounted frequent wars they had in former times among themselves and even enacted for his movie cameras mock battles so convincing that some Mbuti were seriously wounded.[18] In any case, all sources agree that physical violence within a single band is practically unheard of. Arguments are brought out into the open and resolved by the whole band; those who prove intractable or are strongly disliked by others eventually join other bands where relatives or friends are members. Each band has a shifting population, and visiting back and forth is common. Harmony within the band is of capital importance to the Mbuti; it is actually the basis of their ethics, one may almost say of their religion. Friction and hostility within the band, especially between husband and wife, are said to be an offense against the forest, against God, who loves peace.

Within the band territory are other modulations of space that have even more immediacy to the Mbuti. There are certain regions that are seldom entered and that are considered to have a heightened sanctity. Among the Epulu there is an especial avoidance of close, dense, and dark groves of trees and bushes; under the lofty green canopy such groves are relatively rare interruptions of cheerful open space. In one such grove the Epulu store the secret paraphernalia of the *molimo* mysteries, away from the eyes of women and noninitiates. Schebesta also mentions that among many bands the sources of streams, waterfalls, and caves are avoided. It is believed that terrifying serpents having the fiery nature of rainbows dwell at waterfalls; one must stay away from such places, for merely to gaze at these luminous beings is to die. (Interestingly, similar beliefs about rainbow serpents are widespread among Bantu peoples of the Congo region, central, and even southern Africa.)[19] From their caves (where the hosts of the dead flit about), the rainbow serpent or monster releases game to the hunters, and they are the guardians of the forest on behalf of the supreme being above.[20] Associated perhaps with such watery mysteries are the streams that flow through the forest, next to which the Mbuti love to camp. Away from their sacred sources and from waterfalls the streams are not terrifying, yet there is something still connecting them with alien holiness. When the *molimo* trumpet is taken from its sacred grove and blown during the long nights of the festival, it is hidden away during the days upstream from the camp within the flowing cool waters. The cold, the wet, the dark, even the demonic, and the remote, participate in each other and in divinity. They are the primordial modality of the sacred, too intense and formless for man to endure.

THE MORNING FIRE CEREMONY

The boundaries between the camp and the deep forest provide an even more immediate expression of a near/far spatial opposition, intermingled with a sense of in and out, human structure as opposed to primal confusion, and home as opposed to territorial land. Here, where the distinctions are of experiential import in everyday life, we find the beginning of conscious ritual acts of demarcation. One cannot step out of the forest world taken as a whole, but the camp is on a human scale; one can walk outside of that. Within it is domesticity and human beings, outside is hunting and animals. The departure from camp on the morning hunt engages all these realities and has achieved ritual definition in simple acts pregnant with meaning.

It is the practice of the Epulu never to step outside the camp in the morning until the night dew has evaporated from the forest, a practice which may at times delay the departure of the hunters until early afternoon. While the dew moistens the forest depths, the night world still rules; but the camp belongs essentially to the warm and day-lit sphere, and the slanting rays of the sun must drive away the night world before it is safe to hunt. In a peculiar way spatial and temporal structures qualify each other here.

The first departure from the camp into the forest has therefore a special significance. The pathway is opened up for the day by carefully lighting a fire under a small, very young tree on the camp's edge. All hunters and women leaving the camp stop for a few moments beside the fire before going on. Turnbull overheard no prayers among the Epulu, but it is common to find that other Mbuti bands observing this almost universal Pygmy rite make invocations to the forest deity or master of animals, calling him "father" or "grandfather" and asking him for game or food.[21] Among the Epulu we do encounter the widespread usage of smearing ashes from the fire on the temples and around the eyes to "see" game better. The Epulu also share the general Mbuti practice of blowing whistles as they leave the fire on their way into the forest.[22]

According to Turnbull, special leaves are heaped on the fire under the tiny tree, to make heavy smoke; this, it is said, alerts divinity to the hunt as it rises and "rejoices" the forest. It is a pity we are not told what are the species of herbs employed or what kind of tree is chosen for the rite. Turnbull devotes no particular attention to the details, but insists:

> There was no great ritual or ceremonial, but somehow this act put the hunters in harmony with the forest and secured its blessing and assistance for the day's hunt. The Pygmies regard fire as the most precious gift of the forest, and by offering it back to the forest they are acknowledging their debt and their gratitude.[23]

Our curiosity is naturally whetted by this little rite, which has such momentous consequences. A closer analysis may disclose its inner logic and at the same time reveal some of the basic symbolic realities of the Epulu universe. In the more northernly reaches of the net-hunting Pygmy cultures (of which the Epulu are a member), more elaboration is given to this ritual, providing a native extension and interpretation of it. There we find that the fire is made in the camp itself, and a circle of vines is carefully staked out around it, symbolically like the forest encircling the campfires. Within this ritual circle long twigs stripped of bark, sometimes with simple patterns burned into them, are laid out in the direction the hunt will take. Any game caught is brought back and placed within the circle before being appropriated by the camp members, divided, and shared.[24] All these practices are variations of the same ritual elements: There are the vines or the tree, symbolically the forest itself; and the fire, whose symbolism is more complex. The symbolic nature of the young tree would seem to be stressed by the perceptual displacement or peculiarity of the obligatory smallness of the tree: it is important, but not in itself, only for what it stands for. The fire beneath it is also touched by this paradigmatic status, as if it, too, represented all fire, including that which warms the forest like the sun. But this fire is domesticated to the service of mankind; the northern variant has it symbolize the fires of the camp. Within this symbolic realm the entire hunt takes place, as the ritual of bringing back the game and laying it within the circle suggests. The physical reality is returned to its spiritual source. At the same time this gives the entire hunt a ritual and archetypal nature. The real hunt occurs within the circle, between the central fire and the forest depths of the vines, along the paths marked out by the peeled twigs and arrows.

There is a certain resemblance between these symbolisms and those of a Pygmy hunting ritual described by Leo Frobenius but not observed by any other investigator among the Congo Pygmies. Before dawn on the day of a hunt, the famous ethnologist observed his diminutive hunters slip out of camp and make their way to a hilltop clearing; there they drew the form of an antelope on the ground and, precisely at the moment that the first rays of the sun touched the design, shot an arrow into it. At the same instant, the woman who accompanied the hunters and had reached out as if to embrace the rising sun, cried out as if struck as well. Later that day, the hunters returned with the buck they had killed, and plastered its hair and blood over the image just at sunrise of the next day, then erased the entire figure.[25] Here again we find the morning presence of fire and sun, a ritual space (in this case, the clearing itself that the hunters swept and smoothed out before drawing the antelope), the use of the arrow, and the theme of the return of the game to the ritual space before making use of it, in a kind of sacrificial rite. This latter rite suggests the sacrifice of the "returned blood" or offering of the vital centers of the quarry back to the divine in gratitude, with the hope that these organs, bones, or blood of life will come again clothed anew in flesh to be victims of the hunter—a rite and symbolism typical of Paleolithic hunters.[26] But to these themes, found also in rites of the Epulu and their northern neighbors, is added an explicitly sexual symbolism in which the rays of the sun, and the arrow of the hunter, are made to be homologous in their penetration of the antelope figure to a sexual penetration of woman. We meet again with this tantalizing symbolic grammar that "conjugates" hunting and sexual intercourse in identical forms.

In these rites there is developed a remarkable emphasis on microcosm-macrocosm conceptions that assumes the superior reality of archetypes over merely banal existence. Two important points need to be made about this. First, it is evident that Hermann Baumann is in error when he asserts that microcosm-macrocosm conceptions only entered history with the rise of megalithic agricultural societies.[27] More and more evidence is being accumulated to show that already Paleolithic man was fully capable of amazingly abstract thought.[28] Second, the emphasis on archetypes expresses a deep-seated dualism basic to religious, and indeed to human, thought. There is another spiritual realm that only symbols can point to, behind and "truer" than ordinary human existence. This is the realm that Eliade, Cassirer, and Durkheim, among others, refer to as the "sacred" as opposed to the "profane." But one separates out the ideal only in order to attain to the real. Realization of transcendental realities permits one to return to everyday realities with an awareness of their own "otherness." That is to say, establishing a relationship with the gods enables the worshipper to sanctify his entire life; the gods assure the plentitude and continuance of the cosmos. If, then, the worshipper calls upon the transcendental beings to participate in the ongoing process of life, he is making a deeply religious plea, which his very faith permits to phrase as a proclamation. The fusion and even unity of "magic" and "religion" that we encounter so widely in the history of religions reflects this longing for the sanctification of everyday life. Human goals are assumed to be acceptable and part of the inner *telos* of the divine.

So we must not be surprised if the morning fire ritual combines magical confidence in human forces and religious humility before the divine mystery. The circle of vines, fire, and arrowlike path traced out in the more northern Mbuti bands, or the ritual that Frobenius witnessed, are certainly kinds of archetypal anticipation of the hunt, apparently with a magical efficacy of their own. Yet in both cases the game is brought back to the ritual space and offered up symbolically to the divine as a sacrifice: magical anticipation and religious appeal are clearly one in the entire ceremony. One does not express gratitude to a process set in motion automatically by oneself. A closer look at almost all so-called magical rites would probably reveal the same interfusion of anticipatory proclamation and humble appeal.

Much the same synthesis appears, at any rate, in the use of the hunting whistle (or "magic whistle") that the Epulu like other Mbuti like to blow at the morning fire and on their way into the forest. The full meaning of the whistle can only be appreciated through an investigation of the various contexts in which it is used; as we have seen, this holds for all ritual symbolism.

The Mbuti cut the whistle from trees with a special affinity to game—for example, trees that antelope like to rub their horns on.[29] As is the case with other medicines, using it awakens its spiritual power: blowing into it invigorates its spiritual magnetism and draws game. But just as its sound draws good game, so it banishes evil powers that make for disharmony. It is often used against enemies and demons, reminding us of the medieval European belief in the power of church bells to banish evil spirits, or even more of the music of Orpheus, which attracted the beasts of the wild and purged them of their savagery. Schebesta was himself greeted with this sound at the beginning of his field research! But the great power of these pipes over evil can also be used for darker ends. The entranced game comes near and the hunter kills it. The sound itself is deadly. The Efe Mbuti say that the ancestor of all Pygmies, Kodzalipili, used the pipe against his disobedient younger son, and the son died. In another mythic quarrel, an ancestor obtained some drops of blood from his wife and placed them in the pipe, much as the hunter places fiery coals in his pipe even today to heighten its effectiveness. But the association of blood (especially menstrual) and impure fire is a very widespread African idea. The pipe reacted against its desecration and pollution by killing the wife. Other uses include the power of the pipe to ruin a rival's hunting luck, or to monopolize the game available to a band of hunters. As is obvious from these examples, use of the pipes shades imperceptibly over into sorcery at one extreme.

There is a spiritual link between the pipe, fire, and lightning, too. The Bakango Mbuti use their pipe to fan the fire. The pipe itself is cut from the Ota tree, a fire-tree that attracts lightning and has power over fire and storm. There is in fact a nearly universal Pygmy use of the whistle to repulse impending storms, probably also implying the power of the pipe to "cast out evil." It is believed that electric storms are the work of demonic beings expressing the fierce, vengeful side of the forest Deity. The storm may be punishment for transgressions either in the hunt or the band. This is especially likely if lightning strikes someone. To avoid such punishment, the Mbuti retreat to their huts, cover their fires, and offer up blood from their own bodies in penitence, with prayers to God.[30] But in case the storm is not intended as punishment, and God is only sleeping or distracted, the pipes are blown to alert him to his children's distress, and to repulse the dark powers that sometimes try to destroy mankind when he is busy elsewhere. The sound of the pipes has a strong effect. The pure, melodious notes cut through the random noises of the forest, imposing momentarily an order that bespeaks divine power. A stillness follows. The Mbuti conceive of "noise" as analogous to chaos, and "quiet" (including both general social harmony and the peace that the pipes bring) as divine. Blowing the whistle will even stop a leopard in its tracks, or will send a wild buffalo lumbering harmlessly off into the bush.

The wide spectrum of uses for the hunting whistle evidently embraces sorcery at one extreme and prayerful appeal to the supreme being at the other. It is as if the latent fullness of this ritual symbol were not expressed adequately in any one use, whether magical or religious, so various occasions were sought to articulate it. One expression, then, is not more authentic than another, but they are all true to the inner nature of the symbolism. The inner pressure of the symbol to seek varying expression is above all a result of the global and indeterminate nature of its meaning. Moreover, all of these expressions are tacitly present at every use. The same hunter who blows his pipe in humble appeal to the supreme being in the storm knows that the pipe's shrill voice once killed legendary opponents in myth, still banishes evil forces and hypnotizes leopards. The multifaceted meaning gives a rich religious intentionality. The divine has not left man abandoned even to its own whims: Humans can fight back with the very power of the holy. The pipe expresses divine mercy, and through it power can flow forth to modify a severe decree. At the same time, even when used in sorcery, the powers of the pipe depend in the last analysis on an appeal to divine beings. Every use of the pipe evokes latent memories of other uses, gives a depth of reality to its power, and adds a community of past voices to each utterance of the pipe.

Thus when it is blown in the morning before the hunt, facing toward the depths of the forest, the pipe politely alerts and humbly appeals to the deity (with the cold, wet departing night analogous structurally to the frightening storms mentioned just before). The evil spirits of darkness are also cast out, and warmth and music are drawn into the forest, making it ready to receive the hunters harmoniously. The pipe quiets the beasts of prey, in addition, and attracts the antelope. The common element in all of these uses is the whistle's musical power to harmonize and reconcile or even break down polarities. There is an obvious continuity with the meanings evident in the construction of the morning fire. Far from being, therefore, an alien, magical element in Mbuti religion as Turnbull tries to suggest,[31] the whistle clearly involves many spheres of Mbuti culture and relates directly to deity. We can also find many analogies between this little whistle and the huge trumpet used as the voice of the divine in the central religious ceremonial, the *molimo*. Like the trumpet, for example, the pipe is soaked in water ("drinks") and burning coals are put into its mouth, recalling the power of domestic fires to cook food (for it to "eat").

It is astonishing how a seemingly simple, even elementary practice like blowing a whistle can unfold itself into a rich layering of meaning when one makes the slightest effort to discover the actual contexts of its use. No doubt this richness of associations is even greater in a culture like that of the Mbuti that has a limited number of actions making up the catalog of its "typical life." Each symbol must therefore touch on and ritualize an even wider area of experience, or, to use another language, each ritual "lifts up" into the divine or the "paradigmatic" (the model reality) a greater weight of the givenness of life than would be possible in more differentiated societies.

We see this again in another ritual gesture associated with the morning fire ritual. When the hunters pause at the fire, they have the habit of taking up ashes from the smoldering herbs and smearing them on their temples to "see" the game better. This simple gesture is revealed as a deeply profound one when we search for parallel contexts in other rites.

The Epulu, we recall, like to bathe their infants, new mothers, and the sick in vine juices to infuse them with the spirit of the forest. The same persons are also made to suffer slits on the body, especially the temple and cheeks, into which an ash paste (of saliva and special herbs) is introduced. The slits heal into permanent welts, which like tatoos are thought to make their owner more attractive both to humans and to the forest. Bits of the forest are now in the body and spirit, joining it to the divine in unity. Illness, it is implied, is a separation of the self from the universe; the cicatrization is an organic and logical mode of cure. In many agrarian African cultures,

similar rites cement blood brotherhood,[32] and are used in the course of
initiation ceremonies, perhaps reflecting general survival of formerly
common hunting practices. It should be mentioned that the Bushmen have
scarring practices identical to the Pygmies, and the first cuts are commonly
made at the time of the initiation and first "kill" of the young Bushmen
hunters.[33] The Mbuti practice of including infants in this rite assures that
the newlyborn will immediately be placed under the protection and healing
power of the forest, and the tone of a whole life is set. The same rationale is
evident in the case of the mother.

Further nuances are revealed in analogous rituals in other contexts. It is
customary for elephant hunters to burn tail hairs of slain elephants to an
ash and to rub the ash on the heart and stomach regions of their own bodies
before a hunt; in this way they tune in to, understand, and finally master the
prey. To let the hairs lie about unburnt, on the other hand, would attract
elephants eager to "smell out" and trample the murderer of their
companion.[34] The most effective hunters burn to ash various parts of the
most prized animals and save the ash in medicine horns (*anjo*). The anjo is
inverted and stuck in the ground near the family fire (again the fire motif,
here probably necessary to keep the medicine "warm" and activated).
Before the hunt the ash is smeared on the bodies of the hunter and his
family, especially on the foreheads, to establish the link to the game. This
practice is considered so powerful it may lead to disputes between hunters
and be a temptation to anjo owners to hoard the game.[35] The Epulu, like
other bands, tell stories of mythic hunters who caused the heavenly
destruction of whole camps through their greedy use of anjo medicines, and
if a hunter gets singularly successful with his anjo the band may decide in
counsel to force the destruction of all horns, to reestablish camp unity.

More effective than smearing the ash on the body is absorbing it into the
bloodstream through cuts. Amongst the Oruendu Pygmies the wife makes
cuts in her husband's skin before each hunt, and introduces medicinal ashes
into the slits in the form of a paste moistened by her saliva. Modifications of
these usages sometimes accompany the celebration of the first kill of a
Mbuti boy; they constitute his initiation as a hunter.[36] There is a special
need for *women* to make these cuts in the hunter's flesh, at least among the
Oruendu.

Of particular interest is the use of the same techniques in Mbuti love
medicine. The very same herbs are used, suggesting a surprising identity in
function. The yearning lover cuts his skin, introduces the ash paste into the
slits, and takes up his wooing again confident of the outcome. It
strengthens the effect of the medicine to have the beloved smoke these herbs
inadvertently with her tobacco (Mbuti women love to smoke) or to mix
them into her food.[37] *The symbolism makes clear that wooing and*

hunting are homologous. As a tacit dimension to the use of ashes by the hunters during the morning fire ritual, it reminds us of the erotic dances and songs the young Epulu hunters like to perform to the moon-lit forest. Not only are the moon and the night forest feminine to the hunters, but so is the forest and its animals during the day. The hunt is an erotic pasttime. Women are somehow related to animals and the wild, which includes the dark, cold, and demonic as well as the divine. The successful hunter, we read, is always regarded as especially virile, and the young women like to flirt with him and win him as a husband. Indeed, before a man can marry, he must prove himself as a hunter, and this has more than economic significance.[38]

ANIMALS, WOMEN, AND THE NATURE OF TABOOS

The implied equation linking women and the animals men hunt is a fascinating one. If we recall Matu, we may even add the forest realm as a whole to the symbolically "feminine," with all that that suggests of the nature of the divine, of death, and of generativity. For clarification of these obscure correspondences, we should first turn to the taboos that govern hunting. In the process we can learn much about taboos as such.

It is common to suppose that taboos aid in separating the sacred from the profane, or in keeping people from intruding on holy things. Neither suggestion helps us understand hunting taboos. Most of these apply particularly to the wives of hunters and involve activities that do not seem especially sacred or dangerous. Schebesta tells us that the night before the hunt no sexual relations are permitted the hunter and his wife. In many camps this applies to the whole band. If anyone violates this rule, at the least there will be poor hunting (the game will flee), while at worst the animals will turn and kill their stalkers. Moreover, while the hunters are tracking elephants, no sex, dancing, or other celebration is permitted in the camp. Turnbull has objected that if these rules were rigidly applied, the Mbuti (who hunt every day) would cease to exist; but Schebesta's specific examples apply above all to major hunts (like those of the elephant), not to ordinary daily sorties. In all, this would seem to indicate that *there is something incompatible between animals and women*; relations with one prevent relations with the other. Moreover, to establish a relationship with game is a direct spiritual communion that human sexuality destroys or even perverts into its opposite (in which the game hunts the hunter). There is a fascinating structural resemblance between these practices and those of one of the most taboo-oriented institutions in the history of religions, the monastery. It may even be said that the severe asceticism that we find in the religions of highly differentiated, technologically specialized societies is really merely the institutionalization and complex development of these taboos so prevalent among hunting peoples all over the world.[39] We find it constantly repeated, for example, in Christian writings (and in the Muslim, Buddhist, and Hindu ascetical traditions), that the pursuit of divine reality and the pursuit of sexual partners are on the one hand incompatible and irreconcilable, on the other *symbolically* similar. One should thirst for Krishna or Christ like the bride for the bridegroom. The flame of divine love rises from the same base as earthly love, but in sexual desire and carnal union this love becomes perverted and evil.[40] What must be stressed about these taboo-norms is that they assume natural equivalence and therefore an ideal incompatibility between the sexual relationship and the spiritual. It is like the prohibition against adultery: since the sexual urge can lead directly to intercourse with persons not one's spouse, and break up one's exclusive marital relationship, the urge is bound by cultural distinctions. If we were to extend the meaning of these taboo-norms into a general analysis of taboos, we would conclude that taboos separate the *dangerously similar,* that which is vulnerable to confusion of categories. In this way the divine order is preserved in the face of threatening chaos. This interpretation leads to very different results than that which sees taboos as separating the profane from the sacred, the banal self from the Wholly Other. It is not the otherness of the holy that is feared, so much as it is the possibility that it may *not* be sufficiently "Other." The continuity between women and nature is a general Mbuti assumption; the ritual chastity before a major hunt is a mode of preserving distinctions between these realms necessary for mankind to survive. Through these ritual symbolisms, culture discovers itself as a distinct realm within nature; the divine order is articulated out of a generalized, tacit unity. The very taboos themselves assume this unity, for it is their foundation and *raison d'être*. They announce and ritualize order, but through them shimmers the liminal holy.[41]

Yet the Mbuti are not ascetics, and neither do they hold that spirit and nature are to be at war continually and ontologically. The continuity of women with the forest, the nonhuman, and the divine, is not evil but good, and has positive significance also for the men. A man with a pregnant wife, or whose wife has just delivered a child, must not hunt until her blood has absolutely ceased flowing and she has put on her loin cloth. In the same way, the husband of a menstruating woman must stay in the camp and cannot hunt.[42] In both cases, the sexual relationship, even if permitted, cannot be fruitful in children, and so the hunt cannot be fruitful either (in providing animal flesh). A good relationship with one's wife is essential to good hunting, and when domestic quarrels grow too "heated," the Epulu say, the "noise" alienates the forest deity and the animals withdraw from the hunters.[43]

There are numerous other evidences of the association of women with the animal realm among the Mbuti. Taking the Epulu as our instance, it is noteworthy that this net-hunting band expects the participation of women directly in the hunt; as the men string out their nets in a great semicircle a half mile across, the women and children line up as the other part of the periphery and then beat the bush towards the nets, flushing the game. The same symbolism is evident during the evening preparations for the nightlong singing of the *molimo* (which may go on for several weeks at a time). When the cooking of the day's game is complete, the men go about from hut to hut as if on another hunt. Sticking a fishing line or snare into each hut, the men receive after a mock resistance vegetables and meat from the women around the fires.[44] The symbolism is made even clearer when we realize that the hut itself is considered by the Epulu to be a feminine realm; only women build and repair huts. Part of the pathos of bachelorhood is that the man has to build and repair his own hut and generally does a miserable job of it! In the women's initiation ceremonies (the *elima),* the girls spend a good deal of time communing with the forest, roaming about in it in bands, and singing songs of praise to it.[45] The young men seek to hunt down the girls, especially toward the end of the elima when they make mock attacks on the older women who form a guard around the initiation hut and the novices within. The attendants may beat off unsuitable young men, but after running the gauntlet of their whips, the chosen young hunter may penetrate the hut and sleep with the initiate if she lets him. It is understood that following the festival they will marry.[46] Here again we see a symbolic equation between women, the forest, and the hut.

But probably the most striking symbolic link between women and the forest realm is enacted by the Epulu during the course of their honey-gathering season. This, the only distinct season to interrupt the yearly passage of time, may last two months and is the high point of the year. It is a time of general relaxation, erotic singing, laughter, and license. There is also much telling of myths and legends (whose contents Turnbull does not disclose) and "honey-collecting magic."[47] Perhaps the honey dance must be included in this last category; in it the men act like honey-gatherers, the women like the bees. The men sing as they form a line and dance through the camp hunting for honey. Either parallel to them or at the edge of the forest, the women line up and buzz like bees, swinging around their "stingers": smoldering branches. The men pretend to discover the bees and make for the "honey" they possess. But the women do not give up their sweets so easily and beat their firebrands together over the men's heads so that embers fall and "sting" them. A good-natured fight may follow, developing into either a tug-of-war between the sexes or the *ekokomea* dance so much enjoyed by the Mbuti—in it sex roles are reversed and grotesquely caricatured.[48] In any case, it is clear that in the honey dance women and their "sweetness" are symbolically unified with the forest food the men hunt. Of special interest, too, is the recurrence of fire symbolism; it is again active on the boundary between realms, representing their fusion or conflict. We recall that in the Matu myth, fire was the possession of the old woman herself, the mistress of the night forest. And this in turn meshes with what one informant among the northeast Efe Mbuti told Schebesta about the sacrifices made when hunting is poor: the offerings are made to the forest deity, the spirits of the forest, *and the old women of the camp.*[49]

Vivid myths among Pygmies everywhere make these identifications clearer. The Babinga of the Gabon-Cameroons area say that God, or Kmvum (Khmvum), was asked for wives by the Pygmy men who had grown weary of their own cooking; Kmvum told them all to hunt, and when they returned with many species of animals and laid them before the Creator, he ordered the game to arise transformed into women. Each woman was endowed with the character of the animal from which she had been made.[50] It is a common Bantu myth that sexuality was taught to them by the Pygmies, or that they stole sexuality from the Pygmies, while the Pygmies have myths relating how God taught them this secret, or how they stole it from the monkeys.[51] Does "sexuality" here mean (the discovery of) women?

Therefore, the use of hunting medicines in precisely the same way for wooing women no longer surprises us. Smearing ashes from the morning fire on the hunters' brows, we can now understand, is an amatory rite: it acts to attract and charm the animal/feminine world of the forest. The use of ashes (from the anjo horn) either to win game or to generate sorcery against an enemy, adds an important new aspect to the same dynamic. And the application of ash paste in slits to heal the sick teaches us that the underlying structure that unifies all of these various practices is that ashes incorporated into the flesh can unify the self and its will with the world beyond the body. These herbs treated in the transformatory fire have the power to bring separate spheres into relationship and make them one. It is clear that in this new unity the power of the will and the clear consciousness of the user of ashes is decisive in determining the final effect on the relatively unaware quarry—girlfriend, enemy, or ill person.

The rituals involving fire and ashes that we have been reviewing so far may be dismissed as mere magic. However, the power felt to reside in the gestures derives from deep resonances of all of the elements in the act with important implicit regions of experience. Myths even if not explicitly mentioned, sexual, healing, hunting, and sorcery dimensions join together in quiet reverberation every time the rite is performed, adding the weight of their separate nuances to each enactment. This unspoken "felt significance" is given direction and conscious meaning by the immediate context. To these components must also be added that of prayer as such. Many bands accompany the application of ashes to the head and body before the hunt with short invocations to the forest Deity. God is appealed to as "father" and "grandfather," and asked to give success in the hunt and health throughout the day. Religion and magic do not exist separately for the Mbuti.

Symbolisms of fire and sexuality are particularly appropriate for the purposes we have mentioned, for they all concern transformations. Whenever the boundaries of distinct categories are breached, and the hunter moves out into the forest, the woman becomes pregnant, the infant enters the world, or the normally well person falls ill, the use of fire and its ashes help guide one across the liminal threshold into a properly "cooked" form. Absorbing the ashes into one's body, one attains sacred form. The sexual metaphor guides the process into humanly fruitful results. Crucial to all this is the will and conscious intent of the practitioner. He can guide sacred power into healing or harming; he selects which meaning will be central, hunting or wooing, bewitching or praying. But in general we can distinguish two types of liminality, applicable throughout African religions: *positive liminality*, which integrates structures and builds up a divine order: and *negative liminality* which destroys order and isolates its victims. Whatever meaning explicitly orders the ritual and words, all of these layers of sexual, hunting, healing, and bewitching symbolism are tacitly present, adding their force. Ritual harmonizes experience even on the preconscious, tacit level, directing man in his world.

The spatial dialectic that we have been reviewing between the Mbuti individual and the divine is obviously a complex one. We may summarize some of the main points. As their attitude to the keti shows, the Epulu do not wish to merge with divine powers, or to enter wholly into the uncontrollable mystical participations of the primal forest. They wish to preserve a self-conscious distance between themselves and the keti. The keti hunter and the Pygmy should not coincide in space as they hunt; there should always be a slight displacement. The Pygmy steers clear of the dwelling places of spirits like waterfalls, deep groves, or springs. To come too close is to die. The primordial forest is the region of cold, wet darkness, and death; the dew must evaporate and the night-beings retreat from the sun before the Pygmy hunters venture forth from camp. In these and other ways we detect a sharp division between primeval sacred power and everyday human life. Yet Matu is not merely a night-hag Mistress of the Dead from mythic times, residing in the deepest forest. She also releases the animals and can be wooed as the moon. As the taboos show, human women are for their part not only of the camp; they are also of the forest.

Both taboos and morning fire ceremony intimate that forest depths and humanity can be brought together in a greater harmony that preserves all things. A transcendental structure can integrate everyday life and primordial beings. The Mbuti must work the essence of the forest into their very souls through vine-juice baths and scarifications. Hunting itself becomes a sacred ritual joining yet preserving realms, especially when linked symbolically with sexual intercourse.

The conception of the forest realm as being like a woman whom the masculine hunter woos is in fact profoundly significant. Love magic and hunting magic are not different types of magic. If our analysis so far is correct, both are ultimately a *religious* "magic" whose aim is finally to bring together in life-giving communion all divine otherness and the everyday sunlit banalities of the hunting band.

The religion the Mbuti actually practice recalls the intellectual and mystical abstractions of Rāmānuja, the great Hindu theologian, although it is very unlikely he would recognize any kinship between his highly sophisticated theology and that of the Pygmies. Rāmānuja, disagreeing with the absolute monism of his predecessor Shankara, claimed that the ultimate goal of life should be not the fusion with the Godhead (Brahman), but communion with God (Ishvara or Saguna Brahman). Although the soul is merely part of God in the same way that the Mbuti is part of the forest, only when the soul becomes aware of God as distinct from itself, yet related, does God become conscious of himself. All awareness requires a subject and object. Thus in the soul's love of God God achieves blissful self-consciousness. Relationship is higher than identity. Later Hindu mysticism frequently made use of erotic metaphors to express the nature of the relationship of the soul with God.

Yet the Mbuti view leads finally to a quite different conclusion than Rāmānuja's. For the Hindu theologian, the result of mystical eroticism is the annihilation of the perceptual world and of awareness of all things in it, while for the Pygmies, the fruit and actual goal of their spiritual communion is the establishment of this perceptual universe and its preservation within a great harmony. Their view of the divine is finally more complex than Shankara's or Rāmānuja's, for it can contemplate the holy as highly differentiated, a network holding both God and man, and even the world in addition.

NOTES TO CHAPTER ONE

1. Another ethnic group, possibly derived from an earlier, less differentiated African stock before the development of Negro and Khoisan races, occupied north Africa, but our

focus of interest is on sub-Saharan Africa here. For detailed discussion of the evidence that the "Bushmanoid" (or Khoisan, Boskop, etc.) and "Negroid" stocks shared most of the continent between them, and for consideration of the possibility that the "Pygmanoid" is a distinct third stock rather than a form of "Negroid" development, see J. Desmond Clark, "Prehistoric Origins of African Culture," *Journal of African History* 5, no. 2 (1964): 163-82; idem, *The Prehistory of Africa* (New York: Praeger Publishers, 1970); Sonia Cole, *The Prehistory of East Africa* (New York: Macmillan Co., 1965); Thurston Shaw, "The Approach through Archaeology to Early West African History," in *A Thousand Years of West African History: A Handbook*, ed. by J.F. Ade. Ajayi and Ian Espie (Ibadan and London: Ibadan University Press, and Thomas Nelson and Sons, 1965, 1969); and the standard histories. However, "the fact is that we simply do not know the racial history of the Negro," Sir Mortimer Wheeler concludes in his "First Light," in *The Dawn of African History*, ed. Roland Oliver, 2d ed. (New York: Oxford University Press, 1968), pp. 5f.; J. Desmond Clark offers the same judgment in almost identical words, in his *Prehistory of Africa*, p. 165. Jean Hiernaux, in *The People of Africa* (New York: Charles Scribner's Sons, 1974), argues for the essential unity of all sub-Saharan peoples, and suggests that the Pygmies differ from other groups only through long isolation and special environment.

2. Edward B. Tylor, *Religion in Primitive Culture* (Part II of *Primitive Culture*) (New York: Harper & Brothers, 1958), pp. 1-9. First published in 1871.

3. Mary Douglas, *Natural Symbols: Explorations in Cosmology* (New York: Pantheon Books, 1970), pp. 14-18, 36, etc.; on p. 16, she writes: "Pygmies move freely in an uncharted, unsystematised, unbounded social world. I maintain that it would be impossible for them to develop a sacramental religion." By "sacramental religion" Douglas seems to refer to spiritualities emphasizing ritual and magic, and using condensed, multi-reference symbols to define realms and categories.

4. Ironically, both researchers reproach each other for studying the most acculturated bands or ideas, each reserving to himself the "real" Mbuti. Colin Turnbull, *The Mbuti Pygmies: An Ethnographic Survey*; Anthropological Papers, American Museum of Natural History, Vol. 50, pt. 3 (New York: Natural History Press, 1965), says Schebesta failed to distinquish between Bantu and Pygmy myths, and did not notice the adversary relationship between Pygmy bands and their Bantu patrons. Schebesta retorts in "Colin Turnbull und die Erforschung der Bambuti-Pygmäen," *Anthropos* 58 (1963), that not only is this not true, but that Turnbull for his part studied one of the more acculturated Pygmy bands, living near to a European mission and trading station on territory bordering a major road; as a result this band lacked the rich mythology Schebesta found elsewhere.

5. Colin Turnbull, *Wayward Servants* (Garden City, N.Y.: Natural History Press, 1965), p. 252.

6. Ibid.

7. Ibid., p. 250.

8. It is striking how universal is the association of these dark, cold beings of the winter with bonfire celebrations or festivals of light. The ancestral dead who are guided to their children at night by lights in the Divali festival rites of India or the Bon celebrations of Japan and China, or even in the Milamala harvest rites of the Trobriand Islanders, remind us irresistably of St. Nick and his trolls who are guided to Christmas eve homes in Scandinavia and the United States by brilliantly illuminated trees and candles in the windows. Like other fire-loving trolls or dwarfs, the Christmas visitors are said to reside in the cold, dark north, or even with other underground beings in caves. Scandinavian folk beliefs link these trolls to the dead.

9. Turnbull, *Wayward Servants*, p. 252 n. 2.

10. Paul Schebesta, *Die Bambuti-Pygmäen vom Ituri, Ergebnisse Zweier Forschungsreisen zu de Zentralafrikanischen Pygmäen*; Bd. II, Teil III: *Die Religion*, Mémoires, Institut Royal Colonial Belge, Section des Sciences Morales et Politiques, Coll.-in-4°, IV (Brussels: Georges van Campenhout, 1950), pp. 155-67, etc. This work will hereinafter be referred to as *Die Religion*.

11.   Ibid., pp. 95, 161-62, 213.

12.   The "Eastern Pygmies" are quoted as saying that when Waka, the supreme being, takes a person in death, "Alors nous enterrons bien pas celui dont il a pris la vie, et ceux qui restent vont plus loin, car il est dangereux de rester sous le regard de Dieu, . . ." according to Mgr. Le Roy as reported in P. Trilles, *L'Âme du Pygmée d'Afrique* (Paris: Les Éditions du Cerf, 1945), p. 139.

13.   This paragraph draws on Turnbull, *Wayward Servants*, pp. 129-31.

14.   Ibid., p. 253.

15.   Schebesta, *Die Religion*, pp. 52f., 188f.

16.   Ibid., pp. 19-20, 48-49; a popularized English version is in Paul Schebesta, *Revisiting My Pygmy Hosts* (London: Hutchinson, 1936).

17.   Schebesta, *Die Religion*, pp. 28-29, 36, 52, 194, 201, 211; Trilles, *L'Âme du Pygmée d'Afrique*, p. 171.

18.   Lewis Cotlow, *In Search of the Primitive* (Boston: Little, Brown & Co., 1966), pp. 50-55. Cotlow gives many valuable ethnological details missing in the more sentimental accounts of Turnbull and Schebesta. This is all the more striking, since the source for some of these details (or explanations of them) was discussion with Turnbull, cited by Cotlow.

19.   Cf. Luc de Heusch, *Le roi ivre* (Paris: Gallimard, 1972), pp. 72-73, etc.

20.   Schebesta, *Die Religion*, pp. 16-20, 31, 41-42, 59-66, 203-12.

21.   Ibid., pp. 67, 72.

22.   Ibid., pp. 105ff.

23.   Colin M. Turnbull, *The Forest People: A Study of the Pygmies of the Congo*, The Natural History Library, Anchor Books (Garden City, New York: Doubleday and Co., in cooperation with the American Museum of Natural History, 1962), p. 96.

24.   Turnbull, *Wayward Servants*, p. 156.

25.   Leo Frobenius, *Das unbekannte Afrika* (Munich: Oscar Beck, 1923), pp. 34-35.

26.   Cf. Johannes Maringer, *The Gods of Prehistoric Man*, trans. Mary Ilford (New York: Alfred A. Knopf, 1960), pp. 90-135, etc.; Joseph Campbell, *The Masks of God: Primitive Mythology* (New York: The Viking Press, 1959), pp. 295-98.

27.   Hermann Baumann, *Das Doppelte Geschlecht* (Berlin: Dietrich Reimer, 1955).

28.   Probably the most striking demonstration of this in recent years is Alexander Marshack, *The Roots of Civilization: A Study of Prehistoric Cognition* (New York: McGraw-Hill, 1972), and the same author's "Cognitive Aspects of Upper Paleolithic Engraving," *Current Anthropology* 13 (1972): 445-61.

29.   The details of this discussion are from Schebesta, *Die Religion*, pp. 108ff.

30.   Such practices are apparently of amazing antiquity, being reported not only of the Ituri Mbuti, but also for the Pygmies of the Gabon-Cameroons area and even of non-African Pygmies like the Semang Negritoes and the Phillipine Negritoes. See Trilles, *L'Âme du Pygmée d'Afrique*, pp. 137f.; Paul Schebesta, *Among the Forest Dwarfs of Malaya* (London: Hutchinson, 1929), pp. 87f., 192; Kenton Stewart, *Pygmies and Dream Giants* (New York: Knopf, 1954); Rodney Needham, "Blood, Thunder and Mockery of Animals," in *Myth and Cosmos: Readings in Mythology and Symbolism*, ed. by John Middleton, American Museum Sourcebooks in Anthropology, Q5 (Garden City, New York: Natural History Press for the American Museum of Natural History, 1967), pp. 271-85. Needham, in the work cited, assumes that this ritual is peculiar to the Malayan Negritoes and the Borneo Penan among whom he had done field work. But it is not only found among the Pygmies of Zaire, but survives in part also among neighboring central Bantu peoples (perhaps borrowed from the Pygmies). The Shagana-Tonga, for example, use a certain kind of flute to quiet a storm, with prayers to protest their innocence directed to the supreme being. Thunder and lightning cause the Ila of Zambia to retreat to their huts and pray penitently to God as they offer special medicines in their fires to mollify his wrath; like the Pygmies (some of whom are located in their area) they believe that community dissension and individual crimes bring cosmic retribution of this sort. The Nuer of the Sudan do not sacrifice their own blood to God during

storms, it is true, but they do offer up in bloody sacrifices a victim from the cattle that symbolically participate in their own identity. See Edwin W. Smith, "The Idea of God among South African Peoples," in *African Ideas of God: A Symposium*, 2d ed. (London: Edinburgh House Press, 1961), pp. 114, 109; E.E. Evans-Pritchard, *Nuer Religion* (Oxford: Clarendon Press, 1956), pp. 53-60.

31. Turnbull, *Wayward Servants*, p. 154.

32. Theorists have hotly debated the sociological significance of blood brotherhood rites for several generations, on the largely *a priori* assumption that this widespread Bantu practice is a survival of the most ancient "magical" concepts of community. See, for a review and discussion of one Zaire Bantu culture's version of these rites, E.E. Evans-Pritchard, "Zande Blood-Brotherhood," in *Social Anthropology and Other Essays* (New York: Free Press, 1962). The central Bantu commonly use scarification with ashes to heal the sick and in initiations. Among several peoples, especially the Lunda and Luvale cultures, these practices have blossomed into an elaborate cult called *ihamba, chihamba*, or related forms. See Barrie Reynolds, *Magic, Divination and Witchcraft among the Barotse of Northern Rhodesia*, Robin Series III (Berkeley: University of California Press, 1963), pp. 63f., 133-38, etc., and Victor Turner, *Drums of Affliction* (Oxford: Clarendon Press for the International African Institute, 1968). For a general treatment, see H. Tegnaeus, *Blood-Brothers: An Ethno-Sociological Study of the Institution of Blood-Brotherhood with Special Reference to Africa*, The Ethnographical Museum of Sweden, N.P. 10 (Stockholm: Ethnographical Museum of Sweden, 1952).

33. Lorna Marshall, "The !Kung Bushmen of the Kalahari Desert," in *Peoples of Africa*, ed. J.L. Gibbs, Jr. (New York: Holt, Rinehart & Winston, 1965), p. 265.

34. Schebesta, *Die Religion*, p. 111.

35. Turnbull, *Wayward Servants*, p. 155.

36. Schebesta, *Die Religion*, pp. 111-12, and Schebesta, *Die Bambuti-Pygmäen vom Ituri: Ethnographie der Ituri-Bambuti, Die Wirtschaft*; Mémoires, Institut Royal Colonial Belge, Section des Sciences Morales et Politique, Coll.-in-4°, IV; Bd. II, Teil 1 (Brussels: Georges van Campenhout, 1941), pp. 113-14; the latter work will hereinafter be referred to as "Schebesta, *Die Wirtschaft*."

37. Paul Schebesta, *Die Bambuti-Pygmäen vom Ituri: Ethnographie der Ituri-Bambuti, Das Soziale Leben*; Mémoires, Institut Royal Colonial Belge, Section des Sciences Morales et Politique, Coll.-in-4°, IV; Bd. II, Teil 2 (Brussels: Georges van Campenhout, 1948), pp. 355-56; hereinafter cited as "Schebesta, *Das Soziale Leben*."

38. Ibid., and also Turnbull, *Wayward Servants*, p. 126.

39. For instances of these taboos on sexuality and on women in relation to the hunt, see Sir James Frazer, *Taboo and the Perils of the Soul; The Golden Bough, A Study in Magic and Religion*, 3rd ed., Part II (London: Macmillan and Co., Ltd., 1927), pp. 190-208.

40. This view of the carnal led, as is well-known, to a remarkably strong misogynist tradition among Christian Church Fathers and theologians. See for discussion, Rosemary Radford Ruether, "Misogynism and Virginal Feminism in the Fathers of the Church," in *Religion and Sexism: Images of Woman in the Jewish and Christian Traditions*, ed. by Rosemary Radford Ruether (New York: Simon and Schuster, 1974), and D.S. Bailey, *Sexual Relations in Christian Thought* (New York: Harper & Brothers, 1959). Precisely the same virulent misogynism appears in the Hindu ascetical literature, even in the writings devoted to the cult of the mother goddess; for a striking instance, see Cheever Mackenzie Brown, *God as Mother: A Feminine Theology in India; An Historical and Theological Study of the Brahmavaivarta Purāna* (Hartford, Vermont: Claude Stark & Co., 1974), pp. 181ff.

41. Taboos will be discussed in further detail in a later chapter; for a general review of theories on taboo and a preliminary phenomenology, see my "Taboo and the Divine Order," *Journal of the American Academy of Religion* 42, no. 3 (September 1974): 482-504.

42. Schebesta, *Die Wirtschaft*, p. 114; Turnbull, *Wayward Servants*, p. 156.

43. Turnbull, *Wayward Servants*, pp. 278 ff.

44. Ibid., p. 317.

45. Ibid., p. 134. The *elima* is second only to the *molimo* in importance, since the male youth have no formal initiation other than their role in the *elima*. The village initiation of the boys of course also serves as a partial substitute.

46. Ibid., pp. 137-39; as well as the same author's "The Elima: A Premarital Festival among the Bambuti Pygmies," *Zaire* 14, no. 2-3 (1960): 175-92, and *The Forest People*, pp. 188-206. It is interesting that a rather similar hunting and sexual symbolism accompanies the initiation of girls among the Kalahari Bushmen, as described by Marshall, "The !Kung Bushmen. . . ," p. 265. Women's initiations are often the most important initiation ceremonies for small hunting-and-gathering bands.

47. Turnbull, *Wayward Servants*, p. 170.

48. Ibid., pp. 172-73.

49. Schebesta, *Die Religion*, p. 34.

50. H.R. Hayes, *In the Beginning: Early Man and His Gods* (New York: G.P. Putnam's Sons, 1963), p. 290.

51. Schebesta, *Die Religion*, pp. 51-52, 193.

Chapter 2

Renewal of Time in Mbuti Religion

Harmony is the deepest longing of the Mbuti. They seek it on a positively cosmic scale. But what is their response when the transcendental order they love is disrupted, when negative liminality threatens to destroy them? The Mbuti have found the answer in extending the transformative logic of the morning fire ceremony; since within it all the universe is condensed, it can provide the terms for dealing with disorder on both the human and the cosmic levels. On the human level, the Mbuti faced possibly their greatest historical challenge in tens of thousands of years when the Bantu peoples penetrated the rain forest and settled there. On the cosmic level, the Mbuti have had from the beginning of time to deal with death, epidemic, earthquake, and perhaps even famine.

The intrusion of the Bantu peoples over the past two millennia into the territories of the Mbuti, and their clearing of the forest for settlement and farming, presented the Pygmies with a serious crisis. The villagers were far more numerous and technologically advanced, and their hardy warriors would surely not brook any opposition. Either surrender (and enslavement, intermarriage, or death) or resistance to the bitter end would seem to be the only options open to the forest hunters; either way the end of Pygmy culture would seem certain. The surprisingly ingenious Mbuti answer, entirely in accord with their traditional modes of thought, shows that a third possibility existed. They applied the hunting-wooing-sorcery-prayer paradigm:

> The Mbuti in their own parlance regard the village as a place to hunt and eat. They say, "in the forest we hunt, in the village we hunt," . . . also, equally frequently, "We eat animals, we eat villagers." . . . Hunting calls for trickiness, cunning, using tactics appropriate to the game, often imitating it and assimilating, temporarily, its personality. Such tactics in the village include bringing in a certain amount of meat as bait, performing some service, and occupying a generally subservient position. When asked why he forced his son to take part in the *nkumbi* initiation at the hands of the villagers, one father said, simply, "When we hunt elephants, we cover ourselves with elephant dung."[1]

During the nkumbi initiation Bantu and Mbuti children are made to undergo painful ordeals and even scarifications together (though the Mbuti fathers try to shield their children from the more arbitrary trials and

41

generally treat the whole thing lightly). From the viewpoint of the Bantu patrons, the Pygmy youngsters who undergo these experiences with their own children are bound by this into a quasi kinship with the villagers. It is a kind of adoption into the village clans, made much smoother by the desire of the Bantu to be on good terms with the aboriginal spirits of the forest with which they believe the Pygmies commune. However, as the tales of Cinderella ought to remind us, not every stepchild is treated equally with one's own, and the villagers tend to view their Pygmy "kin" as subservient clients who are obliged to work in the plantations, hunt food in the fearsome forests, and run errands. From the Pygmies' side, on the other hand, the new tie with the villagers is very much analogous to the elephant ash he carries with him into the hunt, buried under his skin. It is used to win over, charm, even hypnotize the quarry, and force him to give up much food and gifts. Quite logically, therefore, when the villagers give "their" Pygmies marijuana to bind them more closely to them, the forest hunters choose to smoke it especially in the morning ritual before going out on elephant hunts.[2]

We have seen already that one of the aspects of the Pygmy practice of assimilating parts of the game, the beloved, or the sorcery victim into the flesh is the assumption that the hunter can thereby consciously control the relatively unconscious or unaware prey. From this comes his power to hypnotize. In relation to the villagers, the correlate of this is the Mbuti assumption that the villagers are less truly cultured, more animal-like or "savage" than the Pygmies.

Latent, therefore, in the Mbuti's childlike subservience to the villagers is a mocking condescension, often expressed in jokes about the villagers. Humor, too, is a defensive technique like the morning fire ceremony that disarms the "other" by humbling oneself to the other's expectations. The Mbuti seek to avoid the burdensome aspects of their subordinate village status by cultivating a reputation among the Bantu as clowns and wastrels, as being as unreliable as carefree children and buffoons. Not too much can be expected of them, the Bantu say, with irritation or half-amused resignation. The Pygmies, besides, are mere savages and creatures of the forest in the Bantu estimation. So there is an ironical reciprocity to these attitudes. Just as the villagers view the forest as a genuine wilderness filled with dangerous animals and terrifying spirits and monsters, the Epulu regard the villages as highly dangerous realms, "hot" (*mota:*.hot, powerful, disordered and even demonic), where sacred things cannot be done or spoken. When they must practice the *molimo*, their major religious festival, the Epulu move far away from the village into their beloved fresh forest glades. The Bantu fear of the forest amuses and gratifies the Pygmies. It gives them a place to which they can escape the villagers' demands, yet enables them to act as irreplaceable intermediaries between the villagers and the forest. The villagers need their Pygmy hunters. Yet the Epulu know that actually it is the sweltering village, steaming in the unshielded heat of the sun, that is really mota. This is not so much caused by the sun, the stagnant water, or the rich smells of the village clearings, as it is by the sorcery the inhabitants supposedly practice. Villagers often suspect each other of sorcery, and heated quarrels break out from time to time. This, say the Pygmies, is just "noise," harmful to the deity and hateful to it. If any untoward things happen to any of their own band members, the Epulu are quick to invoke the same village sorcery. They refuse to entertain aloud the thought that one of their own number might be a sorcerer; even if the suspicion is strong enough to lead them to avoid quietly one of the band, they will publicly blame the village. Thus, ironically, the village disorder preserves the harmony and quiet so essential to the forest band. To use an appropriate metaphor, the Epulu use the ash of the fiery village to harmonize themselves with the forest Deity.[3]

THE MOLIMO FESTIVAL AND THE TWO MODES OF LIMINALITY

If the morning fire ceremony is a "threshold" rite of the sort made familiar through van Gennep's *The Rites of Passage*,[4] the molimo festival, picking up and reweaving many of the same symbolisms, may be called a grand threshold rite, guiding the Epulu through the darkness of death, illness, bad hunting, or disunity in the band into the renewed light of the divine order. All of these symptoms of negative liminality, or the presence of the demonic, are signals to prepare for molimo celebrations.[5] Disorder in the camp is an extension or even a cause of disunity in the divine; therefore, restoring the rift between one Epulu and another, between camp and forest, and finally and most audaciously between aspects of God himself are all aimed for simultaneously in the molimo.

A fundamental assumption of the molimo is that the normal order of life is a positive good. Morality exists in the very fabric of things. God cares for man and will restore normalcy if only man fervently entreats him. If anything bad happens, one common explanation is that it is simply the result of insufficiently alert consciousness, on God's part and man's. The normative order must be made explicit again; meaning must triumph over meaninglessness. God was asleep, so things went wrong. Order implies clear awareness. Chaos is a primordial nescience or unconsciousness. As one elder of the Epulu explained to Turnbull:

> Normally everything goes well in our world. But at night when we are sleeping, sometimes things go wrong, because we are not awake to stop them from going

wrong. Army ants invade the camp; leopards may come in and steal a hunting dog or even a child. If we were awake these things would not happen. So when something big goes wrong, like illness or bad hunting or death, it must be because the forest is sleeping and not looking after its children. So what do we do? We wake it up by singing to it, and we do this because we want it to awaken happy. Then everything will be well and good again. So when our world is going well then also we sing to the forest because we want it to share our happiness.[6]

Among the Mbuti, despite their carefree buoyancy, there is noticeable a great stress on conscious control, or at least a suspicion of states that involve loss of self-control. Perhaps extrapolating from themselves (as is suggested in the passage quoted above), they assume that for God, too, confusion and demonic disorder are only the consequences of falling asleep. In any case, one could hardly hope for a more explicit statement that there is something in the nature of consciousness itself that is essentially bound up with the divine. The mystical assumptions underlying this ritual view of life are perhaps not after all so far from those of Indian and Tibetan yogins.

But unlike the mystic's ecstatic abstraction from the world, the Mbuti see spirituality and fullness of being in the normalcy of perception and form. Joy is normalcy. God is benevolently near when normative structure prevails; the Epulu call such harmony "quiet": "Joy . . . is *ekimi mota,* or 'powerful quietness.' Joy is an intensification of quietness and is brought about by the occurrence of the norm."[7]

Disorder, however, is "noise," *akami.* Since God is involved in all life, "noise" in the camp is disorder in God as well; it torments him, and he punishes those that cause it. Disasters befalling the band are divine punishment for nonnormative behavior in the group—an alternative theory used often in addition to appeals to God's inattention or to village sorcery. Especially disobedience by youths, quarrels between spouses, adultery, incest, hoarding, or bragging, all actions that divide the group passionately, are likely to generate the wrath of God. Chaos will then break loose upon the entire universe just as it has already in the camp. Terrifying electrical storms, sometimes killing the guilty, or earthquakes demonstrate God's rage (or his "sleep," this phraseology assuming Pygmy innocence and God's mercy—unknown to him his servant spirits have gotten out of hand). However understood, such catastrophes show clearly that God has withdrawn himself from his children. The animals disappear from the forest (bringing poor hunting), illness or death strikes, and the Mbuti feel themselves totally isolated (as the unfortunate, the ill, and the dying do in all cultures). They say that God has "closed the forest" to them.[8]

The thunder of the storms may be the maddened trumpeting of the giant elephant thought by many bands to be the Master of Animals. His back holds up the sky, and his male powers assure the fecundity of all elephant herds; in some myths, this monster Piombo or Pi-obo maliciously trampled to death the ancestor of all Pygmies.[9] Or the thunder may be the voice of the rainbow serpent, who from her waterfall caves or watery abode releases the stored animals to the hunters, or blasts her unwary victims with a single glance of her mysterious body. The chameleon (multi-hued like the rainbow) may be her gentler side.[10] Ordinarily God restrains such monsters as these, but when akami disturbs him, he releases them to punish the evildoers.

The contrast between the chameleon and the rainbow serpent (or python-snake, as it is usually thought to be) is significant for an understanding of the Mbuti relationship to the divine. In its benevolent form the holy appears to man in diminutive size, as a frail little creature, helpful and kind. In terms of body space, the Mbuti immediately feel secure mastery in its presence. The chameleon can be easily incorporated into a Mbuti-sized world without loss of proportion. It merely offers orientation within that world, directing the hunter to the game. But when reciprocity between man and God is destroyed by "noise," the divine swells out of control and splits the Mbuti world asunder. Before the terrific elephant, vast rainbow, or python, it is the Mbuti who is diminished and incorporated into a nonhuman space. Human proportion is lost. (We can extend these remarks to the general tendency in the history of religions to indicate nonhuman holiness by outsized temples, cathedrals, pyramids, and even palaces, while the preservation of a human holiness and proportion is indicated by humbler shrines. Ritual architecture has its own language.)

The sense of displacement by the ferocity of the divine and the loss of control over one's own existence are also indicated by the first preparations for the molimo festival. When akami builds to a peak, the Mbuti acknowledge the presence of negative liminality by moving camp. If a death has signaled the need for a molimo, the corpse is hastily buried and its hut pulled down over it before the camp and its spiritual disorder is abandoned. Not fear of the dead, but rather fear of the too-close impingement of the disordered side of deity, dictates this flight. It is also common to blame this disorder on the villagers and their sorcery and to leave the vicinity of the villages.[11]

Following a death, and until the new camp is established and the preparations for the molimo completed, it is permissible for the women of the band to give vent to all their sorrow in keening laments and gashing themselves. The men are not expected to expose their natural feelings so freely, however, and when the molimo itself commences it is forbidden for anyone to demonstrate any sorrow. The time has come to rejoice the forest, and a certain gaiety is obligatory.

It is necessary to have a good supply of meat before the molimo can begin, and at the new campsite the men are constantly going out to hunt; one common reason for holding the molimo is poor hunting, so ready availability of game is not only necessary for the celebrants but is also a propitious sign of the renewed intimacy with the forest deity. When sufficient food is gathered and all of the shelters are up in the clearing, the molimo begins. For sometimes over a month, the days to come will be filled with concentrated hunting and the nights with continuous singing.

As was remarked earlier, the highest aspiration of the Epulu is to exist in a state of joyful normalcy; for them, this state is expressed in song, and in a happy Mbuti camp there is always the sound of singing and laughter. The dances fill hours—acting out the hunt, recounting quarrels or anecdotes, dramatizing myths, or simply in play. Mutuality is what sustains this state of contentment, and when it breaks down between themselves and their "father" the forest-deity, it is necessary to reestablish it through even more vigorous expressions. Turnbull conceives of the constant singing as the expression of the natural spontaneity and joyfulness of the Epulu, but his own material shows a darker side, a compulsory aspect to this celebration in the face of death, dissension, and disease. The natural sorrow all band members must feel on the death of one of their number is forbidden expression once the molimo begins. Anyone among the men who succumbs to the exhaustion all feel from hunting throughout the day and singing throughout the night, and falls asleep during the nightly reception of the molimo monster, will be killed.[12] Of course, this is probably one of the rhetorical flourishes the Mbuti delight in, but it certainly suggests a demonic side to the beloved molimo spirit. It also evidences the high value given to consciousness. Demonic chaos is equated to sleep. This attitude is in sharp contrast to the tendency in many other cultures to respond to misfortune by seeking refuge in possession trance, alcohol, or drugs.

The songs of the festival therefore court the divine; many center on sexual metaphors. Soothed by the loving songs, the forest will receive the hunters again like a woman opens to her husband, generating life, light, and food to replace death and hunger. Renewing the fires at the heart of reality, the molimo singers peal out their love into the endless darkness beneath the canopy of trees, interfusing the wilderness with joy and harmony.

The molimo symbolisms are astonishingly similar to those of the "high" world religions that govern festivals of midwinter. Like Christmas, Chanukah, the Hindu Divali and the Bon festival of east Asia, fires burn throughout the night to celebrate the triumph of light over darkness and life over death. We can now trace these winter solstice festivals back to Paleolithic times.[13] The molimo celebration of the fundamental graciousness of reality is a version of one of the most ancient rituals of mankind.

Throughout the night, the molimo spirit trumpets back the songs of the men, echoing first from one side, then from the other, sometimes from afar, sometimes from just beyond the flickering fires. Weaving man and divine into unity, the spirit fills the world with song. The trumpet seems to be performing a double role in the ritual, representing sometimes the forest to the little band, sometimes (or perhaps simultaneously) the band to the forest. Occasionally, the monster-trumpet penetrates right into the circle of light around the fire, the trumpet being borne by youths into the flames themselves to be "warmed," and for the same purpose rubbed on the chests of the singers or passed over their heads. Thus the spirit comes to be domesticated and brought into warm fellowship, and at the same time mankind is purified and transfused with divinity. During this time, however, the women and children must stay in the huts and never even glance at the creature roaming so near by: for them to see it means their death. At dawn the "vengeful" molimo makes one last raid for the night before withdrawing before the sun (thus at this point showing its kinship with the evil beings of the night and the morning dew); the women are often surprised as they have begun to emerge from the huts, and the roars of the monster sends them scurrying back into their shelters accompanied by male laughter. But the molimo "animal" is violent and harsh now, tearing through the camp, surrounded by wild, exhausted youths, ripping down leaves from each of the huts in a mock battle. Troublemakers may have their shelters utterly destroyed in this punitive attack.

We see in these contradictory actions something of the complexity of the molimo spirit. The ferocity of the spirit is most evident just before dawn, as the light is about to triumph over the night, but during the darkest hours the molimo is caressing and kindly. Always it stands for positive liminality and the integral totality of divinity, controlling and subduing on behalf of man the demonic powers of darkness when they are seemingly most intense, chastising man when all nature at dawn seems to be welcoming him. To the uncontrolled extremes of the premolimo condition, in which unmitigated hostility warred with culture, the spirit brings modulated mercy and justice, mutuality, *ekimi*: Articulated structure is extended into the very heart of the liminal.

The concluding nights of the molimo give a fascinating demonstration of this process. Only then do the women begin to take an active role in the nightly rituals of the festival, as if displacing the molimo spirit from the focus of life. One evening, as Turnbull looked on in astonishment, the old lady who was the leader of the women's initiation edged out of the group of Epulu women and danced up to the men around the fire. Though supposedly women were forbidden on pain of death to do this, the men did not even look up, and went on singing as though she were not there. As they sang, she danced around them and looped net twine over them, "binding" them. They were only released after "paying" her to release the molimo: she had tied it up, yet almost as if she had rights of ownership to it the men *paid* her for it. Then she and younger unmarried girls did a dance around the fire apparently symbolic of wild animals fleeing through the forest.[14] The next evening, the girls came out in the same way and remained dancing around the fire when night fell instead of retiring to their huts before the molimo spirit. The old lady finally approached the fire itself, with gestures Turnbull interpreted as filled with hesitation, envy, spite, and desire, until she knelt down and actually crawled directly into the flames, still dancing! In its midst she stood up, dancing wildly, scattering the logs in all directions. The sacred molimo fires, lit at the beginning of the festival and jealously guarded throughout the long days and nights since, were in danger of going out.

> The men hurriedly gathered up the burning logs and rebuilt the fire, dancing a wild erotic dance around it as though the sexual act were fanning the flames to life. Some of them danced right through the fire in this way, apparently without burning their feet. On other occasions I have seen them during a *molimo* dance pick out a red hot coal and handle it, even putting it in the mouth, until it has ceased to glow.[15]

The old woman was not so easily defeated, however; the molimo spirit that charmed the men and to which they made love advances during the nights, neglecting their wives (chastity is required throughout the molimo), now had a determined rival. Again and again the woman danced back into the fire, scattering it, and again and again it was built up out of the erotic heat of the men. Finally a younger girl joined the woman's dance. The girl was Kondabate, married but still childless, the belle of the camp, who was already being trained by Kelemoke, the older woman, to lead the elima and other women's ceremonies. They danced in perfect unison, even to the twitching of their heads, through a complex hour-long scenario that used twine, knives, and other aids to imitate animals circling outside the fire, just as animals in fact did circle outside the camp during the nights. The dancing evinced long preparation, and Turnbull received another shock when he noticed that all the women of the camp were now gathered nearby, singing with perfect familiarity the "forbidden" molimo songs, even leading the singing of the men. Again there came the hesitant approach to the fire, and the old woman plunged into the flames, in full trance, the flames licking her waist. She stood there for a time, legs apart and straddling the flames, then whirled and scattered the fire amongst the men encircling the fire. And again the men danced the fire to life. Eventually, the women retired into their shelters, and the men rearranged themselves for a night of song as if nothing had happened.[16] During the few nights remaining to the festival the strange drama was frequently repeated.

Turnbull confesses his confusion over the meaning of these rites, but adds:

> There is an old legend that once it was the women who "owned" the molimo, but the men stole it from them and ever since the women have been forbidden to see it. Perhaps this was a way of reminding the men of the origin of their molimo. There is another old legend which tells that it was a woman who stole fire from the chimpanzees or, in yet another version, from the great forest spirit. Perhaps the dance had been in imitation of this. I did not understand it by any means, but somehow it seemed to make sense.[17]

We would certainly like to have more information about those "old legends" that Turnbull mentions so casually, but we can agree that there is a latent logic to the constant juxtaposition of fire, sexuality, animals, light, and dark in the final nights of the molimo. It is clear that women have proprietary rights over the molimo and can absorb it into themselves as if fusing with it (old Kelemoke opened herself to the flames when she straddled them, taking their heat into her sexual parts). The men had to "pay" the women for the use of the molimo. And the chastity taboos also point to an identity of molimo spirit and women.

The final dance of the molimo brings all of these themes into yet clearer focus. In it, the molimo trumpet repeats exactly the motions of Kelemoke and her assistant, as if expressing the same drama on a different level. After especially intense singing (the women and children again hidden away), the trumpet invaded the camp, trying to attack and destroy the fire before the dawn came. The youths battled the spirit, breaking hot coals over the trumpet. Sparks flew everywhere. Just as dawn came the molimo reached the fire and scattered it, with the youths helping now to scatter and trample the fire. Then the molimo retired to the forest for the last time.[18] Human and nonhuman finally took their proper places in the divine order, harmonized with each other but apart. Life had replaced death. The molimo, we can say, voluntarily withdrew behind the women, permitting them to come forth anew as the conservers of the ordinary round of life.

The metaphoric participation of the women in the molimo monster is despite everything an astonishing fact, for it seems to contradict much else characteristic of the molimo monster. Women are residents of the camp, the molimo of the deep forest; women are active at day, while the spirit is abroad only at night; and women are forbidden to see the monster or to keep their hearth fires independent of the molimo fire. Moreover, the molimo itself is often identified explicitly as male, over against the female fires. As Turnbull notes:

> Fire is primarily connected with women: The hearth is often referred to as the vagina; the association of fire and blood is considered particularly dangerous.

Thus the association of the male molimo trumpet with the fire and ashes gives the trumpet phallic significance in this context.[19]

In this sense, when the trumpet penetrates the camp molimo fire it is engaging in symbolic intercourse, fecundating the domestic fires that at the end of the festival will be absorbed into the realm of women. But at the same time fire is associated with the molimo monster itself. It is said to breath flames of fire; fire is its element. Like the village, the molimo spirit is mota: hot, dangerous, even vengeful. Rituals right at the start of the festival underline the identity of fire and molimo spirit. Turnbull describes vividly how, during the first night of the festival, a procession of youths emerged from the obscurity of the forest into the light of the new molimo fires. At their head was a youth holding burning embers in each hand, raising and lowering them alternatively. The dancer gave the impression in the darkness of "some monster with fiery feet taking gigantic steps, scattering a path of glowing sparks in its wake."[20] Behind the leader came a group carrying a seven-foot-long bamboo trumpet on their shoulders, with the most skilled singer blowing into it at the far end. Passing majestically through the entire camp, the trumpet came at last to the central fire and was handed through it again and again, circling over the heads of those sitting there. The young men leapt about and performed erotic dances around the fire, miming a myth of the theft and "taming" of elemental fire to human use, while the older men around the fire sang vigorously the molimo's praises. One youth would snatch a burning log and make off with it only to be pursued, caught and dragged back by another. So the primeval fire of the divine (the molimo spirit) was ritually brought within the camp circle and assimilated into the human, tamed, and controlled fire.

The beginning of the festival seems to suggest the phallic aspect of the molimo; the end equates the molimo with the women. Actually, we may have the answer to the nature of the spirit in concluding that it is both male and female. In almost every area of symbolism the molimo is the unity of opposites. For example, despite the molimo's apparent unity with the fire, it confronts man as an emissary from the cold, dark, wet regions of existence. Between molimo festivals the trumpets (there may be several) are kept very deep in the forest, hidden within particularly dark and dense groves high up in the branches. Upon lowering the trumpet from its intermediary (rainbowlike) position between earth and sky, the hunters conduct it back to camp, immersing it in the waters of every stream they pass. "The youths said in a joking way, 'The animal is drinking—if it drinks it sings better.' "[21] After each night's use, the trumpet is submerged upstream from the camp, to cool its fiery heat. We recall in this connection the headwaters residence of the monster python rainbow serpent that the trumpet is supposed to represent. Yet the rainbow is made of fire, and needs the replenishment that the celebrants offer it from the camp fires. Coals from the blaze are placed in the trumpet's "mouth" while the trumpeteer simultaneously gives the most powerful blasts he can. The flying sparks give the impression of a fire-breathing monster. Supplying the monster with the more domesticated heat from the campfires can only moderate the savagery of this strange being that is a mixture of water and fire, of heaven and earth, and of hot and cold. To compound confusion, from the trumpet's mouth comes the roar of a leopard, perhaps followed immediately by the trumpeting of an elephant. Sometimes it bellows threats from the night darkness and at other times repeats the melodies of the songs the men sing as if forwarding them even deeper into the mysterious depths of the universe. Is it a monster agent from God or a spokesman for mankind? The spirit combines all opposites and therefore is the best guide to reconciliation. It builds up the campfire and society through extension from its own *coincidentia oppositorum*.

The monster spirit represents primordial modes of being, existing prior to the universe of order; its dominance in the molimo expresses the spiritual consequences of the social breakdown, death, or despair that precipitated the festival. In light of this primordial liminality of the spirit, it is obvious why there is such confusion concerning its sexual allegiance. Turnbull writes of the phallicism of the trumpet, but the rites make very clear that more is involved. At evening appearances, one youth may sing into one end of the trumpet, while at the other a dancer may mime a ritual intercourse with the coal-filled "mouth." Here the coals are equated to the fire in the womb of women—the same fire that binds women so closely to the domestic hearth. The uterine fire, stoked by intercourse, produces live flesh, human children; the campfire produces cooked flesh, food; while the inner heat of the forest produces universal life, plants, and animals. The dancing youths therefore are not only intensifying the responsiveness of the divine to humanity, but are also increasing the game animals, and in addition are assuring the fertility of their women. This is truly cosmic love!

The polarity within the spirit is therefore only being reproduced on the human level when the Mbuti engage in erotic dances together, in tugs-of-war between the sexes, and in constant sexual bantering. The obligatory chastity makes clear the purely symbolic level of these acts. But the climax of the struggle, and at the same time the definitive victory of the women, comes at the very end of the festival when the women scatter and destroy the molimo fires. Women are the divine within the sphere of human society. Though one sex, they are the source of both. Their triumph is that of the molimo, despite the seeming war between them and the molimo spirit for the men's affections. The whole ceremony is to normalize the universe, creating out of extreme antitheses the gentler modulations of a humanized divine order. The polarities of man and divine give away, or flow into, the more fruitful encounter of the sexes.

The molimo is, then, a kind of meditation in action on the meaning of chaos. Disorder is seen to have two poles; one within the human heart, and the other in the furthest reaches of being itself. The Mbuti must transform their own dangerous, almost uncontrollable, passions into a yearning for peace and harmony, if they expect the wildness at the center of the universe to respond and to be subdued by divine love. The only way to conquer the violence within is by submitting to the transcendental source of order that dwells beyond, who is encountered as the forest diety. The use of sexual metaphors weaves these two extremes together. All passion is directed to the divine through the molimo spirit; the relation of mankind and spirit is sexualized, and in this way the raw desires are disciplined and ritualized. Sensuality is made spiritual. But at the same time, spirituality is made part of the sensual; meaning permeates the instinctual life, and the desires are brought under sacred norms. The result is *ekimi mota*, "intense (hot) quiet," joy in one's innermost being, which is the goal of life for the Mbuti and which can only be expressed in joyful songs of gratitude to the forest deity, dances, and a deep-welling tranquility felt as one goes about one's daily tasks.

The ritual of the molimo ends in making a ritual of the whole of life. The basic human relationships, and their preservation within the divine otherness of the universe, are all established in the ceremonies. The models for living are richly presented and celebrated. Understood in this light, it is easy to see how the molimo infuses hope and desire to live in band members desolated by death, disease, dissension, or poor hunting. The ritual genuinely accomplishes healing simply by its enactment.

There is one last aspect of this process of normalization that we should mention briefly. That is the way in which the molimo festival establishes the proper social roles and their interrelationships. The group cannot survive without cooperation; the ritual requires the active participation of everyone, and thus automatically brings about the state praised in its songs. Simply to perform the ritual, in short, is to accomplish one of the chief goals of the ritual. In a larger sense, since the ritual is a profoundly symbolic mode of activity, simply to do the ritual is to generate and sustain the symbolic world that is the goal of the enactment. This is the "performative" aspect of ritual that has been well analyzed by several writers.[22]

Quarreling in the band between husband and wife, parents and children, and different families may have precipitated the "closing of the forest"; but in the festival there may be no arguments between the sexes, the different age groups, or families. The youth must show deference to the elders, and during the required daily intensive hunting the men must work together.

Only then will the molimo spirit permit much game to be caught. Even the new molimo fires stress the obligatory cooperation and unity of the band, for the previous fires must all be extinquished and rekindled from the new festival molimo fire; in the subsequent days of the festival each family must donate coals daily to the central fire from its own hearth. Each age group has its characteristic role in the ritual: The hunters conduct the molimo "animal" on its nightly tours into the camp; the youths rampage through the morning camp bearing the trumpet, "stirring up trouble" as their age-group is supposed to do but only as an expression of the justice of the molimo spirit. (Thus the Mbuti turn the disorderly behavior of youth into the service of norms, a trick at which they are masters.) The clash of the generations has its paradigmatic expression in the mock battle the elder brothers may put up to the morning raid of the youths. The elders lead the all-important singing and oversee all activities, while the women assume their essentially mysterious role of "hiding from" the molimo spirit (and deferring to the men) while all the time embodying the molimo. At the end, the women assert their real mastery by absorbing the powers of the spirit into themselves, permitting normal life to resume. As Turnbull remarks, the molimo festival enacts a perfectly Durkheimian recreation of society and the moral sentiment. Every person reassumes his or her "type."[23]

CONCLUDING REMARKS

Over a century and a half ago, Wilhelm von Humboldt (in the summary of Ernst Cassirer) suggested that

> man puts language *between* himself and the nature which inwardly and outwardly acts upon him, that he surrounds himself with a world of words in order to assimilate and elaborate the world of objects, and this is equally true of the configurations of the mythical and aesthetic fantasy. . . . In the very first, one might say the most primitive, manifestations of myth it becomes clear that we have to do not with a mere reflection of reality but with a characteristic creative elaboration. Here again we can see how an initial tension between subject and object, between "inside" and "outside" is gradually resolved, as a new intermediary realm, growing constantly more rich and varied, is placed between the two worlds. To the factual world which surrounds and dominates it the spirit opposes an independent image world of its own—more and more clearly and consciously it confronts the force of the "impression" with an active force of "expression."[24]

Though despite the venerable antiquity of their culture the Pygmies cannot be said to represent "the most primitive" manifestations of religion (and besides, the pejorative connotations of that word are unfair to any contemporary society), we must admit the penetrating nature of the basic insight. We have seen that ritual is precisely that intermediary language which in the most fundamental way creates a universe for the Mbuti, a world in which they can live. For the Mbuti, the paradigmatic expression of this humanizing power is the myth of the theft of fire, enacted again and again in their molimo. That myth, the aversion to coinciding in the hunt directly with the keti spirits, the flight from places where one of their number has died, the conception of catastrophe as the overwhelming closeness of the nonhuman divine, even the peculiar way benevolent forms of the divine connect with and slide over to mythic demonic beings, all articulate what might be called a terror of raw sacrality. The liminal purely in itself acts on the human order as an uncontrollable destructive force: it is chaos. This destructive aspect of the liminal we have termed negative liminality. The rainbow serpent, monster elephant, and Matu, Mistress of the Dead and of the night, all have the power to blight and destroy with a glance; they also bestow good fortune in the hunt to their chosen servants. The Mbuti must therefore take care that the better aspect of divinity looks down on him.

The entire ritual of the molimo can be viewed in this way, as a propitiatory rite of *désacralisation*, to use Hubert and Mauss's vocabulary: To remove the holy from their midst and restore the harmonious human condition.[25] This, to be sure, differs from Turnbull's rosy picture of the molimo, but as we have seen, he ignores its darker, less spontaneous, side. We must see the festival as similar in structure to the *nkumbi* initiation in Mbuti eyes. The Mbuti submit to this rite of entry into village society in order to benefit from the villagers without warring with them.

The molimo has as its aim the attainment of positive liminality: The divine is brought into a structured and sustaining relationship with the human realm. There is here not simply the love of the divine, and religious flight from structured society and the merely human condition, but rather the reverse, a terror of the starkly unconditioned divine and a love of structure.[26] The divine is brought into union with the human condition through the expulsion of negative and chaotic elements to remote realms. The assault of the women on the molimo fires represents the triumph of the human sphere and its sacrality over the unmitigated furnace heat and non-order of the divine-in-itself. But the molimo spirit is represented as finally approving and encouraging this assault, even imitating the women's attack on the festival fires itself at the conclusion of the rites. The molimo holiday must end, and the daily and human sacredness of the women and their world must take over. Only through an aggression on the divine can the human condition as such be instituted and maintained, as the Mbuti myths suggest, and thus in the final analysis divinity desires and permits its own displacement from the center of things. In the myth of the theft of fire related earlier, the forest deity calls after the fleeing Pygmy thief, "Doru, my brother, if you had only asked, I would have given it to you!" Divinity itself in its mercy permits a distance to be established between awareness and its physical environment in which consciousness and human culture can flourish. The structure that contains all of these elements is sanctified by God. This is what the molimo songs celebrate, and this is their goal.

The Mbuti are not the only African people to stress the danger of divinity's unrestrained proximity. An even more explicit statement of this comes from the Fang, among whom the Gabon Pygmies live; according to their hymn,

> Nzame [God] is on high, man below.
> God is God, man is man,
> Each is at home, each in his own house.[27]

Far from being a cry of despair (as some have asserted), this is a glad proclamation of God's mercy in removing himself from direct intervention in the world he has created and sustains. Man can be man within a structured divine order in security, despite the divinity's ability to destroy everything in a moment.

The Bushmen of the Kalahari Desert, the only other large group of hunters and gatherers in Africa, stress the frightfulness of meeting God (≠Gao!na, in the !Kung language) directly, or even his assistant ‖Gauwa, Master of the ‖*gauwasi* (spirits of the dead):

> /Ti!kay, who claimed that he himself had never seen ≠Gao!na, said that even a big medicine man is apt to be frightened when he sees ≠Gao!na for the first time and might say, "What does this man want? He is bad. I don't like him." . . . [When curing, however, and filled with power,] he would keep a "tight heart" and take a stick and would rush at ≠Gao!na and hit him and yell, "You sent a bad sickness. You must take it back." And the sick person would get better. . . .
>
> [Much more commonly shamans meet with ‖Guawa and his spirits of the dead while in trance at medicine dances; these spirits are even more brusquely dismissed.] They rush out into the darkness, where ‖Gauwa and the ‖gauwasi are lurking. They hurl burning sticks and swear at them. "Filthy face! Take away the sickness you have brought." "Uncovered penis! You are bad. You want to kill us. Go away." "Hishe, you are a liar. This man will not die."[28]

Similar motifs, though of course usually less forthrightly expressed, can be found throughout central and southern Africa. Among the Zulu, the doctors who have special powers for dealing with thunder and lightning (the weapons of the heavenly judge Inkosi Epezulu) cry out and pray during storms, *Hamba uKosi yenkosi, hamba uSomnganiso, hamba uGugabadele*: "Move away, thou Lord of the lord, move away, thou greatest of friends, move away, thou Irresistable One."[29] The Konde of Malawi fear God's appearances to them, for he comes only to punish evil, in the form of lion or snake, earthquake or lightning bolt; "Hence what the people desire above all things is that God should go away again. 'Go far hence, O God, to the Sango, for Thy House is very large,' is a prayer that is not seldom heard on the lips of the Konde when they think that God is near."[30] The Ila of Zambia believe that when God approaches too near to a person he falls ill, so they pray: "Leave thy child, that he may trust Thee, Eternal One!"[31] The Louyi of Zambia even have a version of the Tower of Babel myth in which mankind sought to climb to heaven saying, "Let us kill Nyambe (God)!" The Swedish historian of religions Olof Pettersson, in a survey of concepts of the supreme being among the southeastern Bantu, has found such "hostility" so commonly connected to a celestial being of thunder in the region that he wishes to isolate it as separate from the supreme being structure as such, hardly ready to believe that God could be viewed in this way. Following these and other subtractions, he unsurprisingly concludes that the supreme being that is left is a very ineffectual figure of little importance.[33] The opposite is the case.

But it would take us too far afield to discuss the whole problem of the High God concept here. For the Epulu, it is clear, God demonstrates his benevolence precisely by withdrawing behind the ritual order he has given to mankind. The order diffuses and defuses his own holiness and power through an entire way of life. Every part of that symbolic order suggests the rest, while filtering the divine totality into a particular mode and function. In this way the details of experience contribute to a general focus of life, creating a deep dispositional meaning felt to be present at every moment and directing the entire universe.

We may take as an example the hunting whistle that the Epulu hunters blow just before entering on the hunt. We can detect in it a lesser version of the molimo trumpet, just as the morning fire is a lesser version of the molimo fires. The music the whistle makes, and the specific power it has over the game and over the powers of the night, are enjoyed by the hunters for its own sake, but latently the full meaning of the molimo festival is evoked. In a simple action a whole perceptual-symbolic world is brought into resonant harmony. When we recall that before the recent decimation of the elephant herds by ivory hunters the molimo was practiced above all before the elephant hunt, we can recognize a yet closer identity of the hunting whistle and the molimo trumpet.

As we have seen, the molimo ritual brings an entire universe into focus, assigning a place for man and woman, for hunter and animal, for age groups and for the inanimate objects of daily experience like the fire and the hut. Aligning all of life with the focus of ritual, bestowing a dispositional order on experience, the smallest aspects of daily Mbuti life are transformed into a form of latent ritualism. For the Mbuti, any more formal ritualism might have the effect of creating a sphere permanently distinct from their everyday life. Thus the triumph of the molimo ritual lies in its informal and occasional nature, for its aim is precisely to restore everyday life to the Mbuti, transformed by transcendental meaning.

NOTES TO CHAPTER 2

1.   Colin Turnbull, *Wayward Servants* (Garden City, N.Y.: Natural History Press, 1965), p. 293, n. 6; Lewis Cotlow, *In Search of the Primitive* (Boston: Little, Brown & Co., 1966), p. 41, quoting a private conversation with Turnbull, reports that the Epulu have just two words for the village Bantu, one meaning "savage," the other "animal."

2.   Ibid., p. 62.

3.   We must admit the identity of the Pygmy view of the village with prejudice pure and simple. By locating negative liminality (the *mota* or "hot") in another people or group, harmony is restored to one's own world. Previous confusion is eliminated; only positive liminality is now associated with one's own sphere. So "good" is reaffirmed, and the structures of the universe secure self-esteem. As with so many other peoples, the dynamic of prejudice is essential to Mbuti culture and religion, providing the necessary shadow to what is highlighted, the darkness that defines the boundaries of the good. For a provocative analogy, see Rosemary Radford Ruether, *Faith and Fratricide* (New York: The Seabury Press, 1974), showing the essential religious role of anti-Semitism in earliest Christian theology and self-understanding.

4.   Arnold van Gennep, *The Rites of Passage*, trans. Monika B. Vizedom and Gabrielle L. Caffe (Chicago: University of Chicago Press, 1960); this work was first published in 1908.

5.   Our concept of "liminality" is indebted to but not identical with the following authorities: van Gennep; Hans Schärer, *Ngaju Religion* trans. R. Needham (The Hague: Martinus Nijhoff, 1963, 1946); W.E.H. Stanner, *On Aboriginal Religion*, Oceania Monograph No. 11 (Sydney: University of Sydney, 1966), and Victor W. Turner, *The Ritual Process* (Chicago: Aldine, 1969). In particular, our distinction between positive and negative liminality, and the emphasis on the existence of structure in liminality, are contributions to earlier theories.

6.   Turnbull, *The Forest People*, (Garden City, New York: Natural History Press, 1965), pp. 89-90.

7.   Turnbull, *Wayward Servants*, p. 289.

8.   See Schebesta, *Die Religion*, p. 85. Turnbull reports the same terminology.

9.   Ibid., pp. 99ff., 205 n. 30; the Gabon-Cameroons Pygmies call him Gorou or Edzingui, according to Trilles, *L'Âme du Pygmée de Afrique* (Paris: Les Éditions du Cerf, 1945), pp. 112-16; this monster leads elephants to the places where the hunters can find them, but demands proper sacrifice of parts of the game. Many Mbuti bands conduct molimolike ceremonies before the elephant hunt, to contact and win over the "king" or "queen" of animals. The Babinga of the western Congo celebrate the appearance of Edzingui (The Spirit of the Forest) after the hunt; he emerges from the forest as a huge masked figure, with bells and music emanating from it. As in the case of the molimo trumpet, women are forbidden to gaze on it; young men screen the spirit, and with songs of praise mime its death and rebirth. By offering itself up as the elephant prey, the spirit shows its love for mankind. See Noel Ballif, *Dancers of God*, trans. J. Cameron (London: Sidgwick & Jackson, 1955), p. 166.

10.   Schebesta, *Die Religion*, pp. 160, 211, unconvincingly argues that the rainbow serpent concepts show a degeneration from an archaic High God religion, to "dualistic" ideas. But the two sides of the divine, beneficent and terrifying, belong to the morphology of the divine as such, as Otto along with Marett and Soderblum have shown. Specifically, concepts of bisexual or doubled good and bad rainbow serpent-spirits seem to be common in the east and

south Zaire regions and east Africa, especially among Bantu cultures showing strong Pygmy influence like the Luba, Vili, Yombe, Zande, and Lese. See Hermann Baumann, *Das Doppelte Geschlecht* (Berlin: Dietrich Reimer, 1955), p. 248. For pan-African incidence of rainbow serpent beliefs, see Baumann, pp. 247-49, and B. Holas, *Les Dieux d'Afrique Noire* (Paris: Paul Geuthner, 1968), pp. 61-66, 103, etc. The belief in chameleons as good divine intermediaries is almost as widespread.

11. If on the other hand *akami* in the band is not too great, Mbuti like to move to the village to return the "noise" to its source. After dwelling a while in the *tupe* ("empty") and *mbafu* ("stupid") village, the band can leave it again renewed and filled with a sense of its own unity and value. See Turnbull, *Wayward Servants*, pp. 294-95. But when akami is totally out of control, the Epulu must avoid the village completely: Simple scapegoating no longer works and the molimo must be performed. A renewed direct relationship to God must be established, cutting across all intermediary lesser forms of liminality.

12. Youths masked with leaves and bearing elephant tusks often precede the trumpet into camp on its periodic raids, embodying the spirit which ferociously "kills" malefactors. But "death" also means "sharp suffering and illness" in the Mbuti language, so perhaps only a beating by the youths or a mystical curse by the molimo spirit is implied by the threat of death to sleepers. Some say the forest will slay sleepers through the agents implanted in scarifications in every Mbuti. This is the most probable meaning. See Turnbull, *Wayward Servants*, p. 280.

13. Elizabeth C. Baity, "Archaeoastronomy and Ethnoastronomy So Far," *Current Anthropology* 14, no. 4 (October 1973): 389-431.

14. Colin Turnbull, "The Molimo: A Men's Religious Association among the Ituri Bambuti," *Zaire* 14, no. 4 (1960): 320. We encounter again the women-game equation.

15. Ibid., p. 328.

16. Ibid., p. 329.

17. Turnbull, *The Forest People*, p. 156.

18. Turnbull, "The Molimo," pp. 333f. In *The Forest People*, Turnbull tells us that the old woman soon moved on to another band, but "before she left us she went to every man, giving him her hand to touch as though it were some kind of blessing" (p. 158).

19. Turnbull, *Wayward Servants*, p. 264 n.9; according to Baumann, *Das Doppelte Geschlecht*, pp. 310ff., fire often has a phallic connotation in Africa.

20. Turnbull, "The Molimo," p. 313.

21. Ibid., p. 316; also Turnbull, *The Forest People*, pp. 72ff. That these drinks are not simply to swell the bamboo, closing cracks and improving tone, is shown by the same treatment given the fifteen-foot metal water pipe used by the Epulu (stolen from a construction site).

22. The analysis has centered on the way language brings about new realities simply by uttering them forth, but all conscious symbolic action has the same power. See J.L. Austin, *How to Do Things With Words*, 2d ed. (Cambridge, Mass.: Harvard University Press, 1975); Ruth Finnegan, "How to Do Things with Words: Performative Utterances among the Limba of Sierra Leone," *Man*, n.s. 4 (1969): 16-35; and Benjamin Ray, "'Performative Utterances' in African Rituals," *History of Religions*, 13:1 (1973), among other studies.

23. Turnbull, *Wayward Servants*, p. 279.

24. Ernst Cassirer, *The Philosophy of Symbolic Forms*, Vol. 2: *Mythical Thought*, trans. Ralph Manheim (New Haven: Yale University Press, 1955), p. 23.

25. Cf. H. Hubert and M. Mauss, "Essai sur la nature et la fonction du sacrifice," *L'Annee Sociologique* 2 (1897-1898): 29-138.

26. This modifies what Eliade calls the "terror of history" present in localized religions. See Mircea Eliade, *Cosmos and History*, trans. W. R. Trask (New York: Harper & Bros., 1959), esp. pp. 85-92.

27. P. Trilles, *Les Pygmées de la forêt équatoriale* (Paris: 1932), p. 77.

28. Lorna Marshall, " !Kung Bushman Religious Beliefs," *Africa* 32, no. 3 (July 1962): 237, 250.

29. E.W. Smith, "The Idea of God among South African Tribes," in *African Ideas of God*, ed. E.W. Smith (London: Edinburgh House Press, 1961), p. 109.

30. Sir James Frazer, *The Worship of Nature* (London: Macmillan Co., 1926), p. 189.

31. E.W. Smith and A.M. Dale, *The Ila-Speaking Peoples of Northern Rhodesia* (London: Macmillan & Co., 1920), II, 210.

32. Frazer, *The Worship of Nature*, pp. 172f.

33. Olof Pettersson, *Chiefs and Gods* (Lund: CWK Gleerup, 1953), pp. 192-204.

Chapter 3

Feminine Symbolisms and Taboo in Hunting and Early Agricultural Religions

The symbolic classifications of the Mbuti might seem to be peculiar to them and worthy of no general attention, were it not that amazingly similar structures crop up upon examination of other hunting peoples' religions. In Africa, the only other hunting-and-gathering culture of any size is that of the Bushmen of the Kalahari Desert of southern Africa. A recent essay on Bushman thought has singled out the sexual symbolisms associated with the hunt as the key to those cultures and saves us the trouble of demonstrating this elaborately here.[1] Only a few important instances, some of which were overlooked in the essay by Daniel F. McCall on Bushman thought, will be sufficient for our purpose.

Among the Cikwe Bushman it is said that the human and the nonhuman natural realm came to be separated, and culture established, through the murder of an elephant woman. It happened in this way: In the dawn of the universe (not too long ago, as the Cikwe conceive of it), Pishiboro, the Creator (and later Master of Animals and Lord of the Dead), had as one of his wives an elephant. Her "animal" sexual voraciousness, however, eventually alienated both Pishiboro and his younger brother, the trickster. The two brothers ran away, but the trickster doubled back and killed the elephant-wife, to Pishiboro's great outrage. In the ensuing argument, the younger brother burst out with the passionate and original proclamation of Bushman culture: "Oh, you fool. You lazy man [the words carry the connotation in Bushman culture of sexual impotence]. You were married to meat and you thought it was a wife."[2] In one burning and contemptuous phrase the human is separated from the nonhuman, man from his Creator.

Notwithstanding his invective, the trickster displayed his own ignorance when it came to skinning the quarry, disregarding Pishiboro's advice to take care to collect all body juices, especially everything from the womb. And the womb juices flowed forth upon the ground and ran away in rivulets, never ceasing until they reached the distant elephant camp and

60

alerted the elephant's kin. In a thundering herd the kinsfolk came to avenge the murder. Pishiboro fled to a termite hill and cowered in its depths (where a divine presence still hovers today), but the trickster killed all the animal warriors in the best epic tradition. And ever since, Bushmen hunters know that they must not permit body fluids from slain animals to run freely upon the earth, or terrible consequences will follow. Body fluids contain a powerful spiritual force, called *n!ow* (the exclamation point represents an alveolar click in the Bushman language); death releases this force in exceptional quantity. If the fluids contact the ground and its *n!ow*, an invisible upheaval affects the whole region, may cause droughts or bring torrents of rain and hail, and even may cause the death of the hunter. *N!ow* pervades the universe in its various modes, which may be divided into the dry, hot forms, and the cold, wet ones. These intersect with male and female qualities in all things (even rain clouds!) to produce myriad gradations in experience.[3] All of these qualities must be carefully kept distinct, and this is the whole purpose of taboos. Taboos for the Bushman act not to keep the sacred from the profane, for the Bushman, like the Pygmy, does not recognize the profane; rather, taboos delineate the distinct paths of the sacred in all of its different modalities and levels, so that they flow harmoniously through the universe creating the entire divine order. To break a taboo is to confuse categories, pollute the universe, breach the boundaries between forces, and create chaotic turmoil.

For example, a menstruating woman should stay away from her husband and ought not even touch his weapons; her doing so would cause his arrows to lose their penetrating power, and they would not even be able to reach their target. Men in the hunting prime of life should not talk of or overhear talk of menstruation; it would drain them of masculine forcefulness in the hunt.[4] In the southern tribes, a menstruating woman can petrify or transform anyone with a glance, or can make the game entirely "wild" (i.e., uncooperative in the hunting *liebestod*). For this reason, she goes about with her eyes fastened on the ground.[5] (Here we find a form of the widespread "evil eye" motif that may help explain some others.)[6] Certainly wives even at other periods of the month have the power to affect their husband's hunting potency. Bad luck in the hunt can be attributed to the unfaithfulness of the wife (though here it is clear that it is the mystical bond between husband and wife that is affected, and the husband too can cause hunting misfortune through his unchastity).[7]

Game and women share a certain symbolic commonality over against men, as the initiation ceremonies for girls among the central and northern Bushmen show. Many authors mention the erotic eland dance practiced among these peoples (including the Naron, Auen, Cikwe—or G/wi—and !Kung groups), in celebration of a girl's first menstruation. Among the

!Kung, two old men don eland's horns, and the women celebrants (setting aside their usual strict modesty) remove the equivalent of their outer garments. The old men must not be kin, so that they are symbolically fully qualified as marital partners (their age emphasizes the purely theoretical nature of this qualification). In the dance the men mime the courtship of the eland with his herd, "dancing among the women with subtly erotic gestures."[8] The underlying meaning is made even clearer by the !Kung practice of scarifying their women on the legs, lower body, and face, "in imitation of gemsbok—big, stately grey antelopes with spectacular black markings."[9]

The !Kung and nearby groups also practice a form of initiation of male youths, centering on Hishe or Houwe, the supreme being in his form as Lord of the Dead and Master of Animals, who is usually represented in these ceremonies as a ferocious woman. The bullroarer is her voice. Again women, animals, the bush, and the divine are identified. On other occasions she is represented by dwarfish demonic figures, by a human couple, or by a lion and lioness together. Medicine men impersonate all these figures; women are not permitted near the circle of initiates. Novices receive at this time incisions above or between the eyes into which are introduced ashes of the main kinds of game.[10]

One last piece of telling symbolism: The northern Bushmen lover explicitly thinks of his courtship as a kind of hunt, judging from his "love magic." The wooer fashions a miniature bow and arrow (made from gemsbok bone, we should note); the perceptual distortion of size (as in the case of the tree in the Mbuti morning ritual) makes clear its symbolic and mystical nature. At an opportune moment, he steals up on his chosen one and shoots the dart into her flank. The same type of miniature weapons are used when doing sorcery against rivals. By shooting one of these tiny arrows in the enemy's general direction, sickness, and even death will surely befall him.[11] Hunting, sexual love, and sorcery—the conjunction of these ideas is not new to us. Their source may lie as far back as the Paleolithic, for cultures as far distant from each other as Siberian hunters and South American forest peoples have been shown to develop the same themes.[12]

But how have agriculturalists developed these ideas? Clearly, farming cultures (like hunting cultures) differ vastly from each other, and their social and technological diversity leads to the expectation of even more dissimilar cultural traits. Yet it is possible at least in Africa to discern some common themes that are variously modulated by the hundreds of distinct and unique cultures throughout the continent. Actually, in this discussion it will be quite impossible to discuss or even to mention the greater part of these societies; our effort can only be directed to the goal of demonstrating what occurs to some of the central ritual themes we have located amongst the Mbuti and Bushmen when they are developed by selected agriculturalist societies. I would maintain, however, that the patterns discovered among these cultures have a wider applicability. Partly for that reason, I would like to turn to a society that is transitional between hunting and farming to examine how they deal with these themes.

AGRICULTURE AND THE TRANSFORMATION OF FEMININE IMAGERY: THE LELE.

In discussing the Mbuti, we began by considering the underlying conceptions of space that received ritual elaboration and which sprang from a preconscious sense of personal orientation. We shall do the same with the Lele, a Bantu people located on the southern fringes of the Congo forest, in the region drained by the Kasai River.

The Lele society presents to a casual visitor the impression of a community given over to farming. The small villages are surrounded by fields carved laboriously out of the forest, and the produce of these gardens is the chief sustenance of the people. But a closer acquaintance reveals that the gardening is done solely by the women, and the chief religious ceremonials and values are centered entirely on hunting. "The village faces its own forest, and through it the spiritual world, as a single whole."[13] The forest is the spiritual Other to the Lele in much the same way it is to the Mbuti. Successful hunting is only possible, for example, when village life is harmonious; the disputes between husbands and wives, or the clash between different clans, disturb the cosmic balance and may even result in the forest being closed to the hunters. Before the hunt, there are rituals to neutralize the machinations of witches and the hostilities between individuals; everyone must confess the rancor in his or her heart, and known witches are sometime called upon to give their blessings to the expedition into the forest. In this way the communal hunts do in fact bring the peace they are credited with causing.

This is no mean feat among the Lele, for each village is an independent political unit (some sections of the Lele, apparently influenced by the neighboring kingdom of the Kuba, do have ritual chiefs, but even these have limited power). Government within the village is by consensus, with clan elders competing ceaselessly with each other and with the younger men for power and prestige.

The hunts, welded together by ritual peacemaking, are obligatory for all villagers, and their success requires that internal solidarity be real in the fullest sense. The future of each village depends on the hunt. A village with poor hunting has many barren women and constant family bickering, the Lele say; the gardens produce little, and mutual recriminations fill everyone's heart with bitterness, hatred, and suspicions of witchcraft;

> A village which has had a long series of bad hunts will begin soon to remark how few pregnancies there have been lately, or a village suffering from an epidemic or frightened by a recent series of deaths will send for a diviner to do medicines for them, saying that the village is spoilt, hunting has failed, women are barren, everyone is dying. Diviners themselves do not confuse the two symptoms. They perform distinct medicines for the separate disorders, but the grateful village whose hunting has been set on a sound basis will praise the medicine, saying, for example: "Our village is soft and good now. Since the diviner went home we have killed three wild pigs and many antelopes, four women have conceived, we are all healthy and strong." These are the accepted signs of a generally prosperous condition.[14]

Violent words and behavior "spoil" a village. The status of the people involved affects the extent of the impurity they cause. The village diviner can spoil the village merely by a rebuke to his wife, an ordinary family by a wife running away in anger (even if she returns penitent the same evening). Fines and purifications may be needed to restore the village's wholesomeness. The importance of family unity and sexual harmony is illustrated by a common ritual enacted before the hunt:

> Each man, as he sets out, takes the machete or knife from his girdle and gives it silently to his neighbor, who completes the exchange with his own knife. The meaning of this action is explained as if one were saying: "My age-mate, you take this matchete with which I may have been hitting my wife," and the other replying: "And you take my knife, in case I have struck my children with it."[15]

These practices may well illuminate the similar Pygmy and Bushman customs of exchanging weapons before the hunt.

Sexual symbolisms color and personalize the Lele contrast between forest and village. This contrast is already suggested by the custom of requiring ritual chastity from everyone the night before a communal hunt; the diviners who lead the village rites must observe this rule for weeks before a major hunt. The forest, the Lele say, views men benevolently but can be dangerous to women and is not their element (as we would say); every third day women must stay out of the forest entirely, and it is in general risky for them to penetrate too deeply into it. On all especially sacred days, women should stay in the village as well; when the new moon appears (associated as with the Pygmies with the forest), at the departure of a chief, a twin birth, when mourning, in menstruation, or in childbirth. No male mourner may enter the forest either, nor one who has had a nightmare. If men transgress important norms, they may have accidents in the forest, but these usually only affect the individual; women's transgressions, however, pollute the entire village-forest relationship.

Mary Douglas, the source for our knowledge of the Lele, concludes from these ideas that "the Lele regard the forest as almost exclusively a male sphere."[16] I believe the opposite is closer to the truth. The much more powerful effect of women's transgressions on the forest suggests that women's nature is essentially bound to the forest realm, and men's only circumstantially. Men, as its opposite, ought by nature to penetrate the forest, while the same kind of jealousy and incompatibility traditionally existing between cowives exists between the forest and women. They encroach on each other's sphere. As we have already seen, it is a major purpose of taboos to *separate spheres too similar to each other in order to affirm their existence on separate symbolic levels*; taboos therefore permeate the relationship between women and forest. According to Mary Douglas, it is a major theme of Lele ritual symbolism: "The separation of women from men, of forest from village, the dependence of village on forest, and the exclusion of women from the forest are the principal recurring elements of their ritual, on which minor variations are embroidered."[17] We have already noted that the male hunters' relationship with their wives has the most potent effect on their hunting luck, and bitter arguments between husband and wife can spoil a whole village. The relationship of man to forest is analogous to that of man to woman, in short, and it is precisely for this reason that good hunting is followed by women becoming pregnant, bad hunting by women's barrenness. The organic nature of these relationships, which to the Lele inhere in the very fabric of things, demands elaborate taboos. We can learn a great deal about the logic of taboo rituals from examining these symbolisms more closely, with the help of Mary Douglas's excellent analysis.

"Noises associated with the day are always forbidden at night: for instance, women must not pound grain after dark."[18] However, drumming (especially on religious festivals) is a night time, masculine activity; the sounds of drumming and of pounding are antithetical to each other, then, as masculine is to feminine. (One recalls the Epulu Bambuti use of the molimo trumpet during the night singing, and its "hatred" of the sounds of women's work or even of the sight of women; the trumpet was hidden from the women who were out during the day.) Pounding, especially of grain and food, and chopping of wood (all common women's activities) are forbidden also on days of rest (every third day, which is sacred to the forest), during the new moon, at funerals, or in villages undergoing special restorative divinatory treatment. On all of these occasions, women are also excluded from the forest. We may see in this a way of organizing a series of "felt significances": Women are felt to be in opposition to men in a way that coordinates with night and day, noise and music, work and rest. Yet the relationships are not simple ones. If they were, women would be merged into their analogous elements night, forest, and music. Instead, the entire taboo system pivots, in a way, on the men. Women are to men as the forest is to men, but women are domestic and cultural, while the forest is remote and natural; the two realms must therefore be kept distinct to preserve the divine order. When men relate to women, their relationship to the forest must be suppressed and made latent, while when they relate to the forest consciously the link to women must be suppressed. A single symbolic continuum is involved, but first one aspect of it is made clearly conscious (suppressing the other aspects into the tacit, "preconscious" dimension), then another. One may observe that women become all the more significant when relationships with them are specifically singled out for taboos, but this conscious awareness is by way of antithesis: the hunter wants to be "perfectly sure" that he is not relating to women while hunting. Nevertheless, the logic of his avoidance and its symbolic structure reveal that latently or preconsciously ("subconsciously," as some would say) he *is* relating to women. The submerged meanings in fact give the symbols their felt significance. While various aspects of the ritual symbolisms are stressed on various occasions, all are present tacitly, creating a background "halo" for the ones singled out consciously.

The symbolic logic of Lele rituals connected with women obviously embraces the entire cosmic order. It is not merely that too close contact of women with the beings of the deep forest might cause the women to be absorbed by the feminine wilderness irrevocably (ending the possibility of culture and humanity itself); there would also be effects on the cosmos as such:

> A menstruating woman was a danger to the whole community if she entered the forest. Not only was her menstruation certain to wreck any enterprise in the forest that she might undertake, but it was thought to produce unfavorable conditions for men. Hunting would be difficult for a long time after, and rituals based on forest plants would have no efficacy.[19]

Just as successful hunting assures the fertility of women and the tranquility of the village in general, so women's conduct affects the forest, the animals, and even the herbs.

Mary Douglas offers two quite different explanations for the taboos surrounding women. One is that through them, the Lele men keep the women under their control.[20] There are numerous difficulties with this functionalist explanation, however. Lele women, by Douglas's own evidence, have remarkable equality with the men;[21] similar taboos can be found in widely differing societies; and if anything the taboos themselves indicate women's power over men rather than the reverse. If women voluntarily abstain from sexual intercourse before the hunt, or stay out of the forest on rest days or during menstruation and pregnancy, they do this out of concern for the well-being of their husbands, children, neighbors, and even the universe itself. They respect themselves too much to toy lightly with their powers. Cross-cultural studies show that while some cultures explain menstrual taboos as the result of women's "dangerousness" and "sacral pollution," others explain the same taboos as springing from women's highly sacred and positive mystical power; however, the rituals, and the association with sacral power, remain the same. The variation in beliefs cannot be simply associated with societies in which women are sharply subordinated to men or are independent from them.[22] Menstrual taboos, and restrictions on sexual intercourse in connection with the hunt, war, or even trade and building enterprises, are so widespread among all kinds of societies as to suggest a very deep prehistory and an association with some of the most archaic and basic spiritual assumptions of humanity.[23]

Douglas's second explanation is more helpful. Taboos separate malformed or anomalous (and therefore liminal) powers or beings from sensitive points in the structured divine order.[24] For example, women are tabooed from eating certain monkeys and the tortoise and may not even touch the Nile monitor lizard or the small pangolin (scaly anteater).[25] Even more animals are tabooed when a woman is pregnant. All of these animals are "abnormal" in one way or another in terms of the basic Lele classification of the universe; they belong to no one realm but combine several. Their wildness or formlessness must be kept apart from women so that women may produce truly human children. In other words, sacred and profane must be kept separate. However, we also read that the Lele not only

> regard the unborn child and its mother as in constant danger, but they also credit the unborn child with capricious ill-will which makes it a danger to others. When pregnant, a Lele woman tries to be considerate about not approaching sick persons lest the proximity of the child in her womb cause coughing or fever to increase.[26]

In short, one kind of liminality must be kept separated from another. The child in the womb is a kind of witch or at least has great mystical power. It is liminal, in passage from one state to another; so is the sick person. It is interesting to add that mourners and the ill are tabooed along with pregnant and menstruating women from entering the forest. Again, one kind of liminality must be kept apart from another, precisely because of their essential similarity. With this insight the food taboos take on another meaning. We notice that all of the animals tabooed to women as such are not merely anomalous but more importantly are watery creatures, according to the Lele. They all are associated with the deep gullies and streams in the forest thought to be the dwelling places of the *mingehe,* the feared spirits of the forest who "hate" women.[27] It is more than anomaly that causes these animals to be tabooed to women. The fish, for example, who belong entirely to the water realm and are not anomalous, are also forbidden to women.

But as we have seen, the forest spirits are symbolically feminine just as are the women: the antipathy between the two is the result of their essential similarity, in the same way that two similarly magnetized poles repel each other.

Taboos help define the realms of the universe, separating out of the primordial divine various modes and levels of sacredness. There is not so much a division between sacred and profane in taboos, in other words, as an articulation of the sacred into a differentiated divine order. The taboos on women reveal their sex to be essentially like the primordial forest and divinity itself, especially in comparison to men. Only by being separated from the forest and divinity do women permit culture to exist.

In a larger sense, the observance of any one taboo implies all taboos and tacitly involves a whole universe of specific distinctions. Each taboo *means* "order" and "pattern." The tabooed person, or thing, is restricted, so that there is room for a universe to exist, and so that "otherness" can be recognized and respected. The otherness that controls and defines an individual may seem on the surface to be merely one object, being or even god (women, for example, avoiding Nile monitor flesh, or the *mingehe* spirits). But more deeply what controls and limits one is a transcendental order, within which one has a specific place or role. Meaning inheres in that order, not in oneself alone. The self is created by and centered in what is beyond the self, through taboos.

To return to Lele taboos on women, it is not even necessary that individual women be able to articulate consciously the insight that they are central to the culture, imply divinity, and precisely for this reason must restrain themselves. The taboos affirm all this through their tacit symbolic associations in the same way that the Mbuti hunting whistle implies the molimo. The felt significance of the taboos underline women's sacral power and link to the forest, each taboo commenting on the others and extending their logic into an entire order. Every woman sustains the entire universe through her smallest actions. Women are taught to have a great deal of respect for their own femininity. Their actions have tremendous consequences for all of those around them; husbands and children depend for their well-being directly on women's continuing solicitude and piety. If, for example, a woman does not keep apart from her husband while menstruating, the husband's hunting will be bad and he may have a serious injury, he may fall seriously ill or develop genital disease or impotence.

Self-restraint (a sense of shame or modesty) and a lively sense of transcendental otherness are essentially intertwined, if this discussion has any validity.[28] Such piety sustains the universal structures, while "shamelessness" or breaking the taboos points to that primordial otherness that lies beyond all structures. The highest Lele cult celebrates precisely this, centering on the ruptures of sacrifice just as the general Lele cultus centers on the boundaries of taboo. Only a few of the hunters attain to the pangolin cult. This animal is apparently the distilled object of all Lele taboos; all symbolic classifications are absorbed into it, and no mere mortal can eat it. But divinity itself can choose a hunter it wishes to honor and offer a pangolin to him, for him to kill and eat.[29]

The Lele say of the pangolin (or scaly anteater), "In our forest there is an animal with the body and tail of a fish, covered with scales. It has four little legs and climbs in trees."[30] The strong identification with fish and spiritual watery beings is clear, but the four legs evoke land animals, and the reference to trees recalls the birds and sky beings. Like humans it bears its young one at a time (not in animal litters), and most astonishing of all, it neither fights nor runs away from the chosen hunter, but curls up into a ball and waits for the spear's thrust. It offers itself to sustain the Lele. All categories of the Lele universe, therefore, are brought together in this liminal being, and in its self-offering to the chosen hunter humanity is allowed to participate in the transcendence of all normative structures, the return to primordial generative formlessness. Yet the cult members are given great powers to reaffirm the normative order by their communal feast on the pangolin sacrifice. Although transcending the taboos that constrain others, they regenerate the structures that are defined by the taboos. The pangolin embodies positive liminality, which contributes to the upbuilding of the divine order. It is in effect the monstrous intermediary between formlessness and form, just as the molimo spirit was for the Mbuti.

After bearing the corpse of the pangolin about the village as if it were a living chief, and singing "Now I enter the house of affliction," the initiates feast on the sacrificial victim's flesh.[31] Thereafter, it is expected, the hunting will be very good, many women will conceive and give birth to children, and the crops will flourish. From the death of the victim (and the initiates who mystically share the affliction) will come new life for all. The cult is the most formidable counterforce to the witches' cult, as well. The latter cult exults in negative liminality: the forest intrudes on the village world only to destroy it. It is interesting to note that while the Pangolin cult allows its male members to contact primordial forces so as to guarantee women's fertility and good hunting (and even the success of the women's crops), the witches' cult affords its generally female members only a negative path to primordiality, as if once contacting that they are tempted to reject the entire divine order. The pangolin cult seems to serve Lele men as a surrogate form of generativity, since they cannot claim the natural powers women possess.

They even do women one better in claiming spiritual control over the women's natural sacred power.

Women are, however, not totally excluded from sacral activity. Their ritual powers are focused on the fields that they cultivate, just as the men's ritual focuses on the forests in which they hunt. Gardening is considered a woman's mystery, and women must observe sexual taboos (abstention from husbands) for weeks while planting groundnuts, until the seedlings appear. In this they duplicate the taboo men must observe regarding sex when hunting, making traps, or gathering special herbs in the forest. It is important to notice that a pregnant or nursing woman must also abstain from sex until the child is well established in life, suggesting that the seedlings in the field are symbolically like the children in the womb and the nursing infant. Women relate to both as 'mothers.' We see here an agricultural identification of women with the earth they tend, a shift away from the hunter's identification of women with the forest. Among the Lele, however, the shift is incomplete, and the stress is obviously still on hunting.

We can conclude our discussion of the Lele by underlining this point: while the Lele resemble the Mbuti in many aspects of their ritual symbolisms, in their cosmology and their attitude to women, it is evident that there are highly significant differences that point to increasing differentiations and new hierarchies of concern. Feminine values are more ideologically subordinated, while the forest has become a darker and more dangerous place, and women are more strictly excluded from it. The forest spirits are more distant and hostile. One may observe that the positive relationship that Mbuti women have with the forest has been displaced among the Lele onto the cultivated earth the women tend. That is, a split is evident in the divine Other that faces the Lele: on one side is the forest, on the other the cultivated fields. The prime focus is still on the former, and the *mingehe* control the fecundity of women and the tilled fields, so men can still aspire to spiritual mastery of generation just by being hunters. But the increased tension (and hierarchical displacement) of these conceptions is evident in the tyrannical hostility of the forest spirits, especially to women, and the contempt the men express for their part about women.

The masculine disdain is, however, only an affectation, or even a defensive mechanism. Competition for women is the chief source of friction among the men; having many wives and many children is the acme of prestige and status. It demonstrates divine favor. Unfortunately for the men, Lele women are independent and do not hesitate to leave disagreeable or despotic husbands. Competition for their favors often frays men's tempers, and they like to talk together of "the weaker sex" as being flighty, frail, and unreliable. Divided as they are over women, such language helps unite the men at least momentarily.

Although their religion is oriented to hunting, the real staple foods of the Lele are provided by the farming of the women. Cultivation is even controlled by women's mysteries. It is evident, in short, that in many ways women are a central nexus of Lele culture. Many tensions come together in them, and only so long as they sustain by their piety and self-restraint the main structures of the Lele cosmos can that cosmos continue to exist at all. We are not much surprised, then, when we are told that when women left the control of the men and the forest spirits and shamelessly entered the missionary schools of the colonial powers, the entire culture of the Lele collapsed.[32]

Lele culture in any case is a kind of ideologically transitional form that in more ordinary circumstances might be expected slowly to culminate in a spiritual focus largely on farming and its mysteries. How fully agricultural societies elaborate their spiritual structures will be the subject we turn to now.

NOTES TO CHAPTER 3

1. Daniel F. McCall, *Wolf Courts Girl: The Equivalence of Hunting and Mating in Bushman Thought*, Papers in International Studies, Africa Series, no. 7 (Athens, Ohio: Ohio University Center for International Studies, 1970).

2. Elizabeth Marshall Thomas, *The Harmless People* (New York: Vintage Books, 1958, 1959), p. 53 (parenthetical remarks are based on Thomas's comments).

3. Ibid., pp. 47ff., 158-62; Lorna Marshall, *"N!ow," Africa* 27, no. 3 (1957): 232-40. "Female" rain is generative and gentle, "male" rain harsh and torrential; the burning hot sun is male; the cool full moon female (the crescent moon male); see Thomas, pp. 96, 147. Right is male, left female, as among so many peoples.

4. Lorna Marshall, "The !Kung Bushmen of the Kalahari Desert," in *Peoples of Africa*, ed. by James L. Gibbs, Jr. (New York: Holt, Rinehart and Winston, 1965), p. 266.

5. Isaac Schapera, *The Khoisan Peoples of South Africa* (London: Macmillan, 1930), p. 119.

6. The sovereign power of the feminine eye was considered an important part of the *beneficient* power of the ancient mother goddesses of the Middle East, as well; see O.G.S. Crawford, *The Eye Goddess* (London: Oxford University Press, 1958).

7. Schapera, *The Khoisan Peoples*, p. 119.

8. Marshall, "The !Kung Bushmen," p. 265; the eland is regarded with awe by the Bushmen as the embodiment of the Master of Animals, according to Laurens van der Post, *The Heart of the Hunter* (Harmondsworth; Penguin, 1961), pp. 212ff. On this ceremony also see George B. Silberbauer, "Marriage and the Girl's Puberty Ceremony of the G/wi Bushmen," *Africa* 33 (1963); for the northern groups, see Laurens van der Post, *The Lost World of the Kalahari* (Harmondsworth: Penguin, 1958), pp. 240ff.

9. Marshall, "The !Kung Bushmen," pp. 267 and 275 n. 9.

10. Schapera, *The Khoisan Peoples*, pp. 122-25.

11. Ibid., pp. 199-200; Barrie Reynolds, *Magic, Divination and Witchcraft among the Barotse of Northern Rhodesia*, Robins Series III (Berkeley: University of California Press, 1963), pp. 85-86, cf. figure 6f on p. 54; Reynolds recalls in this connection the "pointing bone"

sorcery of the Australian aborigines. Also see W.H.I. Bleek and L.C. Lloyd, *The Naron* (Cambridge: Cambridge University Press, 1928), p. 28; and van der Post, *Lost World*, pp. 245ff.

12. See, for example, Z.A. Abramova, "Paleolithic Art in the U.S.S.R.," *Arctic Anthropology* 4 (1967): 83f; G. Reichel-Dolmatoff, *Amazonian Cosmos: Sexual and Religious Symbolism of the Tukano Indians* (Chicago: University of Chicago Press, 1971). On Paleolithic religious ideas, see especially André Leroi-Gourhan, *Les religions de la préhistoire (Paléolithique)*, 2ième ed. (Paris: P.U.F., 1971). In all these cases, women are identified with the prey men hunt; the kill is a *sexual penetration*, producing dead flesh, food, in the hunt, children in marriage; and women control the transformative fire of the hearth and the womb.

13. Mary Douglas, "The Lele of the Kasai," *African Worlds*, ed. by Daryll Forde (London: Published for the International African Institute by Oxford University Press, 1954), p. 13.

14. Ibid., pp. 13f.; the distinction between the common beliefs of the villagers and the attitudes of the diviners is an interesting one, and leads one to ask where the diviner gets his differing viewpoint. Perhaps like many African diviners the Lele practioners gain their knowledge from "abroad," for divination in central Africa is often an intercultural science, with the basic techniques and ideas widely diffused. These and related topics are pursued further in Chapter 11.

15. Ibid., p. 14.

16. Ibid., p. 4.

17. Ibid., p. 6.

18. Ibid., p. 12.

19. Douglas, *Purity and Danger* (New York: Frederick A. Praeger, 1966), p. 151.

20. Ibid., pp. 149-53.

21. According to Ibid., p. 151, Lele women quite readily divorced their husbands if they were not satisfied with them; since the women produced the main staples of Lele diet and largely controlled their use, they had semi-independent means and status. As a result, Douglas observes, the men were reduced to a constant "wheedling" tone of voice whenever they spoke with women.

22. See Alice Schlegel, *Male Dominance and Female Autonomy* (New Haven: HRAF Press, 1972), pp. 89-90, 93; also see Philip M. Bock, "Love Magic, Menstrual Taboos, and the Facts of Geography," *American Anthropologist* 69 (1967), 213-17, and Michelle Zimbalist Rosaldo's "Theoretical Overview" in *Woman, Culture and Society* edited by herself and Louise Lamphere (Stanford: Stanford University Press, 1974), p. 38.

23. See works cited in the previous note; for further documentation, see Sir James Frazer, *Taboo and the Perils of the Soul; The Golden Bough*, Part II, 3d ed. (London: Macmillan & Co., 1927), pp. 145-57, 225 n. 1, 190-204, etc., and Hermann Heinrich Ploss, Max Bartels, and Paul Bartels, *Woman*, 3 vols. (London: Heinemann, 1935), *passim*. A recent but simplistic study is Janice Delaney, *The Curse: A Cultural History of Menstruation* (New York: E.P. Dutton & Co., 1976).

24. Douglas, *Purity and Danger, passim*, and esp. pp. 95, 166-68 on the Lele.

25. Mary Douglas, "Animals in Lele Religious Thought," in *Myth and Cosmos*, ed. by John Middleton (Garden City, N.Y.: Natural History Press, 1967), pp. 234ff., reprinted from *Africa* 27, no. 1 (1957): 46-58.

26. Douglas, *Purity and Danger*, p. 95.

27. Douglas, "Animals," pp. 235ff.

28. See the valuable study by Carl D. Schneider, *Shame, Exposure and Privacy* (Boston: Beacon Press, 1977).

29. See Douglas, "Animals," pp. 237ff., 241ff.; *idem, Purity and Danger*, pp. 168-74, on the pangolin cult.

30. Douglas, "Animals," p. 237.

31. Douglas, *Purity and Danger*, p. 169.

32. Mary Douglas, *The Lele of the Kasai* (London: Oxford University Press, 1963), pp. 60 and 264ff. This is of course not to deny economic and sociological factors in the Lele collapse. Douglas gives full details on this in the above work. Our attention however is directed to the spiritual factors which also contributed.

PART TWO:

SPACE AND TIME IN AGRICULTURAL RELIGIONS

Chapter 4

Maiden and Serpent:
Rituals of Space among the Ila

We have been moving in our discussion from relatively undifferentiated societies to more complex ones. It becomes correspondingly more difficult to treat religious structures comprehensively. When we dealt with the Mbuti, it was not too difficult to show that the immediate experience of sensory reality flowed into and confirmed the general sense of the cosmos, and that the Pygmy individual and the Pygmy universe were unified through ritual symbolism. We cannot attempt the same close analysis of symbolisms with the Ila; our discussion will have to be less complete. Yet the Ila world too can be deciphered through its central symbolisms, as we might call those symbolisms that reveal an entire religion and cultural possibility. For the Epulu Mbuti, as we saw, the molimo trumpet and the fireplace provided a rich depth of meaning, especially in the light of the organic reality of sexual complementariness and the cosmological structures of in and out, light and dark, cold and hot, up and down. In a sense, the ritual symbols of fire and monstrously serpentine trumpet brought together and gave an order to the organic and the cosmological levels of experience. The Ila also make use of fire and serpent symbolisms, but, as we shall see, their cosmos is more varied and its resultant unification more difficult and problematical. In our treatment of the Ila, we will have to concentrate on the structures of that cosmology, for here we discover the contours of Ila experience most quickly, and here too is one of the fundamental foci of their ritual.

THE ILA UNIVERSE

The Ila are a group of related peoples occupying the basin of the Kafue River and its hills to the north, in central Zambia.[1] The greater portion of the Ila migrated to this region several centuries ago upon the breakup of the great Lunda empire in southern Zaire. Their culture therefore has continuities with those of southern Zaire, but more recent events have left their mark. The history of the Ila migrations and of the generations spent in the Kafue River Valley is still preserved in the oral traditions of the Ila and their neighbors. This history is one long chronicle of merciless war and decimation, which largely accounts for the relative sparsity of population in the exceptionally fertile valley at the time Smith and Dale lived among the Ila as missionary and administrator respectively (the "ethnological present" used throughout these pages refers to that period alone, of course). *Bwila*, the term Smith and Dale use for the area, is mainly an extraordinarily level riverine plain covered with lush vegetation. The plain is flooded in the long rainy season toward the end of summer, and Ila villages are located on summits of hills or on mounds in order to escape the high waters. Before the appearance of European hunters and weapons, the plain teemed with wildlife, and hunting and fishing were important supplements to farming. The fertile plains support large herds of cattle, too, around which much of the interest of the Ila centers, and which made the Ila a standing target for neighbors' raids.

The Ila share many characteristics with their neighbors, and are part of a larger cultural province fanning out from southern Zaire to Angola in the southwest, and to the eastern coasts below the Zambesi River in the southeast.[2] These are generally matrilineal cultures, organized loosely into villages of unstable population with the chief (male) authority exerted on the village level. Generally there is no political unification beyond the village, although many cultures have traditions strongly influenced by the ancient kingdoms of the southern Zaire savanna or of Rhodesia, as we shall see. The royal traditions persist—or, equally likely, find their source—in the customs surrounding local village headmen and regional rainmakers. Clan kinship governs village life, with the ancestors acting through the headman and family elders to supervise conduct within the kin-group and even the locality. The villages of a region may feud together, but are generally unified spiritually through cultic worship together at regional sacred shrines and groves to ancestral culture-heroes (often the first founders of villages in the area) and nature spirits. The hereditary shrine priests are *rainmakers* (to adopt for a moment a common phrase from European travelogs), often inheriting their position as the headmen of the clan that first settled in the region; the spirits of the grove are the clan ancestors, who first fecundated the land and continue spiritually to do so. But over them, and central in the regional cult, reigns the supreme being, a stronger figure than many Westerners have realized. As we shall see, sexual symbolisms are strongly emphasized throughout this culture-province, providing a pervasive code interrelating many levels of experience. Women, for example, are associated with the earth and farming; the men leave the cultivation of the earth to their wives and concentrate on war, herding, and the hunt.

Comparative study of world cultures has shown that where hoe cultivation is the method used to till the soil (as in the central Bantu area), women do the main work of farming. Men slash away and burn over the brush to clear new fields, but for the rest are engaged in "manly" tasks. In plough cultivation, however, men take over the more strenuous farming also, depriving women of a chief source of independence. In Africa, ploughs are mainly used north of the Sahara. Hoe cultivation tends to exhaust the soil; fields cease producing after a few years requiring the village to move to a new site. Hoe societies tend to stay at a subsistence level, with little craft specialization. The historically later plough method permits permanent settlements, development of food surpluses, and craft differentiation. In Africa, hoe agriculture tends to be associated with matrilineal systems of kinship and inheritance, and this is especially true in the regions least affected by centralized governments, namely amongst "segmentary" societies in Zaire and the savanna stretching south and east from there (i.e., central Africa), as well as in the Cameroons-East Nigeria area, and among the Voltaic peoples of Ghana and the Ivory Coast. Where men are engaged in hoe agriculture, as in the west African savanna, patrilineal inheritance is more common.[3] Interestingly, some studies show that where women have control of the means of production and maintain rights over its distribution, they tend to have more independence from male dominance.[4]

Needless to say, these comparative and historical remarks, both in regard to the central African culture-province and larger world patterns, have numerous exceptions, but they are useful in putting the Ila into a more general context. To a remarkable degree, in fact, the Ila bear out the comparative studies, and their religious structures illuminate much in at least central African cultures. In this discussion it is chiefly their cosmology that will be analyzed, with points of resemblance to other central African cultures occasionally pointed out to deepen our understanding of the Ila. Particularly interesting for our discussion will be the role of ritual in delineating the boundaries between various spheres and levels of religious life and in providing a sacred path through the divine order.

THE ILA HOME

The first, and in some ways deepest, reality for the Ila is their parental home. It is very likely that in a culture's concept of the space of its homes, profound clues are given of their attitude to human existence and the nature of the universe, for what is true at this level of the Ila is true for us all. The Ila differ from us, however, in explicitly conceiving of the home as a sacred space. We find, for example, that symbols of serpent and maiden that perhaps fascinated us as children in folk tales but had no deeper significance are associated with the home for the Ila in a way that has profound meaning.

The Ila house varies from region to region, but is generally a circular structure of wood and thatch, with the thatched roof often reaching to within two feet of the ground. The space between the deep eaves and the wall of the hut provides an airy, private veranda in which it is pleasant to sit on hot days. The men build most of the hut, but women alone plaster around the doorway, for in a sense the hut is the woman's space. Around the doorway the women shape various figures, especially

> three lumps of clay representing the two mammae with an *impande* shell between. On some huts outside is a representation of a rayed sun. Others have representations of the Itoshi monster, with its flat head and the fins with which it grasps its victims.[5]

As we shall see, the Itoshi monster has very great importance in Ila religion. It is a serpentine being, associated with great ancestral and nature spirits, which dwells in pools and rivers. It controls fertility. The impande shells are complex symbols too. When worn around a man's neck, it would seem to represent the sun (essence of masculine potency), while between a woman's breasts it suggests the life-filled womb and sexual union. Of course, the "heat" of the womb and of sexual generation are similar forms of energy to the Ila.

Some designs over doorways show the impande shell flanked by two breasts, with all this enclosed by the undulating body of the serpent. This form is also common inside the house on the cornice over the family granaries or grain bins, as if these androgenous or womblike beings shape the grain into food or quicken it into vigorous seed. The bins are also decorated with designs of game, thus linking together all the forms of food under the serpent/breasts/womb symbols. The Itoshi serpents and feminine powers provide the food of bush and field together. We find the same serpent and maiden forms molded over the fireplace, where raw flesh and plants are transformed into food by the hearth fire, and on the marital bed, where living children are generated by sexual heat.[6] The special association of these generative powers with femininity is shown by the emphasis on breasts and impande-shell womb in all these designs. The granaries, in addition, are prominently decorated with pairs of breasts molded over the swelling "belly" of the bin, while circling its girth is the undulating serpent. The granaries, in short, are like pregnant women, filled with seed.[7]

The Ila conception of pregnancy helps explain these symbolisms. They say that within both men and women are tiny serpentine creatures that are the actual genitors of life. These *bapuka* (singular: *mupuka*) dwell in all the most important organs of the body and activate them, but their presence is especially important in sexual matters.[8] There is a mupuka in the male genitals that secretes the semen, which in entering the womb is received and worked on by the woman's bapuka (women have two bapuka in their womb, one an "inert" male, the other an active female). The latent androgeneity of women is already suggested rather clearly by this symbolism. The female mupuka of the womb is "The Moulder": it receives the semen with its (flat?) head at the orifice of the uterus and shapes it slowly into the foetus, mingling with the semen the menstrual blood it produces.[9] Difficult childbirths are caused by the reluctance of the mupuka to release its creation, and infant deformities are the result of the mupuka's habit of partially devouring its own children as "food." Food, game, and children are obviously allied realities. The mupuka of the womb and the Itoshi monster of the (feminine) earth's rivers and pools are also symbolically allied. So at least the symbolisms would seem to suggest, although Smith and Dale merely report the data without probing into symbolic meanings.

Returning then to the symbolisms that underlie the home, we can now understand that the home is actually a living presence likened to a woman's body, within which the occupants dwell protected and invigorated. The breasts and impande shell that surmount the entrance, and the bapuka that entwine around it, seem to suggest that the opening into the hut is like one into the womb, while within, as we have seen, the hearth fire, the marital bed, and the grain bins all participate in the same generative power. The Ila even have a practice of placing an earthen pot on the top of the center post that projects above the roof, to indicate that the owner of the hut has killed a man, a lion, or a leopard, while two pots show two victims, and so on. These pots evidently represent the heads of the prey, or at least medicine containing their essential life is placed in the pots, for those not possessing such quarry will crown their huts with the heads of other game they have killed.[10] Here again, and most vividly, we discover the equation of game and women. But in any case, with the spiritual power of sacrificial victims protecting and inspiriting the hut, with heads, breasts, bapuka, fire and womblike bins, one can only admit that the home is imaginatively like a living being, a female but also androgenous as women latently are. Here the husband and wife live, the wife dominant in her hut like the female mupuka in the womb, with their children growing up and shaped by the food and care given them by the mother. The wife is dominant, because not only are the Ila polygamous (meaning the husband invites his wives to sleep with him in rotation in his own separate hut, making him a little bit of an outsider in his wives' huts), but in cases of divorce she takes with her the children and many of the things of the hut.[11]

Within this divine space, an extension of their mother's body, the children grow up. To leave this space is to leave a mode of the sacred, and is a kind of birth or transition into the less secure outside world. The threshold therefore has special significance. The husband offers to his ancestors on the right (male) side of the threshold, the wife to hers on the left (female) side. At this intermediary threshold between structured spheres the living-dead ancestors, who are intermediary themselves, come close to their living kin—as do other intermediary beings, like witches (who like to put evil medicines in the thatch near the entrance way). The Ila prohibit lingering near entrances, especially by children, for they believe the jealous ghosts hover there trying to get into the house and will seize one's inner forces and cause a fit.[12]

It is significant that it is at thresholds that the *ancestral cult* is centered. At the time of the harvest, for example, before any of the food is eaten, a man must sacrifice to his ancestors some fresh cobs of corn, which "he places above the door and in the rafters."[13] Smith and Dale uncomprehendingly inform us: "It is bad form to celebrate the harvest in this way in the absence of your wife."[14] But of course as the cultivator of the food she is necessary to the ritual, and in receiving the ancestors' blessings she shares with the family fields the hope of future fecundity.

Yet if the ancestors dwell at the entrance way, they are not absent from the inward parts of the hut. Here again we must reconstruct meanings. Smith and Dale tell us that every hut has its fireplace, and its fire is never permitted to go out. Even after funerals, when the outside fires are put out, the hearth remains untouched: "For a hut to have no fire in it is reckoned very bad, not only for the convenience of the living, but also for the comfort of the family ghosts who live in the hut. The coldness and darkness of a fireless house has a special name—*kanekezhi*."[15] The special importance of the fire is made clear by the taboo on taking a firestick from one hut to another: "should this be done the lady of the house would *skikula*, i.e., get out of favour with her husband and be divorced."[16] If the force of the ancestors is in the fire as would seem to be suggested by all these details, we can understand the nature of the outrage: to mix fires is to confuse the ancestral essence and mingle it with other families! Similarly, a menstruating woman may not tend the fire. Fire is the very heat of life itself; a new fire is made by twirling a "male" stick in a "female" piece of wood, and the flame is their union and energy.[17]

The fire of a hut is peculiarly that of the husband's ancestors, it would seem, although the wife shares in and is directly affected by its beneficent power. This would seem to be the reason why a wife must return to her own kin and parents to give birth to a child in this matrilineal society. The afterbirth of the infant is buried in her mother's hut, too, and the infant is placed for a few moments on the mud floor of the hut before being bathed and wrapped in cloths, as if to restore it to its source.[18] There is also a ritual involving guests jumping over the threshold, in this way "catching" the diseases that linger there and removing them from the vicinity of the child as they leave the hut.[19] These rituals, along with others not described here connected with births, show the close symbolic bond between domestic space and organic (or body) space. They also demonstrate how intimately ritual shapes and bridges intermediary periods and spaces.

The rituals governing pregnancy, marriage, and initiation of both girls and boys show in detail how the liminal moments of spiritual movement from womb (or childhood home) to the larger cosmos are symbolically mediated. It is fascinating to see how thresholds and fire serve to transform (or "cook") the not-yet-formed to the formed, and how both serve to define feminine space.

There is a kind of antipathy between the not-yet-formed (the primordial) and the formed (the cosmically structured), and even between various kinds of liminal formlessness. The taboos on pregnancy vividly demonstrate this. The pregnant women must never enter the hut where a woman is still recovering from childbirth, lest the born infant "shatter" from the "wars" (of the infants, it would seem). If a pregnant woman passes through a calabash garden, the gourds will also shatter or spoil; if she passes under trees laden with fruit, they will drop their fruit prematurely; if past a litter of pups, their heads will split; if past a nest of eggs, they will crack.[20] Similar realities must be ritually separate.

The role of women in wedding ceremonies is particularly ritualized, for similar reasons: the bride is separated from her mother's "space" and is made the center of a new but symbolically similar "space" serving the husband's kin. Movement into the new hut and creation of its own generative fire is therefore the climax of the marriage ceremonies. These ceremonies are generally only the last acts in the drama of the bride's initiation, signaling her complete transformation into an independently adult woman, separate from her mother.

We cannot describe the full ceremony of initiation here, although it is undoubtedly the most important ritual moment of an Ila woman's life; later on we will discuss the very similar rites among the Ndembu, a people near to the Ila. In fact, women's initiations are basically similar throughout the matrilineal central Bantu cultures, indicating their importance. For us the main points must be that everywhere the novice is separated from the mother, taken from her hut, and in the bush and later in an instructress's hut reshaped into the archetypal fertile woman.[21] The movement in space is also a spiritual one, completed by the wedding.

At the end of the initiation proper, the Ila wedding is enacted by carrying off the girl to the groom's hut. He too is "caught" and carried over the threshold, and the marriage is consummated. Afterward the husband drapes a string of beads measuring the same length as his bride over the bedpost, and repeats the same obviously sexual symbolism with the fire by placing a hoe (symbolically phallic) in the flames. Henceforth the hut fire will consist of the joined essences of bride and groom. At early dawn, the bride arises and cleanses the sexual fluids from her husband's body, together with his pubic hair and hair from his chin which she must pluck away.[22] The wife must always cleanse the husband this way; we are not told what is done with the fluid, but among neighboring peoples (as we shall see) it is collected in "marriage pots" as a medicine assuring the well-being and fertility of the fields and of the couple.

Remarriage also has its appropriate symbolism, centering on fire. The fire in the widower's hut (which retains the powers of the deceased wife) must be put out prior to the ceremony. The bride-to-be is "seized" and carried into the hut, while a sherd is placed on a fire to heat outside. At the moment of intercourse, the bride signals to those outside with a cough, and they put some dry grass on the red-hot fragment of pottery and carry it inside as it bursts into flame. "Then those two lying on the bed move apart, and the people light a fire from that of the sherd; that fire is thus a new one and the woman becomes new. So they sleep."[23]

Just as rituals of initiation of the young girl and of remarriage have a spatial logic, so does the boys' initiation. Here, too, ritual serves to dramatize the transition from one sacred sphere to another, in this case from the mother's hut to the *kraal,* the realm of the men. Of course, the boys have gone back and forth in the kraal before; much of their childhood is taken up in watching over the cattle in the fields during the days and guiding them back to the kraals at night. Their time is already spent in a separate universe, then, defined by the cattle that are so important to the adult men. Nevertheless, a gulf separates the initiated youth from the company of the mere boys who play and while away the time in the fields. The initiated youths are young men and involve themselves with men's affairs, albeit on a low level. The boys' lives still center emotionally and symbolically around their mothers.

The formal request the boys make to their elders to start the initiation sum up its spatial symbolism; they go as a group, and say, "Take us to the cattle outpost and let us *shinga* (i.e., be initiated."[24] So they are taken there, and they sleep. Next morning, after they milk the cows, the boys must run a gauntlet of initiated herdsmen who have sticks, lumps of dry dung, and stones. "The goal which the boys must reach is the bull of the herd, and until they succeed in striking the bull they continue to be beaten. Once a boy has touched the bull he is free."[25] Thus the boys join the male realities, which are appropriately symbolized for herders by the bull.

Like many central and east African herders, the Ila glory in their cattle. The cattle provide the prestige of Ila men, and they talk tirelessly about them and their physical features with each other.[26] The chief of a village likes to hear his cases in the kraal, and there the men meet friends and discuss their affairs.[27] Women, on the other hand, are centered in their huts; we can sense a kind of contrast between particular family spaces and the more universal village space. One is female, the other male, one sustained by organic links, the other by nonorganic social ones. However, in the course of a girl's initiation, the women too gather and move as a party from enclosure to enclosure, and come to the cattle-kraal, where they stand singing just outside the inner fence in front of the men's principal hut for a few minutes.[28] Girls, too, move from the personal "organic" space of their mother's hut to the larger society of women in the course of initiation; this space of all women, however, is located above all in the bush and not in the kraal as for men (see our earlier brief description of the girls' initiation).[29]

Why do the Ila so ritualize the transition from the organic space of the hut to the larger social space of adulthood? Several reasons have already been suggested: the need to give a positive order to the intermediate, liminal moments of life, to dramatize the entry into new spheres of life—spheres that have spatial correlates in Ila thought. These dramatizations also underline the assumption of new social roles and statuses.

But the ritual has an additional value. In relatively undifferentiated societies like that of the Ila, the spheres of life, and the spaces they occupy, overlap each other considerably. For example, even as a child the Ila male knows the kraal and enters it, while after initiation he shall certainly continue to visit his mother frequently and in general to continue the customary round of life. Spiritual transitions and levels might tend therefore to get confused, and psychic spaces might tend to dissolve into the common, intermingled spaces of everyday banality, if they are not given clear definition by ritual. Following initiation, the young man's life is supposed to be centered on the male world of the kraal, the young woman's on the world of her husband's relatives and other adult women. The "coming-out" ceremonies at the end of initiation announce this change for all to see.

Functionalistic social anthropologists have demonstrated the usefulness of ritual to clarify different and competing social roles in societies where the same people meet together every day.[30] In a religious sense, the important point to stress about this is that the social imperatives in ritual are secondary to the spiritual imperatives. There are cosmological implications to the ritual that the social aspects merely interpret. The social groupings actually take on their special value from the cosmological classifications. By participating in an initiation ritual together, for example, the Ila villagers rediscover each other as parts of a larger universal order. It is largely for this reason, perhaps, that ancestors and culture-heroes are the guides through most ritual celebrations: they are already integral parts of the transcendental order, yet are still tied through their descendents with the social world and everyday concerns. Rather than simply socializing the cosmos, they cosmicize society by providing the transcendental models that humans must follow. The living also enter that deeper reality when they perform the rituals, a reality all feel to be the source of social and perceptual contexts.

This is one of the most important attributes of ritual. It places each participant within transcendental value. Even if on the ordinary level of daily intercourse I tend to define my neighbor in egoistic terms in relation to my desires, when we both engage in ritual together I am brought into a realization and sustaining enactment of his existence as part of the universe. This is independent of our personal wants. Even the emphasis on the role-relationships that control our ritual cooperation raises us from the merely egoistical to the transcendental level, since we enter into these roles to sustain an order beyond ourselves. We submit finally not to a social order but to a cosmic community of spirits and norms, anchored in mysterious power.

So it is that the rituals surrounding the Ila home, marriage, and initiation restore people to themselves, by locating them in the ultimate, enduring realities. These realities are beyond the control of the ego, and embrace all persons equally even while placing them in differentiated hierarchies. The independent existence of the neighbor is also restored to us; only as both self and neighbor are situated in a more ultimate reality can they really confront each other. Not even death ends the relationship when it is grounded so deeply. As ancestors, individuals continue to confront the living and each other. They endure only if the cosmos does. The social structure, in short, is made real and normatively corrected by reference to the ultimate religious structures and transcendental intentionalities.

This remains true when we turn from the Ila home to the village and regional levels of Ila experience. Symbolisms of the home are in fact repeated on a wider scale, making the land itself a larger home for the Ila. The resonances echo throughout Ila life.

THE ILA VILLAGE AND COUNTRY

Like many other central Bantu cultures, the Ila do not lay out their villages haphazardly. Instead, the village is conceived of after the plan of the family compound, which itself reflects the structure of the hut. The coalescence of family and wider social patterns is not surprising, since, as was mentioned in the introductory remarks on the Ila, the basic principle of their society is the kinship group. The village is in a sense a vaguer kinship group, a generalized family, over which the chief is a putative grandfather, although different clans do coexist in one place. The chief has essentially paternalistic relations with the villagers; he is expected to give a great deal of his time to them, resolving their problems and conflicts, hosting them at feasts and ceremonies, and appealing to his own ancestors on their behalf. Like fathers generally in this matrilineal society, the chief cannot be a despot. He governs through consensus. The elders of other families are consulted, and if they disapprove too strongly of the chief, they can move from the village and he will lose his "subjects."[31]

Every village is made up of several fenced-off family compounds. In the compound area one usually finds a number of huts in a half-circle, with the hut of the chief wife of the father in the center facing the entrance to the enclosure. Extending to each side are the other wives' huts and the dwellings of adult sons and others. The fence around the outside extends full circle to the entryway opposite, and before the huts another fence protects them from the cattle, who are driven into the central area of the compound every night. Ideally, the father's hut and that of his chief wife should be to the east, and the entryway to the west, and this is the position of the chief's compound area. In the village of Lubwe, of which Smith and Dale give the plan,[32] the chief's compound enclosure stood on the east side of the village somewhat apart from the other enclosures, with a small fenced-in group of hut shrines to the chief's ancestors just outside of the entryway to his compound, to the left. About twelve huts extended in a circle within the compound, a regular little village in itself. But Lubwe village stretched in a vast circle around the chief's compound, encircling it on all sides and including about 250 huts. The population of these villages can rise to as many as three thousand people. Often a chief will govern several villages scattered throughout a district, their sizes varying from just a few huts to quite large communities. In any case, at Lubwe the encircling huts were themselves grouped in compounds, so that the village plan resembles a necklace with many large circular beads strung along it. Each large family with cattle had its own cattle enclosure. But in the central space was a large, open field, criss-crossed with paths. The outer fence of the village was of bushes and stakes placed close together to serve as barriers to hostile invaders. The entrance to the village was through a gate in the western side of its circumference. In all these details the Lubwe village is typical of others.

Just as the threshold has a special ritual significance for the home, so does the entrance to a village. The Ila first establish the entrance when they start building a village, making an offering to the spirits that will henceforth protect it, including Leza the supreme being, the communal ancestors that guided the people in their previous village, the lineage ancestors of the chief, and their important spirits. The entrance always points to the west and to the setting sun (this is so precise that one can tell the time of year a village was built by the direction its entrance faces). East and west are really spiritual modalities: the newborn infant is formally presented to the east and to the west as the midwives set up a ioud lululooing and clapping of hands (to frighten away evil spirits?); the dead are buried with the face "to the Creator," i.e., to the east and the land of the dead; there is also a vague tradition that the Ila came from the east, while all state that the rains come from there.[33] Clearly the east generates all good things and life itself, and the Ila say explicitly that in the farthest distance to the east the earth meets the sky, sloping away from that high point continually down to the west.[34]

While the east brings light and life and gives access to heaven, the west is the reverse. Why then does the village face that way? We can only guess, but it is likely that those who move from the warmth and security of the village into the uncertain (and especially in former days often hostile) outer world, are symbolically moving from light and life to darkness and demonic conflict, while those who enter the village reverse the process. The village is thus symbolically the land of the east, of God and the spirits, and the location of the chief's enclosure to the east in the village is a spatial affirmation of his spiritually sustaining and guiding role for the village, as if he were an agent of the divine among mankind. The groves of trees that are planted on either side of the entrance to the village provide a residence to the spirits that protect the village and prevent evil powers from entering it. Smith and Dale therefore seem to be in error when they suggest that the chief has his hut facing to the west simply because it gives protection from the winds which sweep over from the east.[35] This indifference to symbolic meanings is typical of our authors and certainly overlooks the placement of the village entrance to the west.

We must not oversimplify Ila cosmology, however. While as we have seen the west is the location of the bush and of witches, and also of all hostile peoples, this is a spiritual or symbolic direction that does not contradict the obvious fact that witches often dwell in the midst of the village (they are *really* of the bush), and that hostile peoples were formerly all around the Ila. The simple contrast of east and west is also modulated by left and right, up (heaven) and down (earth), and by the various times of the sacred cycle of the year; in this web of interpenetrating meanings, which like a mystical grid surround the Ila and provide pattern to their lives, no one symbolic set exists independently.

There is a great deal about Ila chieftainship that we are not told by our authorities (like all ethnographers, they have their weak points), but at least we are told enough to know that we do not know. It is evident, for example, that the chief has a spiritual link to the land itself and its powers of fertility that the Ila regard as organic and substantial. We learn also that when a chief is chosen (generally from among the descendants of former chiefs), he must go through a series of rites that in effect make him a "warlock," or witch of benevolent sort. The medicines he is fed and provided enable him to fend off the evil efforts of chiefs and witches from other villages or districts and to preserve the health and fertility of his people, herds, and land.[36] Some chiefs accumulate such a lot of these medicines that their very being is changed, and after death they are tranformed into water spirits or serpentine water monsters, or Itoshi. A dramatic account is given of one chief's burial, in which a reed extended down to the corpse's ear as it lay beneath the earth; from the decaying body an Itoshi and many serpents emerged, wriggled up the reed, and the serpents scattered in the bush, while the miniature Itoshi was carried off to the dead chief's hut. There it was fed on lizards and fish until it was fully grown, and then it was taken to the river accompanied by all the chief's relatives in procession. This was apparently a customary occurence with the chiefs.[37] A chief can eat bits of Itoshi, or lion, leopard, elephant, hyena, or wild dog, depending on the kind of being he wishes to be reincarnated as after death.[38] Such reincarnated chiefs continue to watch over their people, though they occasionally demand the tribute of human lives. These guardians can reside in pools, groves, or anthills near their villages.[39]

These beliefs seem to be especially strong in the Nanzela area of Bwila. Funerals of chiefs here used to involved human sacrifices to accompany the corpse: a deep pit was dug with a mat on the bottom, on which dead slaves were laid. The chief's body was laid on these corpses, with his wives on either side, and at his head and feet some of his children. Passing strangers, it is said, were also killed and added to the grave, and lesser wives would sometimes leap in to be buried alive.[40] But by Smith and Dale's time there were only large sacrifices of cattle at funerals; the corpse would be dressed finely, treated as if alive, and asked if it was content with the village celebration before it was buried.[41] Among another segment of Ila, Smith and Dale detect a Luba influence (the Luba empire of southern Zaire influenced many of its neighbors). The chief of the Lusaka region was believed to incarnate Chinenga, their ancient founding chief and evidently their culture hero. At the hut shrine to Chinenga, periodic libations of medicines were made, which increased the spirit's powers and that of the living chief. At the shrine was an image of the ancestor, surrounded according to Smith and Dale with guns, drums, and other chiefly property. More commonly, the Ila build little shrine huts over chiefs' graves as a temple to their spirits; there offerings are left at the time of harvests, hunts, and other enterprises controlled by the spirit.[42]

There is a kind of correspondence in all of these rituals to a single symbolic logic. The chief is an intermediary figure in many ways, and these rituals merely develop the consequences. He defends the village against witches and outside enemies and therefore must know and master their alien powers. He is the priest of the village to the clan and village ancestors, to the regional spirits, and, on the occasion of the great festivals, even to God, Leza. We have seen that the location of his huts within the village announces a kind of symbolic equivalence to the role of Leza in the greater world. He has a close relationship, above all, to the mysterious powers of the land, which is made clear for all to see after his death, when he is tranformed into the masters of the animals (the lion, elephant, and especially the Itoshi monster). In this guise he continues to control the fertility and fate of the village. In a sense, the chief is the masculine power of the universe made concrete. We see this already in his right to preside over all law cases in the men's own cattle kraal.

But where is the actual connection to the earth and the feminine powers, then? The missing link in our information is the role of the chief's wife, about which Smith and Dale tell us very little. Here we would be completely at a loss, were it· not that the Ila owe many of their chiefly institutions to the Lunda kingdom of southern Zaire and share their features with many other central Bantu societies. Some of these societies have been very well reported on in this matter. I would like briefly to review some of their symbolic structures and rituals, admitting that in any case no culture is entirely like another, and that in this instance all assumptions about Ila practice must be hypothetical.

One of the best studies of the rituals of village headmanship, among a people culturally close to the Ila, is that by Ian Cunnison on the Luapula of northern Zambia.[43] The Luapula are also a matrilineal people of Lunda origin, and among them the wife is extremely important to the headmen of villages:

> Briefly, where a man's position implies mystical care of land and people he can effect this only through his marital relationship. And the chief wife is identified in speech with her husband: *mwadi e mwatu* ("the queen is the king") is a phrase often heard in connection with Kazembe and his first wife. The mystical dangers from dead lions can only be annulled by "owners of the land," and then only after intercourse with their wives; and both spouses have to step on a lion-skin to purify it and the country. A man can rule his country only when it is "hot," and it can be made "hot" only in this manner.[44]

(The reference to lions reminds us that in the Luapula view a man who kills a lion is like one who killed a man, for the lion is a "king of beasts," and together with leopards, elephants, "pythons" (cf. the Ila Itoshi), and other such royal beasts are believed often to be reincarnations of former kings or powerful medicine men. The continuity here with the Ila is of course clearly a strong one.)

The rituals incumbent on the Luapula village headman, to maintain the proper "heat" in his land, are merely extensions according to Cunnison of the normal Luapula marriage rituals. Each Luapula wife has as one of her intimate articles of toilet a marriage pot, in which after every act of intercourse she washes herself together with her husband. (We recall the similar duties of the Ila wife.) In this way the couple avoids retaining the impurity ("heat," "dirt") of their sexual fluids and of intercourse in their daily social contacts. A person still impure from intercourse can badly affect the young, sick, and others in vulnerable states. The marriage pot's "heat," however, as the most intense mingling of the forces of the spouses, powerfully affects all extensions of themselves; for example, the fertility of the fields is dependent on the proper fusion of the sexual polarities of the owners. In the same way, the marriage pot of the village headman and his wife affects the entire village; the couple have medicines related to the village in it, or hanging from a calabash suspended from their hut rafters, mostly composed of leaves and roots of certain trees in the vicinity. The sexual powers of the couple affect the vegetation of the entire land through this pot and control its fertility. It is important to note that this pot is kept by the wife; her power is direct, and great, and we are told that only through his link to his wife can the chief or king be honored with the title, "the Land"—for *mwadi e mwatu:* the queen is the king.[45]

The ritual washing of the couple in the pot after intercourse keeps the village hot and dynamic. At important rituals, especially those of the founding of a village, ritual intercourse of the headman and his wife and even by the villagers in general is essential, and the use of the pot is also required. When a headman's wife dies the calabash containing the village medicines also dies, "and the villiage is said to 'become cold' and 'die.' "[46] Cooked food, the earth and its food crops, the female pot and the headman's wife, fire and the "heat" of transformation, are interconnected. "To put a pot on the fire" has the same meaning as "to rule" (illuminating perhaps the Ila rite of widow remarriage, in which grass is burned on a heated potsherd and with it a new fire started in the newlywed's hut). The same phrase is used for "opening up new land." The marriage pot regenerate the land also by participating in the *nshipa* medicines buried in the headman's hut at the founding of a village. These medicines, gathered from the herbs of the land, ward off all evil including the sorcery of rival headmen. The *nshipa* is perilously close to sorcery itself, since it also draws people from other villages to settle in its own.

If a headman's wife dies, her pot and the village medicine must be thrown away, and the village itself must be renewed. A new wife is found as soon as possible, and meanwhile a caretaker and his wife take over the rituals, and her pot becomes the "village pot." When a new wife comes, the whole village must be chaste their first night (perhaps to focus the cosmic and the newlyweds' sexual energies); the next morning the village turns out to see the wife putting her pot (now the village pot) on the fires. Food cooked in this pot is shared by the newlyweds' relatives.[47]

Such symbolic structures help us understand otherwise peculiar practices of the Ila and confirm the similarity of basic cosmology. Smith and Dale tell us, for example, that pregnant wives and their husbands keep medicine pots near their beds, the power of which affects both them and their children. We are also informed that women who commit abortion must be put outside of the village in a little hut (to the west!) and day after day must wash themselves in a newly prepared medicine pot; such women cannot use pots for cooking. When such a woman returns purified to the village, all the villagers must wash in a special medicine pot and drink the water to avoid being affected by her misdeed (which otherwise would spoil their fertility and the land's).[48] When the Ila move to a new village site, the villagers proceed to the new location in procession led by a woman or child bearing a "pot of medicine"; this pot is put inside a small circle of posts at the side of the future gateway, and blood from a sacrificed ox is added to its contents. Then the spirits are invoked; the posts will later sprout into a sacred grove to the protecting spirits.[49]

The Ila lack genuine kingship. It is clear from these accounts however, that the ultimate logic of their ceremonies goes back to rites of kingship; the Ila admit this themselves in tracing their society back to the Lunda kings. When we turn to ceremonies of kingship still practiced or recently practiced by other Lunda peoples, we find that the ideas of priestly leadership, or "divine kingship" as it has sometimes been called, provide a complete code that deciphers Ila conceptions of chieftainship and its relation to the earth. Fundamentally, the earth is a feminine space, and the institution of ancestral kingship (and male authority) is likened to a marriage—a marriage instigated by heaven, which begins real time. That is, "male" heaven, kingship, culture, and the ancestors (and therefore time) are brought together with the feminine earth, nature, and sacred space. Here again cosmological ideas are used to guide as closely as possible the community's social behavior.

The specific details supporting these conclusions are fascinating, and although constituting a slight digression should be mentioned here. Not far from the Ila to the west are the Lozi or Rotsi people, who also trace themselves back to the Lunda. Here elaborate rituals of kingship are still preserved:

> Lozi nationhood is generally referred to in three terms: the nation (*sicaba samalozi*), the land (*bulozi*), and the kingship (*bulana bwamalozi*). Nation, land, and kingship participate in one another and the systems of relations centering in all the concepts interpenetrate inextricably in reality, though they can be

isolated in analysis. For the Lozi themselves they are absolutely identified: each is always referred to in terms of the others. The land is *mubu wamulena* (soil of the king), and the king's most specific title, used otherwise only for the Princess Chief, LITUNGA, means "earth". The king is MBUMU-WA-LITUNGA, "great-one-of-the-earth"; the Princess Chief is LITUNGA-LA-MBOELA, "earth-of-the-south". . . . . Lozi emphasize all the time: "the king is the land and the land is the king". Similarly the nation *sicaba*, the Lozi people *Malozi*, are the king. The king is saluted as *malozi*, as are his councillors in council and his people *en masse*.[50]

The king is the unity of the people, culture, and the land. He is truly semidivine, a priestly figure as much as a political one. He sustains the land and the people through his relationship with his ancestors, and after death he returns to the earth and is worshipped at shrines.[51] All use of the land is at his pleasure, all wild and domesticated products of the earth are his, and tribute is therefore obligatory.[52] He is *mushemi*, parent, to everyone, and like the Ila of their chiefs, the Lozi think of him as "my father" and "my mother." That is, the king embodies the principles of kinship and is everyone's ancestor.[53] Therefore, his ancestors are also everyone's ancestors and can affect the fertility of the entire land. "When the king dies, the nation falls into a coma," Lozi say; fires are put out throughout the kingdom, at least in theory, until his successor with the help of the priest of Mbuyamwambwa ("wife of God"), lights new fires with frictionsticks. This fire is distributed to all the villages to rekindle their fires; then food is cooked and people warm themselves by "the fire of King so-and-so."[54]

Already in this account we see dual sexual oppositions suggested, in which the king is symbolically complementary to the land and needs the services of the "wife of God" to light the generative fire and renew life. The symbols are made clearer by Lozi political geography. The kingdom is divided into two parts, north and south, without any external geographical necessity for this division.[55] The division is caused by cosmological imperatives. Each province has a ruler; the northern king (called "the Great One of the Earth") is politically primary, while the southern ruler ("Earth of the South," or "Princess Chief") is dominant in a priestly way. Despite the title of "Princess Chief," the southern ruler did not need to be female until recently, we are told, but at the same time we are informed that the founder of the southern part was female, and the two halves of the kingdom are symbolically wed to each other, or, in another symbolism, the south is the mother to the living king and the north. The capitals of the two provinces lie close to each other on either side of the border; the major shrines to the royal ancestors are mostly in the southern realm. The southern king is said to be the younger brother (Mwanambinji) of the first Lozi king, Mboo. Between the grave of Mwanambinji in the southern realm and that of Mboo in the northern lies the shrine of Makono, their mother, "where the king gets his kingship."[56]

Whenever the king and princess chief move they should maintain their relative positions faithfully, the king always to the north, the princess chief to the south, and the other lineage chiefs sited geographically in relation to this axis. When they travel southward, the princess chief leads, and the reverse holds when going north.[57] Despite occasional civil wars the southern ruler is excluded from true kingship (rule in the north), on the grounds that *women* cannot rule.[58] This alone would be enough to verify that symbolically the south is female. The task of the princess chief is to preside over the priestly functions. Mwanambinji was reputed to be a great medicine chief when alive, and is now chief of the spirits of the departed kings.

Gluckman tells us that the relationship between the two rulers forms the pattern for everyday Lozi marital relations: the husband "owns" the wife and is her "lord," but she is "a different kind of lord" to him.[59]

In effect, then, the Lozi have the structure of semidivine or divine king symbolically wed to the priest(ess) of the earth, which is so common in African religions. It is interesting to observe that the wedding of these two polar figures can be represented through ritual intercourse, or symbolisms of war and conquest, possession, and/or death. These associations are hinted at, for example, in the Lozi installation ceremonies, when the priest of "the wife of God" escorts the king to Makono, the home and ancestral grave of the divine queen-mother, "to fetch kingship."[60] Is the King the symbolical husband, or the son, of this original ancestress of the royal family? Perhaps both. We further read, "The king spends the night in vigil by a small lake out of which comes a monster to hold communion with him."[61] The reappearance of the Itoshi being certainly confirms the existence of levels of ritual symbolism not fully reported to us.

The theme of conquest is one that constantly reappears in myths and rituals of kingship in central Africa. The first divine king or culture-hero invaded the land, which had already been passively governed by the earth-spirit, and defeated it, thus instituting culture and time. In some cultures, the earth-spirit is said to transform itself into a great serpent or python, and go down into a lake or river, or a shrine, where kings must still contact it through mediums or even human sacrifices. Such beliefs are found, for example, among the Shona cultures of Rhodesia. The Korekore (of Chakoma district) say that Nyanhehwe, the ancestral culture-hero, defeated Dzivaguru the earth serpent in the beginning of time. It was a battle of brute force and medicines against the primordial magical power of the earth. Dzivaguru finally agreed to cede authority to the invader, and even shared mystical secrets before retiring into the mountain pool where his shrine is still located. Before disappearing, he instructed mankind on social laws and the proper cult for obtaining rain from him. We are told that the culture-hero henceforth viewed the earth as his "wife," which was only a symbolic sexual attribution since the embodiments of the first chief must regularly offer virgins to the spirit as its "wives." In any case, the conquest is symbolically a sexual relationship, as both of these facts indicate.[62] The mock war of the Lozi kings, in which the northern great chief and symbolic male engages in battle with the princess chief and symbolic female during the course of the installation, must also be seen in this context. As with the Shona, the female is the one associated with the earth, the land and the aboriginal; the male is the conquering hero and ancestral king who institutes real history. The first remains present to us through her priests and mediums and is associated with pools; the second is embodied in the present king. It is clear that the basic symbolism is common to a wide range of central Bantu religions.

An instance of the same symbolism among a people closer to the Ila culturally and geographically is the Ndembu kingship. There, too, we find two chiefs, one political, the other priestly, though both have religious and secular aspects. As we have come to expect, the priestly chief embodies the aboriginal Mbwela people and is their senior headman; he represents the land and confers chiefly status on the ruler.[63] It is said that the Lunda royal ancestor Kanongesha conquered the Mbwela in a fierce struggle but then entered into a ritual relationship with the Kafwana, the head of the Humbu branch of the Mbwela. Kafwana is called *Mama yaKanongesha*, "*Mother* of Kanongesha," since he kills and *gives birth symbolically* to each new chiefly embodiment of the paramount chief.[64] He teaches each new Kanongesha the witchcraft proper to a chief and presents him with the "supreme symbol of chiefly status among tribes of Lunda origin," the *lukanu* bracelet. This is a circlet made of human genitals and sinews soaked in the blood of male and female slaves sacrificed at each installation.[65] The bracelet was originally owned by the ancient Lunda kings, it is said. The Kafwana hides it during each interregnum of primordial chaos to protect the land he "owns." The paramount chief makes daily invocations to the lukana, at dawn and sunset, for the fertility of the land and all beings on it. It recalls the marriage pot of the Luapula and Ila peoples to us. Interestingly, like the charmed pot, the lukana is controlled by the "feminine" aspect of the king; he wears it on the left arm. Moreover, when the novice chief is "killed" and "reborn" as archetypal king under the Kafwana's guidance, the chief's senior wife or a ritual substitute who takes part is also called *lukanu*.[66] Time itself emerges in the person of the culture-hero/chief from this primal birth and initiation.

Examples from other Lunda peoples could be given, but the pattern should be dramatically clear: "feminine" primal space and "masculine" time (embodied in the royal ancestors or culture-heroes) thematically structure many central African religions, including that of the Ila.[67] Sexuality is a transformative pattern that deeply shapes reality. Just because the pattern is so similar on so many levels, and these levels interconnect through human awareness of them, ritual control is needed to keep the levels ordered and distinct.

Ritualization of these symbols makes two seemingly contradictory statements at once; that processes in different realms *are like each other* and even in some sense identical, and that they *are different* and are to be separated from each other. That is, ritual creates a *symbolic* universe in which to live. For example, calling a human being by the name of a symbol (e.g., the ritual wife of the Ndembu chief is his *lukanu*) affirms a continuity, but the physical difference between the person and the symbol also states a discontinuity. The spiritual reality is indicated by the physical one but is really beyond it. The two are not the same, yet they are organically connected. This perceptual world rises out of the spiritual one and is fundamentally shaped by it. Moreover, slaves are physically sacrificed to invigorate the *lukanu* bracelet. The metaphor is not a "mere" metaphor, but a sacred reality.

The difference between perceptual and spiritual reality is made clear in a number of ways. One is to distort perceptual realities when one wishes to point to their symbolic status. The shrines that the Ila erect for dead chiefs are very tiny structures that no living person could use; the embodiments of "female" sexuality in ritual are often actually male (as in the case of the Lozi princess chief or the Ndembu Kafwana). This acts as a ritual "heightening" of symbolic realities. Or, sharp distinctions will be made in the ways in which everyday life is related to ritual acts; in short, taboos will demarcate and separate the two realms. Thus, ritual taboos on sexual behavior indicate that the ritual action is structurally a transformation of a sexual type that must be distinguished from merely physical sexuality. Hence hunting requires sexual chastity among the Ila, although some Ila hunters underline the continuity between realities by believing that intercourse gives luck on the hunt—and if a hunter dreams of having incestuous relations, he *ought* to go and hunt (to get the bestiality out in the right direction, so to speak)![68] In fact, the list of activities that require ritual chastity is practically a compilation of those processes the Ila conceive to be analogous to each other and that therefore demand clear separation: going into battle, fishing, hunting, going on journeys (all of these illuminate the themes of wandering, hunting and military invasion and conquest in kingship myths), sowing seed, threshing grain, storing it in bins or making beer from it, smelting iron, and when the wife is pregnant, nursing her baby, or menstruating.[69] All of these are liminal occasions of transformations, and the various varieties of transformation must not be confused: e.g., human sexuality belongs in the village, not in the bush where one kills or travels, or in the fields where one plants and the ancestors (and God) fructify the land.

A compact instance of all these points concerning ritual symbolism is the Ila method of ironsmithing. Here we see as well how actual women are dismissed by Ila men in their appropriation of feminine mysteries, a consequence of the separation of symbolic and literal realities.

Smithing in many African cultures is a sacred process deeply shaped by cosmological conceptions. In a number of west African religions the first smith was the demiurge or agent of God, the trickster, or the first culture-bringer. Among the Dogon of Mali, all of these terms characterize the first smith, who is said to have stolen fire and the seeds of all life from heaven and carried it to earth in an ark that was also his furnace and anvil. This ark was "feminine," and was really his wife; when he hammered it the vibrations produced life in all directions.[70] Among the Yoruba of Nigeria, Ogun the ironworking trickster deity has phallic and serpentine associations (serpents are also associated with Dogon smiths as well).[71] These instances should demonstrate the remarkable tendency to sexualize the smith's mysteries in many African cultures, but the symbolisms are if anything much more clear in Bantu societies. Among these cultures it is common to find that all implements in the smithing process are shaped in sexual images: the main furnace of the Chokwe of Angola is shaped like a woman squatting in childbirth, as is the furnace among the Shona several thousand miles to the east; genital symbols on smithy bellows in Uganda intimate that these bellows are phallic in relationship to the fire that melts the ore.[72] So in a great triangle from Angola to Rhodesia, and north to Uganda, many of the same ideas reoccur.

Here we need only discuss the Ila practices.[73] Smithing is for them a highly esoteric art, preserved by smithy clans whose secrets are closely guarded. Since smithing involves use of the earth's products and creation from its depths of human and cultural shapes, it needs special medicines and can be done only in the spring when the earth is ready for cultivation. At this time, the smith builds a miniature village in the bush, in which "husband" and "wife" procreate not human children, but refined iron ore. The camp is laid out to the cardinal points, the anthill supplying the clay, to the east, the shelter for the workers to the west within the enclosure. Anthills, as we have already noticed for the Ila, are the homes of generative spirits and even Itoshi. It is appropriate that they are to the east, "ruling" the workers. Within the shelter, the smith or "doctor" has his place just to the right of the entrance looking out, while his "wife" sleeps to the left. This symbolism, so clear to us from hut architecture, makes clear that the workers are symbolically the "couple's" children. In accord with the emphatically symbolic nature of these equivalences, however the smith's "wife" is really his chief male assistant; women must not enter the area, especially menstruating women. If any of the workers should dream of women and have an emission, he must inform the smith who will have to go through an elaborate purification of him: the smithing symbolism is as far from pornography as it is possible to be. The "doctor" himself, as well as his workers, is tabooed; he can have nothing to do with women during the operations, a state represented as well by his uncut hair and unshaven face. The women of the village have taboos on them, too: they may not wash nor anoint themselves, nor beautify themselves; "They are, as we were told, in the same state as recently bereaved widows."[74] The sharpness of the symbolic distinctions could not be clearer.

Nevertheless, the women from the village prepare the clay from which the kilns are to be made. These kilns, as we shall see, are symbolically female themselves. The kilns are arranged in a line from east to west on the *southern* side of the enclosure (i.e., the left-hand, *female* side when facing west: the same side as the smith's "wife" sleeps on in the shelter). The lower part of the kiln bulges out, and is called the "belly".[75] The entire structure is built up to a height of about five feet. When still incomplete, a boy and girl from the village are brought out to stand in its interior and crack beans in their mouth; the men greet the crackling with shouts acknowledging the crackling and roaring of the fire. Without a doubt, the young couple are the *bapuka* of the kiln womb; their rite "is supposed to conduce to the proper smelting of the iron," and after the children return home they are regarded as betrothed.[76] Even the spouts that are inserted into the kiln have symbolic meaning as vaginal openings; the poles that place them into the clay wall are smeared with symbolic semen. There are openings into the furnace from each of the four directions, but the greater number of spouts were placed in the western side, for here the ore will flow forth. When the actual firing of the ore rocks is done, songs of strongly sexual content are sung. Special medicines are also part of the fuel; it is said that these medicines actually transform the ore into smelted iron. The "doctor" and his "wife" must share in the placement of these medicines in the furnace.[77]

Following the smelting of the ore into iron, the metal is worked into tools by the smith.[78] This last stage can be done later on, in the village, but it still has a symbolic structure that makes the task a kind of ritual. The bellows consist of two shallow wooden bowls, to the top of which are strapped leather coverings and long-handled sticks that can be used to pump air in and out of the bowls. Wooden tubes project from the bowls, which join together in the unnecessarily flared opening to a baked clay funnel leading to the fire. By working the sticks up and down, air is driven into the funnel and from there to the fire, causing the lump of iron to melt down so that it can be shaped by the smith. I would like to suggest that the symbolism of all of these objects is sexual; there must be two bowls with leather covering, like the testicles, which have tubes that are joined together and enter the funnel like the male organ in the female. That the funnel is clay is perhaps also symbolically meaningful (as we shall see in further detail shortly, clay is feminine). The fire that transforms the raw ore would in this interpretation equate to the "heat" of the womb. The smith creates cultural objects in the same way that women create children.

SUPREME BEING AND THE EARTH:
THE PROBLEM OF THE ONE AND THE MANY

We have followed the permutations of body symbolism from the natal home to the larger village, to chieftainship and even to ironsmithing, watching it become ever more separate from actual physical realities, ever more metaphorical and abstract. At the furthest reaches of the Ila universe these symbols become very diffuse and generalized, and we find that the organizing ideas at this level are centered on another kind of reality, the unitary idea of God. It is as if we have to do with two different kinds of logic here, one ascending from the body, the other descending from unitary intellectual/spiritual insights. To understand this other level, we must start by discussing the Ila view of God, although as we shall see the two logical networks must and do join together and merge.

The Ila religion is essentially a monotheism, although with various "refractions" (to use the terminology of Evans-Pritchard). On the regional level preside the great ancestors of the Ila, whose spirits (*muzhimo*) may be recognized by all or many villages as culture-heroes active in the creation of the world and of man. These great spirits rule the lesser ancestors and are ruled in turn by Leza, the supreme being. They receive annual festival recognition and thanksgiving for the rain, prosperity and crops of their districts; some are worshipped by the entire people, however, and the greatest of these is Bulongo, "the earth only."[79] "He is the muzhimo of the whole country: there is no community that does not pray to him."[80] He has no groves; only temporary huts are built to him for the annual ceremonies, but his power is recognized everywhere. At Mala, an ancient village of the Ila, his priest is an old chief of the lineage of Shimunenga, the main culture-hero of that region, and recognized by many Ila elsewhere. It was Shimunenga, the most powerful of the ancestors, who first ordained the annual worship of Bulongo. Thus the chief of the ancestors, who instituted time and history, also regulated the relationship of mankind to the earth and space; his representative today continues his primordial role. Interestingly, the chief of Mala district who inherits Shimunenga's political power is not the same as the priest who heads the Bulongo cult: the worship of the earth and of the nearer, more politically active ancestors is separated, although kept in the same primordial clan.

Despite Bulongo's universality ("in all the world his existence is recognized—everywhere")[81] he speaks to men through the culture-hero Shimunenga, whom he seizes as a medium is seized by a spirit. (In other Ila districts other demi-god ancestors take this role.)[82] Shimunenga in turn seizes his human medium, and informs mankind in Bulongo's name. Despite this complex communion between the chief ancestor and the earth, Bulongo does not belong to history, is not a person, and was here before the first ancestor (one informant differed, saying Bulongo was an ancestor prior even to Shimunenga, the aboriginal possessor of all prosperity and riches). But all agree that Bulongo is beyond all other beings and dwells in the presence of God; Bulongo is the privileged "friend of God" and is prayed to as God's emissary. Bulongo is more likely to answer prayers for rain than God, one Ila stated, but he added that when Bulongo is invoked at the end of the cold season, it is really Leza who responds and makes the rain fall; Bulongo merely intercedes for mankind.

Primal as Bulongo is, and lacking clear distinction from Leza, it is not even clear what sex he/she has. Bulongo "is not a person," yet in relation to Leza the spirit is feminine, while in relation to mankind the spirit is sometimes considered the masculine extension of Leza. At the beginning of the universe, Ila say, Bulongo (literally; "clay") and Leza ("sky") joined in sexual union, and from their intercourse came grain and all things. This myth of the union of heaven and earth is of course one of the most archaic and widely diffused myths of planting cultures, both in Africa and beyond.[83] One of the first fruits of this union, for the Ila, was the culture-hero Shimunenga and the other ancestors who continued the creative work of

Leza. Addressed as male, Bulongo is chief of the ancestors of mankind. But the Ila also include Bulongo in the vague generosity of primordial being that is Leza; at one of the great village centers already referred to, Lubwe, Leza is called Bulongo-Namesi (Namesi means "rain-giver," an attribute of the sky), indicating the inclusion or unification in the high god of the entire universe of space and time. For as the Ila say of Leza, he is Namakungwe, "he from whom all things come."[84] He is "the Master of All," the source and controller of the power in all things. The power of the various spirits and ancestors is ultimately Leza's; the Ila admit that they address God through these lesser beings to show respect, just as one petitions a ruler even in his presence in the third person as "his majesty."

For example, if a murder has been committed, there must be a blood offering to the district's spirit, usually Shimunenga, as the embodiment of Bulongo, the earth, for the earth hates shed blood. Ten to twenty of the killer's cattle must be sacrificed to the ancestors, and two must be offered directly to Shimunenga. All the people share the flesh, and the heads are deposited at the grove. In the distribution of the meat the village chiefs and lineage heads all receive specific portions, so that the entire community with all its subdivisions is reconciled and reintegrated.[85] So we see that when the levels of the divine order are ruptured by an infraction, the entire community is involved and restitution of order requires a great sacrifice engaging them all. In the feast of reconciliation at the district shrines, celebrated in honor of the culture-hero and the earth, the various groups that embody these realities must enact a common drama together. In these rituals a politically fragmented society is religiously unified.

We can easily see how divine kings, as embodiments in their societies of the culture-hero, continue this unifying function in the ceremonies of marriage to the earth at their installation and in their ongoing cultic relation to earth-priests.

Unity, however, would be impossible without the prevading presence of God. For the Ila, Leza is the operational idea permitting all these transformations and integrations. Shimunenga's priest receives two oxen and conveys their shadow-soul (*chingvhule*) to Shimunenga, who in turn brings it to Leza. God, then, is the real recipient of sacrifice. In explaining this to Smith, the old priest to Shimunenga "went through the action of Shimunenga approaching Leza with the offering in his hand."[86] The resemblance of other culture's divine kings and Shimunenga is striking. But it is clear that even the communal demigod is not transcendent enough or distant enough from the disturbed divine order to heal its divisions, without recourse to more primordial realities.

Leza can be approached directly, however. Many Ila offer personal, direct prayers to him every morning when first leaving their huts; the liminal passage from home to world thereby is guided by the most positive orientation.[87] Prayer here serves the same transformatory and mediatory function as sacrifice. Similarly, prayers to Leza begin hunting trips or fishing and are made whenever bad luck strikes.[88] As is so common in the history of religions, the Ila refuse to make any sharp distinctions between "religion" and "magic" and pray to Leza when making medicines. Medicines have only the power Leza gives them, and unjust use of the charms would make their force recoil on the user. Prayers to Leza are made before using hunting, fishing, healing, antiwitchcraft, or other medicines.[89] All these instances show us that Leza is particularly available during moments of liminality, at the interstitial points in the divine order. Leza guards and preserves the structure of the world, moving his creatures from one stable level to another in harmony and security. He withdraws behind the divine order and permits it to continue, only intervening when movement from one level to another is needed and thus showing his compassionate self-restraint yet omnipresence. Thus it is that Leza is appealed to directly in times of greatest trouble. Relatives pray over a person having a lingering illness: "Was it not Thou who createst him on the earth and said he should walk and trust Thee? Leave Thy child, that he may trust Thee, Eternal One! We pray to Thee—Thou art the great Chief!"[90] In a peculiar way, in Leza's remoteness is evidenced his compassionate presence.

When order threatens to disappear entirely, and everything loses normative form, he is appealed to again to remove himself from his confusing unmediated nearness to man. Barren women pray directly to Leza, for he is the author of barren destiny, and he can heal it.[91] The year itself hinges on liminal moments when Leza is especially near: the period of the rains begins with a three-day interdiction on all work in the fields, for these first rains are the fluid aspect of Leza giving life to the earth; to cultivate the earth would hurt him.[92] But the regularity of these liminal moments signifies their controlled, restrained nature, the benevolent face of Leza. Leza is even more overwhelmingly near in the catastrophes that break into time and destroy the everyday order; epidemics, earthquakes, and severe lightning storms are his judgments. On such occasions all villages join in public and private prayers directly to him for mercy and forgiveness, for all mankind is then caught up in the liminal breakdown. The Leza affirm, however, that the normative order is more basic an expression of Leza's purpose and nature than chaotic disorder, when they interpret even drought and cataclysm as judgments designed to bring mankind back into a greater obedience to Leza's norms. The same is indicated by Leza's decision to enter directly into chosen mediums and proclaim his general dissatisfaction with the deeds of the Ila, the need for renewed sacrifice, and repentance, or even new commands or norms (either taboos or cultic practices). In this way, prophets transmit to the people new customs and values, founding them in God.

Leza is in short the transcendental one, present in all his raw power in the breakdown of the divine order, but mirrored also in the benevolently sustaining patterns of everyday normalcy. The entire world witnesses to him. So overwhelming is his presence and power that he cannot be confined to any one grove or cult-center, and he needs no special priests to intercede between the individual and himself. Therefore he seems to have little cult, but this is deceptive. Leza relates to the individual and the whole of the world directly; neither needs cultic expression. The structures of society, and particular subgroups of the divine order, have each their own governing agents that express the unitary power of God while locating and legitimating particular parts of the whole. The cult of the communal demigods, the family ancestors, the medicines, and the annual festivals are all in their totality aspects of the larger cult to the supreme being. They do not exist independently of Leza.[93]

There are yet other ways in which he enters into Ila life. The personal guardian spirit (the "namesake" or reincarnated ancestor who dwells within the descendent and is worshipped by him), and the destiny discoverable through divination, both come together in Leza. Thus the guardian spirit and destiny on the personal level, the family ancestors on the kinship level, the communal ancestors and culture-heros on the regional and "national" levels, and his own epiphanies on the cosmic level, all present Leza's active governance of the realms of existence.

An apt form of the diffraction of Leza's power and life through the various levels of the universe is the Itoshi monster we have referred to several times. It is always associated with watery places; water is Leza's own vivifying essence, his "sperm." Perhaps Leza's most characteristic medium of expression is the rain. He is called Namesi, rain- or water-giver; one says, "It's raining," by saying, "Leza is falling."[94] People are sure of Leza's compassionate nature for one reason above all others: he causes the rain to fall regularly regardless of the sins of men. However evil or good people are, the rains always come in due season.[95] Moreover, the proper method of praying to Leza is to fill one's mouth with water and squirt it out as an offering or put medicines in a pot of water, pray and pour it out on the earth. Thus one communicates with God.[96] Daily prayers at dawn, or prayers on special occasions, are especially effective if they are offered near to rivers or streams, and when one comes to a river on one's traveling, it is a good opportunity to fill one's mouth with water, squirt it out, and pray somewhat as follows: "It is Thou who leadest me. Now may I return with Thy prosperity from the place where I am going, O Leza! Go on shepherding me well, my Master!"[97] It would seem that in the vicinity of the river one is closer to Leza, or even in his presence.

It is therefore very significant that in the pools and rivers that rise and overflow in the rainy season rule the water-monsters, the bapuka or Itoshi, who oversee communal life and sanction behavior. Each community has its guardian spirits, some apparently simple nature-spirits, others once human beings, great chiefs of the village who emerged after death from grave-shrines as pythons and were escorted to the pools by priests. The Itoshi observe the doings of mankind, and drag evil people into the water, but they also reward the good by controlling the rains and granting fertility to the women. Smith writes:

> All rivers and lakes in Africa are probably thought to be inhabited by similar monsters. In the Victoria Nyanza there is Lukwata. The Bathonga speak of the Maloa in the Zambesi and the Barotsi of the Lengongole. . . . It is to this class of creature that Itoshi belongs. It has been described to us as big as a very large Ihunga thorn-tree, with the body of a crocodile, the head of a man, and the fins of a fish, and upwards of fifty feet in length. It is generally invisible to all but those who have the proper medicine; should it appear to others it means death.[98]

Smith's generalizations concerning all Africa rivers and pools may be too enthusiastic, but he is certainly correct about the idea being pan-African. We recall the Dzivaguru of the Korekore Shona, the molimo rainbow-serpent of the Mbuti Pygmies, and even the partly related pangolin of the Lele, for it is a watery beast with scales. The veneration of the water-serpent is widespread throughout west Africa as well, often associated with the rainbow.[99]

The monstrous, intermediary nature of the Itoshi is extremely important. It is ancestor, culture-hero, nature-spirit, and water beast. It joins together the living and the dead, man and animal, heaven and earth. It belongs, for example, to the primordial past when deformed monsters roamed the earth, before the culture-heroes established order. Often the Itoshi is a transformed ancestral chief, or even a trickster/culture-hero itself, who as master of the dead rules the spirits of the dead in villages below the water. But this transformed human who is also a nature spirit and animal controls the living as well; he permits ancestral spirits to reincarnate in the womb and supervises the fertility of the fields as Leza's agent or embodiment on earth. The bapuka or Itoshi of the womb, we recall, represents the ancestors; the woman's womb is analogous to the earth-enclosed pools and rivers in which the great Itoshi dwell. The Itoshi, in short, it appears to be the primal form of masculine fecundity, the phallic refraction or extension of the primordial, vague presence of Leza who is "at home" in nature like a chief with his wife.

Within the Itoshi all time is summed; as we have seen he is past ancestor-chief, but also source of future children and crops. This reveals the nature of time as a field within which Leza acts. We have discussed spatial concepts among the Ila; we must now turn to time.

NOTES TO CHAPTER 4

1. Our source for most of what follows is E. W. Smith and A. M. Dale, *The Ila-Speaking Peoples of Northern Rhodesia*, 2 vols. (London: Macmillan & Co., 1920), one of the major older "classics" of African anthropology. Unfortunately, most recent anthropological studies of particular cultures are either so "professional" and specialized or so generalized that a sense of the unity and interrelatedness of the entire culture is lost. However, it is precisely this cosmological integration that we are seeking to discover at this point in our study, and for this we must turn back to the older studies. Smith and Dale's investigation is useful also because it draws our attention to the cultures extending from southern Zaire through a large portion of central Africa, a vast area but remarkably homogeneous in basic outlines. There emerges therefore in our description a continuity which is not only geographical with the Zaire Mbuti, Lele and Lega. As the next note will elaborate, the Ila are offshoots of an important Zaire culture, the Lunda, an important source of many central African cultures.

2. On the essential unity of this culture-province, see the general agreement of Jan Vansina, *Kingdoms of the Savanna* (Madison: University of Wisconsin Press, 1966); Hermann Baumann, *Les peuples et les civilisations de l'Afrique*, trans L. Homburger (Paris: Payot, 1948), pp. 146-70 ("Zambesi circle"); George Peter Murdock, *Africa: Its Peoples and Their Culture-History* (New York: McGraw-Hill Book Co., 1959), pp. 271-73, 290-302 ("Central Bantu" culture province); Jacques Maquet, *Les civilisations noire* (Paris: Horizons de France, 1962), pp. 16, 121-30 ("Granary civilizations"). Also see Wyatt MacGaffey, "Comparative Analysis of Central African Religions," Africa 42, no. 1 (January 1972): 21-31, and even more Luc de Heusch, *Le roi ivre, ou l'origine de l'État* (Paris: Gallimard, 1972), showing the pervasive presence in this area of essentially the same values and mythic-ritual symbols. Beatrix Heintze adds another dimension in her *Besessenheits-Phänomene in Mittleren Bantu-Gebiet* (Weisbaden: Franz Steiner, 1970), pp. 252-58, demonstrating the strong influence of Intralacustrine cultures on possession-trance ideology in this area, and reminding us of Herskovits's delineation of a cattle-"spear" cultural continuum stretching down into central Africa from East Africa. Heintze suggests that the Intralacustrine circle forms together with the Zaire-Angola-Zambia cultures and those extending in the southeast through the Shona region of Rhodesia, a "great triangle."

3. These remarks reflect Jack Goody and Joan Buckley, "Inheritance and Women's Labour in Africa," *Africa* 43, no. 2 (April 1973): 109-21; Ester Boserup, *Women's Role in Economic Development* (London: St. Martin's Press, 1970); and the works by Baumann and Murdock mentioned in the previous note. Also see the recent, elaborate study by Jack Goody, *Production and Reproduction* (Cambridge: Cambridge University Press, 1976).

4. Cf. Judith K. Brown, "A Note on the Division of Labor by Sex," *American Anthropologist* 72 (1970): 1073-78; Alice Schlegel, *Male Dominance and Female Autonomy* (New Haven: HRAF Press, 1972); and Peggy R. Sunday, "Toward a Theory of the Status of Women," *American Anthropologist* 75(1973): 1682-1700.

5. Smith and Dale, *The Ila-Speaking Peoples of Northern Rhodesia*, Vol. 1, pp. 119f. (hereafter referred to in the form of "Smith and Dale, I, 119f.").

6. Ibid., I, 119-21.

7. Ibid., I, 136f., 139.

8. Ibid., I, 224-28.

9. Ibid., I, 227-28. The reader may be struck by the attribution of separate will to what one might think merely expressions of the single self, in this case the sexual powers. Sterility in

women, or impotence in men, is for example blamed on a lazy mupuka. But it is common in Africa (and in many other culture areas) to conceive of the self as composite, the communion of many individual forces, such as the names (public and esoteric, each with its own force and characteristics), the ancestral character reborn in the self, the destiny given before birth by God, often in the form of a specific soul, the special aura or charismatic power some leaders have, and so on.

10. Ibid., I, 118.

11. Ibid., I, 284-87, 380-85.

12. Ibid., I, 121; II, 122-23, 166.

13. Ibid., I, 140.

14. Ibid.

15. Ibid., I, 142.

16. Ibid.

17. Ibid., I, 143.

18. Ibid., II, 9.

19. Ibid., II, 11.

20. Ibid.

21. Ibid., II, 18-26; the Ila call the girl's initiation, or the climactic part of it, *chisungu*, as do many peoples in Zambia. For a detailed discussion of another culture's version of girl's initiation, see Audrey I. Richards, *Chisungu* (London: Faber & Faber, 1956), dealing with the Bemba of Zambia.

22. Smith and Dale, II, 25 n. 1, 55, 59.

23. Ibid., II, 60.

24. Ibid., II, 28.

25. Ibid.

26. Ibid., I, 27-33.

27. Ibid., I, 113ff.

28. Ibid., II, 24.

29. Also see our discussion in chapter 7 of the very similar initiation of girls among the Ndembu of Zambia.

30. A full bibliography of representative studies is hardly necessary here. An excellent recent version of this approach is Max Gluckman, *Politics, Law and Ritual in Tribal Society* (New York: New American Library, 1965), with particular application to African cultures; also see the more general discussion by John Beattie, *Other Cultures* (New York: Free Press, 1964).

31. Smith and Dale, I, 298-308; on the chief as "father" to his "children," see p. 307.

32. Ibid., I, 112.

33. Ibid., I, 109, 112 ff.; II, 9f., 119.

34. Ibid., II, 218.

35. Ibid., I, 109.

36. Ibid., I, 300-302; II, 129ff.

37. Ibid., II, 114.

38. Ibid., II, 125-26.

39. Ibid., II, 131.

40. Ibid.

41. Ibid., II, 110 n.1.

42. Ibid., II, 169-71.

43. Ian Cunnison, "Headmanship and the Ritual of Luapula Villages," *Africa* 26, no. 1 (January 1956): 2-16.

44. Ibid., p. 13.
45. Ibid.
46. Ibid., p. 12.
47. Ibid.
48. Smith and Dale, II, 5-6.
49. Ibid., II, 176.
50. Max Gluckman, "The Lozi of Barotseland in North-Western Rhodesia," in *Seven Tribes of British Central Africa*, ed. Elizabeth Colson and Max Gluckman (London: Oxford University Press, 1951), p. 19.
51. Ibid., p. 61.
52. Ibid.
53. Ibid., p. 21.
54. Ibid.
55. Ibid., pp. 25f.
56. Ibid., p. 26.
57. Ibid., p. 27.
58. Ibid., p. 28.
59. Ibid., p. 43.
60. Ibid., p. 47.
61. Ibid.
62. Michael Gelfand, *Shona Religion* (Cape Town: Juta and Co., 1962), pp. 146ff.
63. Victor W. Turner, *The Ritual Process* (Chicago: Aldine, 1969), p. 98.
64. Ibid.
65. Ibid.
66. Ibid., p. 100.
67. The pattern holds in Rhodesia, as the Shona instance illustrates, and also obtains for patrilineal peoples such as the Thonga of Mozambique; see Henri Junod, *The Life of a South African Tribe*, 2d ed. (London: Macmillan & Co., 1927), I, 291ff.
68. Smith and Dale, II, 44, 135.
69. Ibid., II, 43-44.
70. Cf. Marcel Griaule, *Conversations with Ogotemmeli* (London: Oxford University Press, 1965), pp. 41-50; notice that the Dogon maintain that within the furnace, or beneath it, is a serpent very like the bapuka who molds the ore!
71. Cf. E. Bolaji Idowu, *Olódùmarè: God in Yoruba Belief* (New York: Praeger, 1963), pp. 85-89; William Bascom, *The Yoruba of Southwestern Nigeria* (New York: Holt, Rinehart & Winston, 1969), pp. 82-83; A.B. Ellis, *The Yoruba-Speaking Peoples of the Slave Coast of West Africa* (Oosterhout, Netherlands: Anthropological Publications, 1970, 1894), pp. 68ff.
72. Cf. Baumann, *Les peuples*, the figures on pp. 67, 87, 143, and 415, and the remarks on p. 166; also E.C. Lanning, "Genital Symbols on Smith's Bellows in Uganda," *Man* 54: 262.
73. Smith and Dale, I, 202-221.
74. Ibid., I, 207.
75. Ibid., I, 204.
76. Ibid., I, 205.
77. Ibid., I, 210.
78. Ibid., I, 211-21.
79. Ibid., II, 193.
80. Ibid., II, 192.
81. Ibid., II, 194.

82. Ibid., II, 181-89: the various demigods are associated with clans, and their worship shares clan fortunes. Besides Shimunenga, Malumbe and Munyama are the principal demigods. Malumbe also enjoys a status like Shimunenga for his people—he helped shape the land, and finally vanished *into a pool* after appointing chiefs (II, 183).

83. Hermann Baumann, *Schöpfung und Urzeit des Menschen im Mythus der afrikanischen Völker* (Berlin: Bietrich Reimer, 1936), pp. 174-77; Charles Long, *Alpha: Myths of Creation* (New York: George Braziller, 1963).

84. Smith and Dale, II, 202, cf. 203.

85. A similar interdependence of fragmented lineage groups and regionally integrative earth-shrines prevails among the Tonga to the south, and resembles the Tallensi structures remarkably. See Elizabeth Colson, *The Plateau Tonga of Northern Rhodesia* (Manchester: University Press, 1962), and Meyer Fortes, *The Dynamics of Clanship among the Tallensi* (New York: Oxford University Press, 1964).

86. Smith and Dale, II, 212; cf. I, 414.

87. Ibid., II, 211.

88. Ibid., I, 162; II, 177, 209f.

89. Ibid., I, 274, 275, 278, 162; II, 209.

90. Ibid., II, 210.

91. Ibid., II, 1, 211.

92. Ibid., II, 209.

93. This recalls the remarkably similar structures of Nilotic religions as described by E.E. Evans-Pritchard, *Nuer Religion* (Oxford: Clarendon Press, 1956) and Godfrey Lienhardt, *Divinity and Experience: The Religion of the Dinka* (Oxford: Clarendon Press, 1961) and *idem*, "The Shilluk of the Upper Nile," in *African Worlds*, ed. by Daryll Forde (New York: Oxford University Press, 1954), pp. 138-63. It would not be hard to show the same structures among many other peoples as well, including such very different religions as the Yoruba and the Mande of Mali.

94. Smith and Dale, II, 204.

95. Ibid., II, 205.

96. Ibid., II, 209, 210, etc.

97. Ibid., II, 211.

98. Ibid., II, 129.

99. Cf. B. Holas, *Les dieux d'Afrique Noire* (Paris: Paul Geuthner, 1968), pp. 61-66, 102, etc. de Heusch, *Le roi ivre*, shows that among the Luba and allied peoples of Zaire and Zambia (including some Lunda cultures), there is an association of rainbow serpents with termite mounds (in which the termites and ants are considered to be the form of the transformed ancestral spirits). The Luba serpents embody the primordial super-masculine but crude trickster ousted from the human sphere by the first king and culture-hero. But the trickster-serpent still rules nature and the wilderness, from within his lodging within the termite mounds. The annual renewal of the struggle between trickster and culture-hero, accompanied by movements of the terrifying rainbow serpent up to heaven and down again, is the cause of the change of the seasons and the coming of the rains. The sacred year, in short, constantly repeats the same divine pattern established at the beginning of time, and thus the universe is annually regenerated.

Chapter 5

The Primordial Madness:
Time and Rituals of Sacrifice

If space articulates the immanent presence of the divine, it also presents the danger of its banalization. There is need for constant renewal of a transcendental perspective, even to keep clearly in mind the holiness of space. This renewal can only occur through rituals of time. The rites of passage we have already discussed show one dimension of this in Ila religion; each Ila person is periodically forced to break out of his habitually established space into more inclusive boundaries governed by transcendental forces. From initiation through marriage to eldership and death, the home, kraal, bush, and entire region are continually redefined, and the purely personal values associated with each are progressively attenuated. In the final stage of ancestor, the Ila joins the other spirits in river or termite hill, in kraal, grove, or children's homes (or all at once); the body no longer proves to be the decisive boundary, and the self is now part of the transcendental cosmos.

Each rite of passage moves the participant from familiar home or village to the isolation of the bush or closed hut, only returning the initiate to the world of the ordinary after a fundamental reorientation of his attitude to that world. Everything is now seen from a new perspective, removed from the thoughtless immersion in things that characterized the old attitude. One now sees the "real" connections between things.

The two attitudes are in truth two different spiritual universes. The egoistic "life-world" is fundamentally spatial, oriented by the body and its inner mental reflection. It is common-sensical, pragmatic, but basically static. In the other universe, however, the ego and body are opened to a transcendental order whose power irresistibly shapes the self through the mysteries of time.[1] It would seem that the more emphasis a person or culture places on time, the more important is transcendence from the material, spatially defined world. For example, the ancient Jews developed an awareness of the distinct natures of time and space, and with their consciousness of history came also a remarkably intense experience of God's transcendence. Much later on, with the failure of extreme apocalyptic hopes in the Graeco-Roman period, some Jews came to separate time and space completely, producing both Christianity with its "fulfilled eschatology" and her yet more radical sister, Gnosticism.[2] In each, to varying degree, eschatological hope was set free of natural and social space, encouraging the sharp rejection of common sense, bodily experience, and an antithesis between spirit and flesh. Spiritualization of time can produce acosmicism.

The Ila are far from such extremes. Their entire effort is put into the harmonization of spiritual realities. The common-sense world and transcendence are fused. As we shall see, perhaps the most characteristic expression of this is the Ila ceremonial cycle of the year, in particular the new year's festival that brings together the symbolisms of the entire ritual calendar.

The Ila, in fact, could not survive without some vision of the union of space and time. They are agriculturalists, settled in semipermanent villages and dependent on crops that mature at differing rates. Their food sources require long-term planning and cooperation among groups. The ritual calendar expresses the aspiration for understanding of the ecological interdependence of their universe and reveals how this mutuality operates. Time must, therefore, inevitably seem different to an Ila than it does to a Pygmy, for the small hunting-and-gathering bands can renew their food every day with little preparatory organization; even individuals can work alone. The famed "spontaneity" of the Mbuti is as much a cultural and spiritual product as the astrology of the Babylonians or the self-restraint of the Ila.

The Ila express the interdependence of all things, and the integration of space and time, through an insistence on the *cyclical repetition* of ultimate realities. A primal order has been established in the beginning of time, and on every level of experience this order plays itself out again and again. An elder participating in the birth, initiation or marriage of one of his grandchildren or great-grandchildren can say with truth that he has seen it all before, many times. His wisdom even consists largely in this, that he knows the fundamental patterns that all lives follow; he sees past the individual ego, even his own, to the transcendental structures. He has attained even while alive to living more in time than in space, and his metamorphosis to ancestor will bring him yet closer to eternity.

To a certain extent, an understanding of time implies a knowledge of the proper spatial definition of roles. Ritual delineates both. For example, in the funerals of friends and relatives that occur more and more regularly as an elder ages, he takes up one after another of the possible "eternal" roles of mourning acquaintance, friend, brother, son, uncle, father, husband—until at last he on his deathbed knows that soon he will occupy the central role in the forthcoming ritual repetition. From standing on the periphery, he has come slowly to the center of socio-ritual space. This understanding fosters acceptance; eternity is near, in the ordinary cycles of life and death.

The eternal patterns have been established since the beginning. Often the entire society celebrates its participation in transcendental time through commemorating the deeds of the common culture-hero. By reenacting his deeds, everyone becomes him, and thus becomes brother to everyone else. The ritual repetition of primal history is particularly striking in the festivals that punctuate the year. We notice it especially, for example, in the new year's festival, and even more among related cultures that celebrate the divine king's death and rebirth.

The underlying African attitude to time and change is one that has been very well characterized by Mircea Eliade in terms of "the myth of the eternal return."[3] In the primordial past the gods and the ancestors did everything for *the first time*, creating the primal images that control the flow of the real. Man sustains the perfection and freshness of those gestures by continuing them, permitting them to take him over and act through him. To forget those first dramas of being is to destroy the forms that hold the universe together. Meaningless chaos is the only possible result. Life lived at its deepest, therefore, is truly a remembering and a *reliving*. Countless others have done as one does now. One's father and mother did thus, and their parents before them. All merge together with oneself in the ritual.

The Ila, and many other African peoples, understand this ritual logic very well. Therefore it is possible to misunderstand them, and to think that they live for the past, that they have no sense of the future. According to one prominent authority, in traditional African religions

> time is a two-dimensional phenomenon, with a long *past*, a *present* and virtually *no future*. The linear concept of time in Western thought, with an indefinite past, present and infinite future, is practically foreign to African thinking. The future is virtually absent because events which lie in it have not taken place, they have not been realized and cannot, therefore, constitute time. . . . *Actual time* is therefore what is present and what is past. It moves "backward" rather than "forward"; and people set their minds not on future things, but chiefly on what has taken place.[4]

However, this view, while having the virtue of directing discussion to an important question, is not satisfactory. It is certain that Africans have conceived of a future, and as one commentator has pointed out, the presence of prophets (and diviners!) in traditional cultures, and the contemporary flourishing of millenary movements, show this clearly enough.[5] At the same time, it is evident as well that the future in the abstract is of no interest to them. As Evans-Pritchard pointed out a generation ago for the Nuer, "time is for them a relation between activities."[6] Time is created by human activities and the relationships that exist in them. "Time of day" is normally measured by the position of the sun or the activity appropriate to that period of the day. The market day cycle, the succession of age-sets or of chieftains, and notable natural events or personal experiences all serve to structure the passage of time. The remote future does not exist, therefore, not because it cannot, but simply because no relationships as yet exist in it and between it and the present.[7]

In the same way, it would be an error to suggest that because egoistic time is periodically abolished in rituals commemorating and reviving primordial events and persons, therefore Africans recognize nothing we would call history or change.

For the Ila as for most African cultures, extensive traditions exist recounting the deeds of past generations. Oral traditions have proven to be an excellent source for reconstructing African history, at least in terms of the past two or three centuries.[8] Moreover, the tales make clear that although the mythic culture-heroes established the basic structures and relationships of life in the distant past, later generations continued to refine and elaborate the patterns so as to result in the humanized complex world of the present. In details, then, structure continues to change and adjust, unfolding the implications of sanctified forms, although in general the divine order is timeless.

Change therefore is only a threat to the divine order until it becomes history. That is, it is dangerous only if it is made central, for then it overthrows the past instead of contributing to it.[9]

What anchors all change, and indeed all time seasonal or otherwise, is God. For the Ila, God is the ultimate rationale for space and time, the true center of the universe. Personal space and time are definitively overshadowed in the wider order of things by a universe centered on the supreme being. All of this can be seen by the specific details of the Ila treatment of time, to which I now turn.

The Ila base the entire year directly on God, just as they say that he is responsible for creation of the universe. Leza is the ultimate ancestor. The year is called quite simply the day of God; if the rainy season is too short, the Ila say that Leza "ties up the day"; at the first downpours of the rainy season, "Leza softens the day."[10] Leza is also the source for each person's destiny, which is directly controlled by God without any intermediate spirits intervening.[11]

Within the eon of the year, endlessly circling through its seasons, each segment is distinguished by the specific activities occurring in it. The spring season (which is around September since the Ila are south of the equator) is *chidimo*, the time for cultivation. *Mainza* is the time of rains. *Mveto*, winter, is the season when the cold winds blow over the slowly draining pools and streams, and people should stay at home. Each season is divided into moon-periods (months), which again are named for the associated activities.[12] In the largest sense, the seasons are the activities of Leza. When it rains, he is inseminating the fields, and the first days of the rainy season are a time for a general prohibition on work in the fields—with Leza's own essence there any cultivation would wound him.[13] The storms are his visible presence. When it thunders, people say, "Leza is thundering"; when lightning strikes, Ila murmur, "Leza is fierce." All things struck by lightning, including humans, have been punished or chosen by Leza. Thunder may bring repentance for evil actions, or a frightened person may shout into the storm his innocence of wrongdoing. Some Ila toss a piece of tortoiseshell into their hearth fire and beg Leza to rain gently on them, for they submit to him as his humble slaves.[14] In fact, the lightning storms are terrific in this locality, and claim victims every year. The hierarchy of powers in the universe is ritually reviewed soon after the beginning of the rainy season, for following shortly after the days sacred to Leza come brief ceremonies acknowledging the communal demigod or regional ancestral spirit (and Itoshi). At this time sacrificial offerings accompany the first sprouts appearing above ground in the sacred groves. The first harvest occurs soon after the beginning of the rains, as if to prove the potency of Leza. The planting is in fact done early and new sowings are repeated frequently thereafter to assure constant food supply. Finally, the first corn that is reaped is offered to the family ancestors in the hut, with the wife present. We can see a progressive specificity to these ceremonies: first prayers to Leza for the rains invigorating the whole world, then to the communal demigods in the groves on the appearance of the crops in the locality, and finally offerings to the family ancestors in gratitude for the family prosperity. The fertility connotations to these rituals are made more explicit by mock marriages the children of the village engage in at this time: with the village chief's blessings, the children go from hut to hut (Hallowe'en style) to demand some harvest food, with which they set up house in specially constructed huts in the bush, pairing off for some days or even longer as if to repeat in the wilderness the first experiences of culture by the ancestors.[15]

In this way each of the three major seasons is marked off by ritual celebrations, so we find rituals of time defining the divine order at its joints just as rituals of space do. Winter, for example, is heralded in May with festivals directed to the communal demigods and the earth (in Mala where Smith and Dale gathered most of their information, the festival was to Bulongo and Nachilomwe). The report of the ceremonies of this festival is fragmentary and scattered over several chapters of other material, and it may be that some of them are repeated before the Ila New Year's celebration.[16] Nachilomwe is Bulongo's embodiment in direct relationship to the culture-hero Shimunenga; she is the feminine earth or the ancestral spirit with the closest ties to it. As Shimunenga's "mother" or "sister" she has powers over women's fertility and the crops and is apparently the center of regular worship in a women's cult we are told almost nothing about.

THE NEW YEAR'S FESTIVAL OF THE ILA

The most significant of Ila festivals is the new year's festival in the spring. Its symbolisms sum up the themes of the other annual celebrations. Smith and Dale give a detailed account of those rituals observed by them at Mala, a large Ila village, from which it appears that the entire festival is a reenactment of myths of founding and of the beginning of time and culture. The ceremonies begin with an invocation to Shimunenga, who as ancestral first settler and hero showed the way to overcome formlessness and to institute human culture, and who as present demigod still guides his descendants through the same drama. The ceremonies center, however, on Nachilomwe and on fertility themes and conclude with an enactment of the political conquest of the land by the young men (who thus embody and reexperience the culture-hero). They charge out of the cattle pens in war regalia, penetrating the primal wilderness around the villages and taking possession of it while the women gather and sing praises to their virility. Giving war cries, shaking their spears, the warriors pair off into opposing armies and "attack" each other again and again in the days that follow. This is also the time when in battle dress the men ceremonially lead the cattle to new pasturage near the river (for the waters have long since receded and local pastures dried up).[17]

Before the festival begins, the medium to Shimunenga communes with his spirit and receives instructions on the order of the rites. The women brew beer, and the shrines are cleaned; when all is ready the dances begin. The men, plastered in white clay (symbolizing the ancestors and their virility?), and the women dressed in their finest, dance and call upon Shimunenga: "Shimunenga, Gatherer of men, Giver of virility to males!" Then, in the most important dances the women gather to sing ribald, "phallic" songs to Nachilomwe at the groves.[19]

The "obscenity" of the songs and dances is very important, precisely because the Ila are ordinarily so puritanical in their language. This is especially true for the women. To refer to a person's genitals is deeply humiliating, and to make mention of the sexual act or one's own sexual prowess is even more scandalous. All of these things reduce one to a mere bodily function, and depersonalize one. The body image is distorted and the ego's control assaulted. Yet there are times when these rules and scruples must be violated. To list them produces a curious concatenation of seemingly unrelated occasions: funerals, ironsmithing, initiations and marriages, as well as the new year celebration. We may say at this point that only one characteristic seems to be shared by them all: namely, they are abnormal times.

Certainly when the Ila sing "phallic" songs, they feel the inversion of things. Other rituals of the new year confirm this feeling. The men roam about the villages in rowdy groups, seeking out prominent men of the community and demanding gifts of them. Now it is not Ila practice to demand of a host that he give one beer, yet this is what is done; and even stranger, the demands are accompanied by insults instead of compliments. Smith and Dale relate for example that such a group came before the village headman Chidyboloto, and sang out the following affront: "Boloto sat as an owl; throw a firestick at him and make him fly away!"[20] The meaning can only be that Boloto is a witch (mulozhi); among the Ila, night-witches are known to fly in the form of owls to their victims; "If you see it sitting on your roof in the dusk, and it wakes up and cries, there will be a death in your home. You are then to throw a firebrand . . . at it to drive it away and take off the spell."[21] (The home fireplace is the place where the protective ancestors dwell, assuring the productive heat of the family; through the firestick weapon they can attack the "cold" witch.) It is true that headmen are always a bit suspect and feared among the Ila, for they must be powerful sorcerers to manage the village medicine and ward off the machinations of rival headmen anxious to draw off village residents and even rain to their own locales. Sometimes maddened headmen may direct their fierce magic against their own people, it is thought.

Despite the deadly insult of the choristers' song, sufficient at any other time to evoke fierce resentment and the imposition of fines, if not worse, the headman had to accept their remarks humbly and even to give them beer in turn. Insults on this day could and did fly in all directions and were aimed at anyone in power by the roaming bands. Later in the day the ethnologists, studiously observing the women's singing at Nachilomwe and Shimunenga's grove, found themselves suddenly the recipient of hymning by a passing group of men. Their songs when translated asserted that "where Shimunenga is, a visitor, however ugly he may be, is not to be beaten!"[22] An embarrassed Ila bystander reassured the missionary and government officer (Smith and Dale respectively) that the Ila meant no ill to them: it was just their way of praying for rain! We can imagine their bewilderment at what such insults could possibly have to do with rain.

But they were to be yet more startled by the events that immediately followed at the grove.[23] At a lull in the singing, a procession of men in their most impressive apparel approached the women, one of their number leading a young ox. To the beat of drums, an equally proud group of women stepped out to receive them, with one of particular elegance in their center. The two parties met, and the man leading an ox presented it to the leader of the women, receiving from her in return a spear. The delegations then broke up with much singing and dancing. In this manner, it was learned, the couple made a public agreement to be lovers, a specially sanctioned relationship that can endure a lifetime without any regard for the marital status of the partners; nor can the legal mates complain. At future feasts it is accepted that the paramours will sleep together, and indeed a man might well be ridiculed at feasts if he had no such lover. It is therefore a very common relationship, an institution of a kind of sacred marriage into which all can enter. It helps to heighten yet regularize the orgiastic atmosphere: "In many points, the annual feast is comparable with the Saturnalia."[24] But ritual license and 'obscenities' also characterize many other ritual occasions such as ironsmithing and funerals. Actions normally prohibited entirely are openly encouraged, and thefts, property damage, and adultery are regarded as somehow a necessary part of the celebration, grievous though these actions may be.

Yet the tone of the annual festival is exultant. Following the day devoted to Nachilomwe, in which all of the events recounted above took place, worship shifts to Shimunenga the culture-hero. Just as in the beginning of time the primordial world of Nachilomwe had no rule or form until the culture-hero brought order and separated out the primary classifications, so the days that follow are less wild, but still preserve the boisterous qualities of the pioneering epoch of Shimunenga. Beer feasts, singing, vigorous dancing, boasts and challenges fill the day and even the night. It is after all Shimunenga's own potency that inspires the drinkers in the new beer that is brewed from the grain. The men parade their cattle before their great ancestor and demonstrate to what a degree they have absorbed his virility with mock battles of glorious athletics and pageantry.

We can feel the power of the Ila festival, but what in fact is the logic behind all this? Why is it so necessary every year to have such strange, upside-down behavior? What is the connection of this with the other festivals of the Ila, with their life-cycle rites, and ordinary day-to-day life? And how is it that such peculiar behavior is thought to regenerate the fields, insure the fertility of the women, multiply the cattle, cause the rains to come, and appease the spirits and God himself?

Our first answer might be that as for the behavior itself, it is indulged in to taste forbidden fruit, for sensual reasons; and as for the cosmic claims, it is grandiose nonsense, mere magic, based on the assumption that what man wants must happen. But without disputing that there are sensual aspects to the new year's festival, it is interesting that the Ila look forward to its completion as if the rites were not wholly agreeable or spontaneous, while the judgment of magic is one from a certain western perspective, which explains next to nothing about the Ila views and in fact distorts them considerably.

Actually, profoundly religious assumptions are involved. The best, or at least most interesting, way to show this is perhaps to begin by showing the universality of the peculiar behavior the Ila display on new year's, particularly in Africa, and then to go on to focus on one of the most studied and developed extensions of its logic, the rites surrounding the death of a divine king and the installation of another. It will be remembered that the Ila have received many of their traditions from a neighboring empire. We shall see that the basic mechanisms and beliefs involved are common to many kinds of ceremonies and depend on certain profound insights into the nature of the universe and human life.

It is impossible not to think of the similarities of the Ila celebration with our own observance of New Year's Eve, especially when we appreciate the fact that such holidays as Hallowe'en (with the mocking of the elders by children) and Christmas (which once had orgiastic features too) are also forms of new year's.[25] In any case, the noise, buffoonery, sexual license and reversal of ordinary hierarchies may certainly be observed in the American celebration at the end of December.

In an interesting article, Edward Norbeck calls attention to African festivals of this sort, pointing out that everywhere there recur the same themes.[26] Among the Ashanti of Ghana and the Ivory Coast, for example, the new year is still a time for masquerading and dancing in the streets, lampooning leaders in songs, rather "loose" behavior and a great deal of gaiety and license. There can be no question that the Mardi Gras of New Orleans and the Carnival of Rio de Janiero partly reflect such African influences, although certainly the medieval Spanish, French, and Portuguese had precisely similar carnival periods. An early Dutch historian of the Guinea Coast wrote in 1705 that it was common to find in coastal West Africa "a Feast of eight days accompanied with all manner of Singing, Skipping, Dancing, Mirth, and Jollity; in which time a perfect lampooning liberty is allowed, and Scandal . . . highly exalted."[27] Among the Ga of Ghana, the festival is called Homowo, and is "the very pivot of tribal life."[28] It is the time (in late August) for families dispersed over many villages to congregate in their home town and offer sacrifices to the clan ancestors from the foods harvested during the previous months. Through the sacrifices, the living and dead are brought into a harmony. As if to underline the importance of the sacrificial motif, when the family members appear at the town gates bearing the produce of the clan fields on their heads, the townspeople race against them in mock battle as if eager to provide human sacrifices to the spirits as well. After the town gates are sealed shut, the people celebrate day and night for weeks. Offerings at ancestor shrines and to the demigods are very important; at these well-attended events, the spirits come so near that they possess many people outright. The streets too are filled with extraordinary activity. Bands of youths press through the crowds singing scandalous songs, mingling them with hymns to the demigods and lampoons detailing the misdeeds of town notables in the past year. Witchcraft accusations, adulteries, thefts and poisonings get a full airing, and the victims, whether justly or unjustly accused, have no redress. Instead, they may be seized bodily and borne about by the street gangs, bound up like sacrificial victims or scapegoats. But the best "victims" are the priests and chiefs, of course, for they embody the entire community. They must even show their full acceptance of their role by giving gifts of food and beer to their tormenters. Sacrificial themes clearly are of central importance in these festivities.

As with the Ila, sexual license marks the Homowo. Costumes are worn by everyone, and "for men to dress as women, wearing women's waist-beads and sailing very near the wind in the matter of decency, is considered one of the pinnacles of comedy."[29] So free was the sexual climate in the old days, especially during the night-long dancing and drinking, that we are told that the sexual act itself "was often publically carried out"; even today men ceremonially embrace strange women boldly in the streets.[30] This is a time also for all quarrels to be patched up, and acquaintances seek each other out in the streets to ask forgiveness for old slights and offenses. The ceremonial sacrifices at the shrines emphasize the unity of the people, the nearness of the divine spirits and the human realm, the intermingling of the living and the dead (ancestors), and the vigorous quality of the current of life that courses through all of them.

Norbeck points out that the same themes may be detected in many other kinds of rituals: funerals, initiations, weddings, and the installation of chiefs and kings. At some weddings, for example, the prospective bride or groom is actually cursed, and mock battles between the hosts and the in-laws are not uncommon. Blood may be drawn in these "ritual" contests. The hostilities end only with the presentation of gifts, recalling to us the Ila rule that the insulted party must respond with gifts. Funerals have no less puzzling features among many peoples. The Ashanti console mourners with obscene jokes, and demand that they act "happy," while the LoDagaba of Ghana even insult their newly dead and clown at funerals.[31] The Nyakyusa of Malawi might be considered to have reached the heights of perverse absurdity in their rituals of mourning. The nearest of kin (the deepest mourners) must have symbolical incest with each other, eat faeces or at least appear to, smear themselves with it and sit in filth. They are expected to become temporarily "insane," in short, and they must act this way whether they wish to or not. The songs sung during the funeral graphically urge sexual intercourse and bestial behavior on the listeners.[32] We may be quite sure in this case, however, that there is no desire for sensual indulgence in these rituals of reversal; if the logic holds as well for the Ila during their new year's celebration, then we must dismiss the thesis that such festivals are just natural concessions to lust or irresponsibility.

THE KING WHO MUST DIE: A SACRIFICIAL VICTIM

The meanings of funerary rituals are more applicable to our topic than one might at first suspect, even in details. For the model (or exaggerated form) of the ritual abasement of Ila chiefs in the new year's ceremonies can be located in the rituals that typically surround the death (often the murder) of a divine king and the installation of his successor. Just as the Ila chief is insulted at the "end of time," for failing to live up to chiefly ideals, the king is often killed or dies an unnatural death when he fails to live up to the ideal of divine kingship established in the beginning of time. This failure and death bring time to an end, in cultures with kingship structures, and there follows an interregnum with precisely the symbolic features of the Ila new year: adultery, confusion, mockery of leaders, general chaos. That is, what happens every year to bring the cosmic cycle to a close is repeated in divine kingship at the end of a reign, as if a reign were symbolically like a year.

The similarities go further: just as the king is the embodiment of the culture-hero and repeats the history of the culture-hero, so too among the Ila each *year* repeats the legendary history of the culture-hero (and even of creation). We have already seen in an earlier chapter that the Ila chieftainship is patterned closely on the divine kingship of the Lunda culture. Other Lunda peoples like the Ndembu and Rotsi(Lozi) also permit chaos and war during interregnums. But these Lunda kingdoms share a remarkable number of characteristics with others scattered from the southern Congo forests to the Zulu of South Africa and to the interlacustrine states of Uganda, Kitoro, etc. Probably the most discussed kingship of this type is that of the Shilluk of the lower Nile. Some have even called it an archaic survivor of the primal cultures behind ancient Egyptian religion.[33]

The Shilluk form of divine kingship has in any case certainly sparked the greatest controversy.[34] The basic traits are clear enough, however: Shilluk kings never die. Each king is really the reembodiment of the culture-hero and first king, Nyikang. Like Shimunenga, he came long ago to the land of the Shilluk (crossing the Nile miraculously), conquered the monstrous beings that lived there, and created out of them humanity. He gave the laws of culture and finally disappeared into the wind before his people's eyes. Within the wind he still roams the land as the vice-regent of God (Jwok), and he also takes on human form as the living king, possessing that king at his installation.

Traditional Shilluk accounts unanimously agree that no king died a natural death. Each was physically destroyed while still at the prime to pass on the spirit of Nyikang unharmed to the successor. So whenever the king's wives determined that he was becoming impotent or sterile, whenever drought or famine afflicted the land and life or general fertility languished, whenever battles were consistently or disastrously lost, or when the king himself fell ill or was blemished in his body, it was time to transfer the spirit to a new receptacle. Accounts differ on how the imperfect body was destroyed. Some tell of mysterious battles at night in the capital, where the king would regularly meet all challengers and demonstrate by his fighting skills his right to rule—or by his death his loss of that right. Some relate that the king's legs would be broken by the Ororo priest-clan (representing the aboriginal inhabitants Nyikang anciently conquered); then he would be walled up alive in a hut with a young wife to die. Perhaps his wives would ritually smother him, or, most often, he would meet death boldly on the battlefield when his time had come. No one but the priests would know of the "disappearance" of the king; the populace only learned of it when his bones were sewn into *the hide of a sacrificed ox* (an important detail, as we shall see) and placed in a shrine.[35] With the announcement, mourning and lamenting filled the land. All building stopped, no weddings or business transactions could be performed, and even the fires in all the homes were put out. War would break out between rival claimants, devastating the land. Adultery, robbery, and even murder had to go unpunished, for there was no law anymore. A year later, after the final traces of the former king's fecundity had been reaped in the crops, the new king was installed. But that, too, was extraordinarily dramatic.

The candidate earned the kingly stool by being "killed." When messengers burst in upon him to announce to him that the priests and provincial chiefs had chosen him, they shouted: "You are our Dinka slave; we want to kill you!"[36] The candidate received this glad news with an obligatory struggle and flight. He fled to the south, where he gathered an army to resist the honor. Then, from the north, an eerie host of warriors descended against him, led by Nyikang himself (resident of the portable effigies of his shrine), and his priests. At every town the spirit army did battle, capturing the inhabitants, taking their cattle, and enlisting their soldiers for further struggle. Finally the two armies met, at the mid-point of the kingdom, and the royal candidate was captured and taken "dead" into the capital. There in seclusion his body was laved by priestesses (the wives of the former king) as if in preparation for a funeral. At last he was carried to the royal stool, and there, hidden behind white sheets, let down upon it, to be seized and revived by Nyikang himself. Trembling, in trance at least theoretically, the new king would issue forth, henceforth to be the embodiment of Nyikang. There would follow further rites, including a ritual marriage with a "wife" from the Ororo clan and a speech before the people in which "new laws" would be issued.

There can be no doubt that, when all the details of this extraordinary drama are reviewed, we must conclude that the divine king is symbolically a sacrificial victim.[37] It may even be suggested that the former king and the new king are versions of each other, the former king being killed actually (the deed being denied symbolically) and the new king being killed symbolically (but not actually). These inversions give redoubled emphasis to the symbolical nature of the entire proceedings.

Only when we understand that the new and the former king are *the same person,* moreover, can we comprehend the meaning of other symbolisms. The failings of the former king (impotence, blemished body, epidemics or drought, etc.) are given their clearest meaning in the treatment accorded his replacement: all of these failures are a kind of *rebellion* from Nyikang. The new king enacts the rebellion explicitly. That is, when the king fails, he is resisting with his mere body the transcendental imperative of Nyikang; he therefore "disappears" (taking on the form at one time of the sacrificial ox, at another of the "Dinka slave" that is in fact killed at the accession of a new king as a scapegoat offering), finally appearing again as the corpselike being that leads the southern army against Nyikang. But he is again captured by Nyikang, placed on the stool and penetrated anew with the culture-hero's spirit. The king is *resurrected* from his temporary death: "the king is dead, long live the king!"

The interregnum, then, is the form rebellion against Nyikang takes: war, murder, adultery, the prohibition on marriages, hearth fires, building. *It must be extreme and larger than life*, to assimilate it to the mythic archetypes. In the myths, however, Nyikang did conquer the aboriginal inhabitants, and so too shall the new divine king. The more monstrous the inhabitants of the land, the more certain it is that Nyikang shall emerge anew. For it was all established like this at the beginning of time. If the day should come (as in fact it has) when the Shilluk do not respond to a king's death with anarchy and upheaval, the king shall not revive; to say that it is normal for a king to die means the rules of normality govern: and in the normal world there is no resurrection of the dead.

The abnormal symbol, in short, must be drastically separated from its too-normal, physical vehicle (the imperfect former king) and given dominance again by forcing abnormality on its physical vehicles until it is firmly reestablished as transcendental and powerful again. When the former king ages, when he loses battles, when he no longer can beget children, the physical actuality, the common-sense world of limitation and mere humanity threaten to conquer the transcendental kingship. It would be the death of the symbol. The king must voluntarily or involuntarily acknowledge the power of the symbolic. He must disappear and reappear as sacrificial ox, as Dinka slave, and triumphantly as new king.

In his career, the divine king conforms to the typical pattern of the myth and ritual of the hero, a necessary part of which is that he "loses favour with the gods and/ or his subjects, and . . . is driven from the throne and city, after which . . . he meets with a mysterious death."[38] The hero as a symbol of perfection cannot die, but if death comes to him as a mere individual mortal, he can at least demonstrate the triumph of the symbol over raw actuality and the ordinary human condition by meeting death in mysterious and "voluntary" fashion. The last favor the hero bestows on his subjects is that he dies for them without bitterness. (For if he were bitter, he would forfeit his status as hero.) In the Shilluk case, the actual death of the king is secret; the people only know that he has "disappeared" when he is presented to them metamorphosed instantaneously into sacrificial bull at a shrine, and (a year later) assumes the form of "rebellious" king.

As Evans-Pritchard so rightly says, "It is the kingship and not the king who is divine."[39] It is fascinating to see to what a degree this means that sacrificial rites must dominate. Sacrifice from this perspective serves to separate the symbol from its physical vehicle, and by the drastic "abnormal" nature of this separation to announce the dominance of the symbolical over the physical. The extraordinary fate of the divine king actually includes both of the major types of sacrifice. A *piacular* logic determines that the former king, the source of drought, epidemics, failure in war, etc., is removed from our midst and installed in a shrine outside the capital, or as "Dinka slave" is simply slain and the body divided in half for the new king to walk through. This removes all negative liminality from the midst of the people, the land, and the (new) king. Only good liminality, true sacred form, is left. But as resurrected king who is restored to his people, inseminating the Ororo "sister" who represents the entire aboriginal population (the subjects bereft of culture) and the "land," and then pronouncing the new laws of life, the king completes the cycle of *communal* sacrifice, in which the victim is returned to the sacrificers at the end to be shared amongst them.

Another typical (indeed, obligatory) characteristic of sacrifice is that the victim be already symbolic. As symbol, it can mediate between the actual world of the sacrificers and the transcendental spiritual world beyond; it is both "us" and "other." The divine king certainly qualifies for this role, being both all-too-human and divine. At the end of the entire interregnum, the king stands forth anew as a figure removed from the common lot of mankind. All the chaos that has swept the land, destroying all normality and the secure everyday round, has been gathered up again into himself. When he is restored to himself, his subjects no longer suffer anarchy; he restrains those forces and releases them only in controlled doses, for the good of his land. The more savage the interregnum, then, the more divine the king, for his power must be greater to overcome chaos. No mere human could by his disappearance cause such terrible confusion and desolation. Thus, when the merely human side again surfaces, the king is certainly most worthy of being sacrificed anew as representative both of humanity and the divine.

I believe these remarks show us the way to unify two very different explanations of such rituals as we have reviewed. Max Gluckman, a leading British social anthropologist, has characterized rituals like the Shilluk royal installation and the Ila new year's celebration as "rituals of rebellion." Also drawing on Zulu spring festival practices in which women dress like men and sing 'obscene' and mocking songs (again rather like the Ila festival, as we shall see more convincingly in a moment), he suggests that catharsis of pent-up resentments by the oppressed is an important function of these rites.[40] He even more provocatively has pointed to the need in relatively undifferentiated societies for people to dramatize social roles and identities clearly in ritual, since in the course of ordinary life they tend to overlap and merge.[41] Zulu women, for example, are in-law wives, clan sisters, and mothers; the Zulu spring festival serves to define them as "women." Thus "rituals of rebellion" emphasize role conflicts. Ritual humiliation of leaders defines the ideal of true leaders, which the leader himself is forced to acknowledge in self-humiliation; while ironically by insulting the leader the subjects reaffirm themselves as a body over against the ideal leadership. Thus institutions are actually reaffirmed, though they seem to be overthrown. According to Gluckman, none of this ritualization is necessary in more differentiated societies where role specialization simplifies self-image. In other words, roles do not overlap so much, so they do not need strong ritual definition. Ritual is reduced to temple and priest cult, while the rest of society undergoes secularization.

Victor W. Turner, a researcher who brilliantly demonstrates how religious and anthropological categories can be used together, has urged that the rituals Gluckman describes actually have precisely the opposite effect from Gluckman's claim, for instead of these rituals defining all the social roles in ideal form, they overthrow them. These rituals revive *communitas*, an abounding sense of social unity and common fate, which may be at the source of social structure but which stands outside of it, and as "anti-structure," even against it. The rituals center on a direct experience of the nonrational, unstructured Essential We or I-Thou of Martin Buber's philosophy.[42] People exult in the freedom from "onerous role definitions"; spontaneity is triumphant. Antistructure permits people to discover their common identity and the consensus society needs to keep together.

The contrast between the two viewpoints seems total. But perhaps they can be reconciled by observing that Turner correctly describes the feeling of spontaneity and release that participants in rituals of reversal experience, while Gluckman correctly describes the structures through which these feelings are expressed. Or, to put it another way, the entry into transcendental *structures* and archetypal forms in such festivals is at the same time a release from exhausting banality, the commonplace, and merely egoistic form of experience, the *merely* normal, which threatens to submerge ideal structure. Everyone is joined by their entry together into transcendental meaning, although their roles in the divine order that is revealed can be quite different. Rituals of reversal present the vision of unity in diversity, or what we have called earlier the liminality of structure.

Thus the insulting of Ila chiefs, as does the drama of renewal of divine kingship, both joins and separates anew the chief and his subjects. The chiefs are ritually humiliated because they are, after all, imperfect mortals; the symbolic chieftainship must be kept unstained. The accusations center on ways in which the ideal chief symbolism was not measured up to by the incumbent. Boloto is mocked as witch, thus serving as scapegoat. A distinction is thus also made between the positive and negative aspects of the liminality of chieftainship, and the negative aspects are publically rejected. The chief participates in this rejection when he shows the hero's sacrificial "lack of bitterness" by returning gifts for insults. Thus he demonstrates that he rises above the negative stereotype and remains worthy to be chief. If he were to become defensive and try to punish his accusers, he would show his merely human vulnerability and his unworthiness to be chief. By a normal response he would cease to be abnormal. Yet as a result of this heroic reconciliation the ideal remains unchallenged, and the merely human is still distinguished from the symbolic. Boloto remains chief by accepting his common identity with his accusers. He too has succumbed to desire, dislike, perhaps even witchcraft. He and his subjects are all one in this, though they are apart in their roles.

Gluckman also exaggerates when, in his earlier writings, he emphasized role *conflicts* as the key. These are not rituals of rebellion so much as rituals of reconciliation (as, to be sure, Gluckman also noted from the beginning). More to the point, it is not satisfactory to explain these cosmological rites in a merely sociological fashion. We cannot forget that insulting the Ila chiefs and even the European administrators brought rain to the Ila valley. Moreover, many of the so-called rebellion themes turn out not to exist, or to be unimportant, in most of these rituals. Thus, as noted before, Edward Norbeck has shown that the same inversions and reversals occur in contexts where rebellion by the oppressed does not apply. Men, for example, more frequently dress like women and enact inverted roles in African ritual than women act like men, yet clearly in most of these societies men are not oppressed by women. Neither is it clear how mourners who sing obscene songs or smear themselves with filth and act "mad" are oppressed by social superiors. Eileen J. Krige, in discussing the Zulu spring ceremony, has shown that Gluckman's thesis does not apply here.[43] It must be understood above all as a *cosmic rite of marriage*, in which young Zulu girls accompany the earth-goddess of fertility, Inkosazana, through a preparatory women's initiation into a marriage with heaven. The result of these cosmic nuptials is that the inseminating rains will fall, and the world will exult in fertility. The entire fertility ceremony is therefore modeled on initiation rites for girls, and in fact girls may be initiated in its course. The elder women hoe the fields like initiating elders teaching their virginal novices the mysteries of sex. The songs are similar to those sung during girls' initiations, heightening feminine sexuality by expressing group 'hostility' to men, and making use of 'obscene' language that in fact is not obscene at all in the context. As a matter of fact, it was not married women whose actions and dress imitated that of men, but the virginal girls who were still pampered "younger sisters" of the fertility goddess. So the least 'oppressed' women acted out the reversals of behavior.

It is because the world of normality is temporarily abolished in all these rituals of reversal, that the basic taboos which help structure that world must be momentarily broken. Every such violation is a symbolic sacrifice, in which the material and visible world is offered up again to the invisible transcendental forms that inspirit it. For a time, primordial formlessness seems to triumph. The Shilluk king commits ritual incest at his installation (by having intercourse with his "sister"), the Nyakyusa mourner wallows in feces, the Zulu girls parade in men's attire, and the Ila shout their obscenities gaily at their elders. Yet in all these instances, sacrifice serves finally to reinforce the taboo-controlled normative order, by establishing the transcendental nature of the cosmic order. The divine order expresses the primordial realm unfolded into human meaning. The taboos are sacrificially violated in order to regenerate them with added forcefulness.

As Smith and Dale acutely remarked in regard to all of the upheavals of the Ila new year, "In normal times the abnormal is taboo, but in abnormal times the abnormal things are done to restore the normal condition of affairs."[44] Or as Monica Wilson observes concerning the "insanity" of Nyakyusa mourners, they act mad so as to fend off genuine madness.[45]

We can conclude, then, from this discussion of the Ila new year and related festivals that the central rite of the holiday is not the obscenities, the festival drinking or mock battles, nor even the mocking of Boloto the village chief. The central act that all of these merely explicate is the sacrifice of oxen at the groves to Shimunenga and ultimately to Leza. Despite appearances, it is not sensuality but symbol that triumphs. Shimunenga and Nachilomwe, heaven and earth, humanity, the land, and even husband and wife are renewed and reunited to start a new year, with all trivialities and commonplaces washed away. Individuals have become types in the festival, the better to perceive the eternal that underlies the everyday world of the rest of the year. With their new vision, the Ila can recognize their ancestors in themselves throughout the coming months.

Time for the Ila provides the sacrificial medium through which transcendental realities can break into the universe of space and transform it. As a whole, time is the form of God's action in the world. The Ila express this in a different and more intimate way in saying that not only the universe as a whole, but even the individual life, is continually controlled by God directly: Leza governs each person's fate. Bad luck or good luck is generally spoken of in terms of God.

In such concepts the Ila merely echo larger Bantu and even African patterns. Geo Widengren long ago showed that the view of God as the "fate-determining one" is the most essential and common attribute of the high god complex throughout Africa.[46] In a more recent survey of east and central Bantu religions, J.V. Taylor claims to find a general association of the multiple souls of the Bantu person with the fundamental realities of his universe. All of these are controlled by the "transcendental soul" or destiny soul, which comes from God directly and returns there after death.[47] (The Bantu, according to Taylor, most commonly recognize three souls: the life-soul, present in the blood, red in color and stemming from the mother; the individual-soul, giving shape through the bones and semen, white in color and coming from the father and his ancestors; and the transcendental soul, transparent and participating in God. The life-soul is linked to the maternal earth, to the wilderness and the unconscious; the individual soul to the atmosphere, community and consciousness; and the transcendental soul stemming from God fuses the other two together.)

SACRIFICE AS THE UNIFICATION OF SPACE AND TIME

We have constantly been encountering repetitions of a few dominant ideas shared with the Ila by very many of their neighbors. These ideas can be expressed in schematic form (fig. 1). We speak here, of course, only of general tendencies. But whatever the variations, we constantly find binary oppositions structuring level upon level of the spiritual universe. Taboos act to keep the levels distinct and to stabilize the divine order; sacrifice destroys and renews them. The two ritual types interact to give the cosmos dynamic continuity.

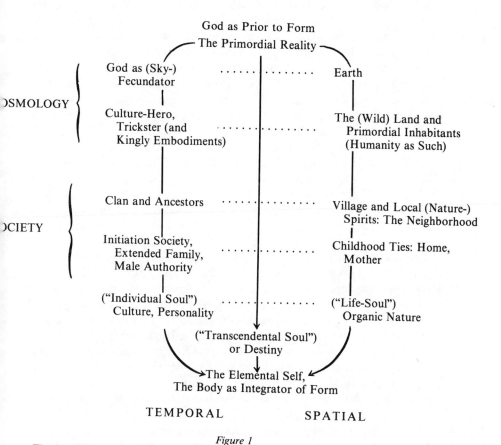

Figure 1

The dotted lines indicate relationships mediated through symbolic sacrifice, generally in terms of sexuality and/or war. Words placed in parentheses refer only to some religions discussed in these pages.

The cosmos is interwoven by the elements of space and time, and on every level these two are brought together in generative transformation producing the next lower level. Very little may be said in myth of creation itself. Accounts are brief and vague if they exist at all. But generally *sexual interaction* involving God or an agent and the earth or other female beings provides the metaphor.[48] As a consequence of the primal union various beings populate the earth, generally monstrous in form. These are beings considered to dwell in the wilderness or forest, beyond the boundaries of culture, constituting a kind of primordial space. There finally appears the culture-hero, who conquers the aboriginal inhabitants and institutes history.[49] Here the transformative metaphor linking cultured time and natural space is that of *war or conflict*, but many culture-heroes are said to settle in a region by marrying a female representative of the land. In cultures with divine kingship structures, as we have seen, these sacred marriages form an important part of installation ceremonies. The king is in fact the living embodiment of the culture-hero, who must repeat the founding dramas regularly to renew time. The king must acknowledge his indebtedness to the earth-spirit (who controls the fertility of the land, and often the rain) by periodic sacrifices—and, when his own life-powers and fecundity begin to fail, by the sacrifice of himself. Thus *sacrificial death* is another transformative metaphor that implies the earlier ones of war and sexuality and repeats their logic. Sacrifice is the chief form of relationship between the clan elders (who here represent not only the living but also perhaps the ancestors as well) and the land and its governing spirits. At harvest time especially, but also at other periods of regular festival or crisis, sacrifices are made by the entire community of elders to the spirits of the earth (often at pools or rivers, to serpentine beings). The village chief, as we have seen, develops the sexual aspects of the basic transformative dynamic in his relationship with his wife, who is linked to the land of the village. The same is true of each family, which in its interaction is really a microcosm of the entire universe and its generative process. The male initiation society teaches men to think of women as primal beings, sacral in nature; the women's mysteries teach much the same of the men, and both reserve a great portion of their attention for sexuality and generation. Often the sexual encounter is referred to in the initiation songs in terms of war, wounding and "death."

Out of the union of initiated adults in marriage come children. They in their growth to maturity, wisdom, and eventually ancestorhood recapitulate most of the stages of creation we have mentioned, in reverse order. The movement to old age and transformation to ancestral status is, in other words, a progressive return to transcendental structures. The child, who fuses in himself or herself the spiritual essences of mother and father but who is finally guided by the fate decreed by God, is the ultimate result of the whole universal dynamic. In childhood, he or she is most closely involved in the home and the feminine space created by the mother. Only through initiatic "death" does the child move definitively out of that space and enter into cultural time, learning the deeds of the ancestors that must henceforth be his or her models. The girl initiate, like the boy, learns that she will from this time forth be part of adult history and concerns; she is part of the women's society and no longer centered on her own mother. Cultural history and concerns replace merely egoistic ones. As young adult, the male enacts another aspect of the transformative dynamic as he engages in warfare with the primordial beings (and peoples) who dwell in the "outer wilderness" of the bush. As we have seen in connection with the Ila, the hunt, the entry into warfare, and even trading journeys into the bush, are all characterized by sexual taboos. In other words, the basic transformative dynamic is controlled by the taboos that surround it. One element is singled out by the taboos and the others excluded.

As ancestor, the person passes entirely over to the invisible world sustaining the visible. But he or she remains in varying degrees still active in sustaining human culture and norms. There has been quite a bit of controversy in recent anthropological writing concerning the status of the ancestors. Igor Kopytoff has revived the older theory of Cullen Young and J.H. Driberg that the ancestors are not so much spirits as merely transformed elders; that is, more secular humans than supernatural beings.[50] It is certainly true that ancestors are generally approached without deep awe, such as we might expect for genuine demigods or God. Yet even with God we often find in Bantu cultures a very intimate and even somewhat casual and spontaneous attitude.[51] It must not be forgotten that in Bantu religions sacral ritual underpins the whole of life, so that it is actually invalid to draw either/or distinctions between sacred and secular.[52] That, indeed, is one of the main points of our study. Society, too, is not the core of African religions, even though it is one of the chief media through which religion is expressed. Everyday life and society as well as the ancestors reflect transcendental structures pervading the cosmos.

The ancestors, however, are closer to those ultimate structures. It is significant that ritual sacrifice is the chief method of coming into contact with them. They in turn often make their desire to communicate known through sickness, sterility, or even death. They are especially present, that is, at liminal points of transformation (such as thresholds). Above all during funerals, and during the great festivals such as the new year's harvest, they return to dwell among the living. It is interesting that just at such times we observe mock battles, 'obscene' songs and sexually exaggerated behavior, ritual sacrifices and a general feeling of reversal and release. All of these forms of "madness" (as the Nyakyusa frankly call them) express the basic sacrificial transformation taking place.

Through such an alternation of "madness" and "sanity," each Ila person is exposed to the deep springs of sacred reality and is guided in directing its flow into everyday life. The Ila world is not "closed," despite the efforts of some ethnologists and theologians to claim that this is the attribute of African spiritual universes.[53] On the contrary, the normative world and everyday pragmatic realities are constantly broken open to the incommensurate quality of existence. Confusion and chaos are directly experienced. Every ritual enactment recognizes not only the rule of normative structure, but also the otherness and mystery of everyday life and the things in it. Ritual is in fact generally evoked by sickness, confusion or death, to establish an equilibrium between formlessness and form. The Ila are keenly aware of this, as their frequent appeals to Leza indicate. God, who is not limited by any determinations, is the direct cause of "luck" or fate. In such a universe apparent contradictions can coexist, and even very different lives are possible. It is the faith of the Ila, disclosed in the logic of their ceremonials, that despite all of this mystery there is a divine order to the world, a transcendental structure to which man can accord himself, within which all opposites of "madness" and "sanity," "abnormal" release and "normal" restraint, nature and culture, man and woman and even life and death, can be reconciled.

NOTES TO CHAPTER 5

1. For excellent phenomenological analyses of the commonsensical ego-based world see Alfred Schütz, *Collected Papers*, Vol. 1 (The Hague: Nijhoff, 1962), pp. 99ff., and *idem* and Thomas Luckmann, *The Structures of the Life-World*, trans. R.M. Zaner and H.T. Englehardt Jr. (Evanston: Northwestern University Press, 1973), pp. 3-44. Schütz terms this level of awareness the "paramount reality" by which all others are measured by effectively operating individuals. However, the very desire of the ego to control all phenomena must ultimately lead to the recognition of its own merely finite condition, for in fact there always remains an uncontrollable element in the experiential world. One may even argue that ego-consciousness itself can only arise out of a prior acceptance of the "otherness" dominating experience. Only that "otherness" offers the self a way of lifting itself from a simple, total and painless immersion in experience and becoming self-aware, knowing the world and the self as object. But whatever the genesis of the pragmatic ego-awareness, its ultimate failure to control all experience must force it to submit to "otherness" if only to assure its own continuance. In short, the commonsensical attitude contains in itself the seeds of its own overthrow. It is not the fundamental reality, even if it seems at first estimate to be dominant.

2. On the birth of Gnosticism from failed apocalyptic Judaism, see Robert M. Grant, *Gnosticism and Early Christianity*, rev. ed. (New York: Harper & Row, 1966), pp. 33-38, a thesis which while controversial is accepted by many scholars. Others believe that Gnosticism was the result of a general and intensifying mood in the ancient world and had gentile roots.

3. See Mircea Eliade, *Cosmos and History: The Myth of the Eternal Return*, trans. W. Trask (New York: Harper & Row, 1959).

4. John S. Mbiti, *African Religions and Philosophy* (New York: Praeger, 1969), p. 17 (italics in text); Rev. Mbiti may be drawn to this viewpoint by the desire to contrast it with Christianity (along the line of the typical "paganism fulfilled in Christianity" liberal missionary approach): see his *New Testament Eschatology in an African Background* (London: Oxford University Press, 1971).

5. Benjamin Ray, *African Religions* (Englewood Cliffs, N.J.: Prentice-Hall, 1976), p. 17.

6. E.E. Evans-Pritchard, *The Nuer* (Oxford; Clarendon Press, 1940), p. 100.

7. See Newell S. Booth, Jr., "Time and Change in African Traditional Thought," *Journal of Religion in Africa* 7, no. 2 (1975): 81-91, an excellent study.

8. See, on this interesting topic, Jan Vansina, *Oral Traditions* (London: Routledge & Kegan Paul, 1965), and *idem. Kingdoms of the Savanna* (Madison: University of Wisconsin Press, 1966); J.D. Fage, ed., *Africa Discovers Her Past* (London: Oxford University Press, 1970); Ruth Finnegan, *Oral Literature in Africa* (Oxford: Clarendon Press, 1972), and David P. Henige, *The Chronology of Oral Tradition* (Oxford: Clarendon Press, 1974).

9. See Booth, "Time and Change," pp. 89-91.

10. E.W. Smith and A.M. Dale, *The Ila-Speaking Peoples of Northern Rhodesia* (London: Macmillan & Co., 1920), II, 204. Hereafter referred to simply as "Smith and Dale."

11. Ibid., I, 357.

12. Ibid., I, 141-42; II, 217.

13. Ibid., I, 139; II, 209.

14. Ibid., II, 204, 220, 261.

15. Ibid., II, 37ff.

16. Ibid., I, 142; II, 189-96.

17. Ibid., I, 131; II, 189.

18. Ibid., II, 189.

19. Ibid., II, 191.

20. Ibid., II, 191.

21. Ibid., II, 88; the owl as witch is a very common African idea. A striking account of such ideas in west Africa, in relation to an epidemic, is in Elisabeth S. Bowen (pseud. for Laura Bohannan), *Return to Laughter* (Garden City, N.Y.: Doubleday, 1964), pp. 198, 251ff.

22. Smith and Dale, II, 190-91.

23. Ibid., II, 67-69.

24. Ibid., II, 191.

25. See Edv. Lehmann. "Christmas Customs," *Encyclopaedia of Religion and Ethics*, Vol. III (1910), pp. 609, 610.

26. Edward Norbeck, "African Rituals of Conflict," in *Gods and Rituals: Readings in Religious Beliefs and Practices*, ed. John Middleton (Garden City, N.Y.: Natural History Press, 1967), pp. 197-226.

27. R.S. Rattray, *Ashanti* (Oxford: Clarendon Press, 1923), p. 151, quoting Bosman.

28. Margaret Field, *Religion and Medicine of the Gā People* (London: Oxford University Press, 1937), p. 47.

29. Ibid., p. 48.

30. Ibid., p. 54. For similar rites among the Yoruba, see A.B. Ellis, *The Yoruba-Speaking Peoples of the Slave Coast of West Africa* (London: Chapman & Hall, 1894), p. 78.

31. Norbeck, "African Rituals of Conflict," p. 217.

32. Monica Wilson, "Nyakyusa Ritual and Symbolism," in *Myth and Cosmos: Readings in Mythology and Symbolism*, ed. John Middleton (Garden City, N.Y.: Natural History Press, 1967), pp. 149-66.

33. For a useful survey of African divine kingship theories, see V. Van Bulck, "La place du Roi Divin dans les circles culturels d'Afrique Noire," in *The Sacral Kingship: Studies in the History of Religions; Numen* supplement IV (Leiden: E.J. Brill, 1959), pp. 98-134.

34. For most of the following details, see Wilhelm Hofmayr, *Die Schilluk: Geschichte, Religion und Leben eines Niloten-Stammes*; Anthropos Bibliothek, Bd. II, 5 (St. Gabriel, Modling bei Wien: Anthropos Verlag, 1925), the fundamental study. Also see C.G. Seligman, "Cult of Nyakang and the Divine Kings of the Shilluk," *Wellcome Tropical Research Laboratories, Fourth Report* (Khartoum; Sudan Government, 1911), Vol. B, 216-38, and *idem, Egypt and Negro Africa: A Study in Divine Kingship* (London: Oxford University Press, 1934). For an excellent general discussion, see M. Riad, "The Divine Kingship of the Shilluk and Its Origins," *Archiv für Völkerkunde* 14 (1959): 141-284. Also of value is Dietrich Westermann, *The Shilluk People: Their Language and Folklore* (Philadelphia: Board of Foreign Missions, and Berlin: Dietrich Reimer, 1912), and J.P. Crazzolara, *The Lwoo* (Verona: Editrice Nigrizia, 1950-54), 3 vols.

35. E.E. Evans-Pritchard, "The Divine Kingship of the Shilluk of the Nilotic Sudan," The Frazer Lecture of 1948, reprinted in *Social Anthropology and Other Essays* (New York: Free Press, 1962), pp. 192-212, has doubted that the king was ritually killed, though admitting that all recorded deaths were unnatural (usually in battle). The doubt seems to be gratuitous, since it contradicts all first-hand field research. See Riad (referred to in the previous note). While the actual deaths were generally not in the public eye, among related peoples eye-witness reports do exist: see Godfrey Lienhardt, *Divinity and Experience: The Religion of the Dinka* (Oxford: Clarendon Press, 1961), pp. 298ff., with references; also note the references of Murdock, *Africa: Its Peoples and Culture History*, pp. 178-80. Also see the following notes, together with Ibrahim Bedri, "More Notes on the Padang Dinka," *Sudan Notes and Records* 29, pt. 1 (1948): 40-57. The sacrificial ideology that governed divine kingship also makes an actual murder likely, as we shall see.

36. W.P.G. Thomson, "Notes on the Death of a Reth of the Shilluk," *Sudan Notes and Records* 29, pt. 2 (1948): 154.

37. For a remarkably similar analysis of the west African Jukun practices, see Michael W. Young, "The Divine Kingship of the Jukun: A Reevaluation of Some Theories," *Africa* 36, no. 2 (April 1966): 150-51, etc.; also see T.O. Beidelman, "Swazi Royal Ritual," *Africa* 36, no. 4 (October 1966), 373-405, and the ingenious extrapolations from the Beidelman article by René Girard, *Violence and the Sacred*, trans. Patrick Gregory (Baltimore: Johns Hopkins Press, 1977), pp. 104-11.

38. Lord Raglan, *The Hero* (New York: Vintage Books, 1956), p. 175.

39. Evans-Pritchard, "The Divine Kingship of the Shilluk," p. 210; also see p. 201.

40. See *Custom and Conflict in Africa* (New York: Barnes and Noble, 1955), and *Order and Rebellion in Tribal Africa* (Glencoe, Ill.: Free Press, 1963), both by Max Gluckman.

41. Gluckman, *Politics, Law and Ritual in Tribal Society* (New York: New American Library, 1965), esp. pp. 284-97, a revision of his earlier theories in response to criticism.

42. Victor W. Turner, *The Ritual Process* (Chicago: Aldine, 1969), and *idem, Dramas, Fields and Metaphors* (Ithaca: Cornell University Press, 1974). Despite the reference to Buber, Turner's theories betray the strong influence of Christian theological assumptions about the divine, and are Paulinian at base. They are most adequate for other religions of salvation, though incomplete even there. Turner shows in the last-cited work, however, the beginning of a reevaluation of his radical antithesis of "structure" and "anti-structure." It is revealing that the first early work of Turner's in which the antithesis was elaborated also contained explicit and lengthy explorations of Christian myths and theology: *Chihamba the White Spirit: A Ritual Drama of the Ndembu*; Rhodes-Livingstone Paper No. 33 (Lusaka: Rhodes-Livingstone Institute, 1962), now available in Victor Turner, *Revelation and Divination in Ndembu Ritual* (Ithaca: Cornell University Press, 1975).

43. Eileen J. Krige, "Girls' Puberty Songs and their Relation to Fertility, Health, Morality and Religion among the Zulu," *Africa* 38, no. 2 (April 1968): 173-98, richly confirmed by the details in Axel-Ivar Berglund, *Zulu Thought-Patterns and Symbolism* (London: C. Hurst & Co., 1976), pp. 63-73.

44. Smith and Dale, II, 84; cf. 111, 113.

45. Wilson, "Nyakyusa Ritual and Symbolism," p. 160; according to a Nyakyusa informant, "All the rituals are the same; if they are neglected men will become mad." This is

one of those statements that shows that informants are sometimes much more profound than their Western interpreters.

46. See Geo Widengren, *Die Hochgottglaube im alten Iran* (Uppsala: Lundeqvistska Bokandeln, 1938), with its extensive discussion of African beliefs in the High God, or the most recent treatment of African forms by the same author, *Religionsphänomenologie* (Berlin: Walter de Gruyter & Co., 1969), pp. 46-53.

47. John V. Taylor, *The Primal Vision* (Philadelphia: Fortress Press, 1963), p. 63.

48. At the same time it is interesting how vague such bodily symbolisms are in relation to creation. The Zulu simply speak of a (phallic) reed out of which mankind emerged, etc. Most Bantu peoples have very indistinct ideas of creation, mainly viewing it as beyond speculation. See A. Werner, *Myths and Legends of the Bantu* (London: Harrap, 1933).

49. Cf. H. Tegnaeus, *Le héros civilisateur* (Stockholm, 1952). See also Luc de Heusch, *Le roi ivre* (Paris: Gallimard, 1972) for a survey of central Bantu myths centering on the Luba.

50. T. Cullen Young, "The Idea of God in Northern Nyasaland," in *African Ideas of God: A Symposium*, ed. Edwin W. Smith, 3d ed. (London: Edinburgh House Press, 1966), p. 39; J. H. Driberg, "The Secular Aspect of Ancestor Worship in Africa," *Supplement, Journal of The Royal African Society* 35, no. 138 (January 1936); also see Meyer Fortes, "Pietas in Ancestor Worship," *Man* 91, no. 2 (1961): 166-91; Igor Kopytoff, "Ancestors as Elders in Africa," *Africa* 41, no. 2 (1971): 128-42. Responses to Kopytoff include James Brain, "Ancestors as Elders in Africa: Further Thoughts," *Africa* 43, no. 2 (1973): 122-33; Victor C. Uchendu, "Ancestorcide!: Are African Ancestors Dead?" in *Ancestors*, ed. William H. Newell (The Hague: Mouton, 1976), pp. 282-96; and Walter H. Sangree, "Youth as Elders and Infants as Ancestors. . . ," in the same work, pp. 297-304.

51. See, for examples, the symposium edited by Edwin W. Smith cited in the previous note.

52. Most assertions of secularity in regard to African cultures merely have in mind the everyday, normal quality of religious life. The only genuinely secular African cultures appear to cluster in Tanzania, where generations of war, Arab slave-raids, and epidemics combined with the rise of long-distance trade to shatter traditional values. See Roy Willis on the Fipa in his *Man and Beast* (New York: Basic Books, 1974), and Gerald Hartwig on the Kerebe in *The Art of Survival in East Africa* (New York: Holmes & Meier, 1977).

53. See Horton, "African Traditional Thought and Western Science," *Africa* 37, nos. 1 & 2 (January and April 1967): 50-71, 155-87, and Horton and Ruth Finnegan, eds., *Modes of Thought: Essays on Thinking in Western and Non-Western Societies* (London: Faber & Faber, 1973), where various contributors discuss the idea; also see the objections by Max Marwick, "How Real is the Charmed Circle in African and Western Thought?" *Africa* 43, no. 1 (January 1973); 59-71, and J.H.M. Beattie, "On Understanding Ritual," in *Rationality*, ed. Bryan R. Wilson (New York: Harper & Row, 1970), pp. 263ff. A number of articles in the latter work deal with this question. The really rather obvious theological bias in Horton's theory blossoms in the enthusiastic version of it by the theologian Philip Turner, "The Wisdom of the Fathers and the Gospel of Christ. . . ," *Journal of Religion in Africa* 4, no. 1 (1971): 56-62, where the supposed scientific "openness" of Christianity (Galileo would have been surprised) is contrasted with the "closed predicament" afflicting African spirituality. There can be no doubt that Horton himself has a theological prejudice against African religions, since in his programmatic article "A Definition of Religion and Its Uses," *Journal of the Royal Anthropological Institute* 90 (1960), 201-26, he sharply distinguishes between authentic religion (characterized by beliefs about and subjective communion with spiritual beings) and mere manipulative religion (which seeks to use the divine for externalistic, pragmatic personal or community goals). The first is typified by early Christianity, the second by the "Pharisees" and the "exclusivism" of Biblical Judaism. In his articles on African religions we discover that the essence of these religions, too, happens to be merely pragmatic and communal. They can even be seriously explained as proto-scientific attempts to understand and control the environment, partly through personifying natural forces. The unification of society and cosmos, however, is what leads to the cognitive exclusivism of the "closed predicament." Ironically, the heavy theological prejudice in all this does not prevent Horton from taking Victor Turner to task, in his "Ritual Man in Africa," *Africa* 34, no. 2

(April 1964): 85-103, for Turner's "Christian" bias. Turner's theories on ritual are said to be too influenced by Thomas Aquinas and the liturgical concepts of the Catholic Church. Apparently Turner is insufficiently Protestant for Horton. In any case, Turner's theories have the inestimable advantage of directing us to an appreciation and understanding of the spiritual dimensions of African ritual, while Horton's more exclusive approach would have us ignore or denigrate these.

PART THREE:

THE STRUCTURES OF RITUAL SYMBOLISM

Chapter 6

Esotericism and Bodily Knowledge

Every moment of awareness is really the synthesis of two forms of cognition, not just one. There is the deductive type that starts from the abstract and general and "descends," so to speak, in increasingly concrete "refractions" into the actualities of earthly life, building up a symbolic hierarchy linking the One and the Many. This we have already seen. And there is another, inductive kind of systematic network of symbols, that starts from the concrete and "ascends" from the Many to the One. The two types together create a complex grid, balanced and infinitely extending around each person; together they comprise each person's entire universe, although different cultures may emphasize one or the other.

Ascending symbolisms, which we can also call "orectic" symbolisms, are based on sensory physical complementaries, such as hot and cold, left and right, darkness and light, and so on—elemental sensual experiences—which in their repetition and interlacing correspondences weave an inclusive and organized sensory-motor order. Psychological studies have documented the slow refinement of the perceptions and organic responses that continues from the first days of infancy and finally produces the vivid, differentiated experiental world of maturity.[1] This tacit cognitive structure, rooted as it is in the sensory-motor apparatus, is an entirely different kind of symbolism from that which moves from rationally deduced, systematically and consciously focussed principles to the multiplicity of things.[2] The latter exults in clear meaning, but clear meaning is often in danger of lacking depth and persuasiveness, or even the sense of living reality. Ascending symbolisms, however, are mainly preconscious, sensory, even aesthetic and intuitive in nature. Yet the systematic knowledge they shape is certainly as meaningful religiously as the more abstract and therefore more often noticed systems, and in fact the inductive and the deductive structures need each other to find completion. The abstract cognitive structures that descend from One to Many lack the specificity and rootedness that only the concrete "ascending" symbolisms can bestow. It is the latter that determines the precise form of shrines and ritual gestures, for only the latter organizes experiential reality systematically, engaging emotions directly.

ASCENDING SYMBOLISM

Few studies of religious ritual have paid much attention to what we have called "ascending" symbolisms; indeed, few studies seem even to recognize its existence. Smith and Dale, for example, in their discussion of the Ila, merely give the outline of ritual action, scarcely noticing whether they deal with "hot" or "cold" realities; use black, white, or red motifs; occur at night or at day, in the shade or light, near fire or in streams; involve rough-surfaced objects or smooth, bitter or sweet tastes; actions of penetration or of enclosure, and so on. Such details as the species of tree branches and herbs used in the ritual, and the sensory and cognitive associations linked with each in the minds of the users, are generally missing entirely from such accounts, although it is becoming evident that they are very important.

Since the 1950s, only a few students of African religions have actually devoted much attention to this area of religion, and interestingly most of these worked in central Africa among peoples not much different from the Ila.[3] Of these the most insightful and stimulating is without a doubt Victor W. Turner, whose articles and monographs on the matrilineal Ndembu of northwestern Zambia have revealed a startlingly complex and interwoven symbolic system collating the most elementary color perceptions, the various species of animals and plants, social kinship, and other areas of daily experience that determine the form of ritual objects and their place in ceremonies. One example from the many Turner provides will suffice to demonstrate this.[4]

The most important transition of a Ndembu woman's life is probably the nkang'a, a puberty rite held when the young woman's breasts begin to swell. This rite generally culminates in the ceremony of marriage in a way quite similar to the chisungu rites mentioned in an earlier connection as widespread in central Africa (although chisungu is generally associated with the first menstruation). The nkang'a has three phases, which as Turner shows correlate closely with the three moments of "rites of passage" delineated by van Gennep: separation, transformation, and reincorporation of the initiate. (However, one can argue that the transformation occurs already in the first part of the nkang'a, and the remaining two "acts" of the Ndembu drama stress reincorporation.) The division into three phases, we can suggest, in any case, is done by the Ndembu themselves, for a different symbolic center dominates each of them. In the first, the dominant symbol is a *mudyi* tree. In the second, the dominant symbol is the seclusion hut built on mudyi saplings. In the third, the dominant symbol is the girl herself, who has her "coming-out" dance before everyone, and is then carried off to marry the groom. Until this point, the girl has been largely passive, and the dominant symbols, the songs, and the instructions have been worked almost literally into her very being; when she dances before the assembled guests, she is more than just a specific young girl, she is the embodiment of Ndembu femininity and of Ndembu society. In a sense, we can say that she is the human form of the mudyi tree.

What, then, is the mudyi tree? Unfortunately, the Ndembu tell no myths to explain to a stranger their actions in this ritual—at least, there were none told to Turner. But informants were very articulate about their associations with the various items used in the ritual, including the mudyi, and by means of an almost psychoanalytic method of tracing associations through to a subterranean logic, Turner was able to discover a great deal about ritual symbolism. He found entire systematic networks of meaning connecting even the smallest items in ritual to each other, an entire universe that dwelt in what he, too, called the "preconscious."

Thus the mudyi tree (*Diplorrhyncus condylocarpon*) is unusual in one respect; the Ndembu say that if its thin black bark is scratched, a white latex exudes in milky beads (hence the name they give to it, the "milk tree"). According to the women, the milk tree stands for human breast milk and also for the breasts that supply it. The connection to the budding breasts of the novice is obvious. But the Ndembu understand this as a spiritual truth that is beginning to actualize itself in the initiate, and not merely a physical, biological process. We can say that process as such is spiritual, to the Ndembu. "The main theme of Nkang'a is indeed the tie of nurturing between mother and child, not the [merely physical] bond of birth."[5] Moreover, motherhood is understood in its widest sense not to refer to the actual mother of the initiate, nor even to her own future generativity alone, but most particularly to motherhood as the source of humanity and of matrilineal kinship. Mudyi represents in this way the organizing principle of Ndembu society. A male ritual specialist explained the matter very clearly (and in the process hinted at a very important mythic model being present after all):

> The milk tree is the place of all mothers of the lineage (*ivumu*, literally "womb" or "stomach"). It represents the ancestress of women and men. The milk tree is where our ancestress slept when she was initiated. "To initiate" here means the dancing of women round and round the milk tree where the novice sleeps. One ancestress after another slept there down to our grandmother and our mother and ourselves the children. That is the place of our tribal custom (*muchidi*), where we began, even men just the same, for men are circumcised under a milk tree.[6]

The initiate returns to the beginnings, and joins all her people through the unifications worked by the mudyi. The tree is a "natural" symbol, located in the wilderness, and the candidate thus enters a primordial, precultural condition at this point. Yet here is the root of all tribal tradition, *muchidi*: "The tribesman drinks from the breasts of tribal custom," as Ndembu say, fusing in one image natural and cultural realms. Nourishing and sustaining his people, the chief is also called the "mother" of his "children" the people, and both he and the human mother are extensions of "mother earth," parent of all life. The mudyi telescopes all these meanings into one ritual focus. Each ritual context extends the semantic web. In all these ways, the mudyi is a typical ascending symbol, accreting around it all chance associations and extending its meaning infinitely, as far as experience will permit. This illustrates a basic characteristic of such symbolism, which we may call its "imperialism." Each sensory symbol is when cognized the center of experience; each seeks to be the *total* meaning of life, subordinating other ascending symbols to itself. As Freud first made clear, all symbols of this passionate, sensory type are essentially ambivalent. Each fragments awareness as it seeks to unify it, by competing with others for supremacy. There is a schizophrenic tendency to this level of cognition, just as there is a paranoiac tendency to focused, systematic "descending" symbolism.

So we find that the mudyi is not a just a symbol of unity. It also symbolizes conflict. It represents the primal matrilineal ancestors in both male and female initiations, but can also mean the unity of women over against men. Both meanings are invoked in nkang'a. Until noon on the first day, the novice is laid on her left (feminine) side beneath the mudyi, while the women sing scurrilous songs about the men (underlining the first phase of ritual separation). But she is turned onto her right (masculine) side in the afternoon, and the songs then stress the integration of the sexes: from the novice will come male and female children, for the mudyi is mother of all.[7] But here the biological mother tries to kidnap her daughter away; in a mock battle, she is repulsed. Now the mudyi symbolizes the conflict between natural mother and spiritual mother. The elders sing instead of the symbolic motherhood that is now in process of giving birth to a new adult person, a woman. The girl who once existed only for herself and her mother is gone forever, to be replaced by a fully socialized, symbolical being able to produce life. The transcendental mudyi is now her mother and her essence.

Precisely this characteristic—that the ascending symbols immediately involve prior sensory experience and the preconscious passionate life—gives them a special depth of "reality," which categories that have been developed solely by rational clear consciousness cannot have. These sensory schemas have immediacy and directness because of the completeness with which since infancy they have been assimilated into the preconscious. At the beginning, the infant may not yet have learned how to focus on particular things, define them sensorily, and "comprehend" them, so that for it their reality was uncertain, but with the maturation these basic cognitive schemas are so well mastered, so true and familiar, that they pass into the preconscious, the "assumed-to-be-true" realm, by-passing the hesitations of clear consciousness. The ritual in stressing these symbolisms borrows from them an air of reality and depth, bending this to its own purposes.

The "imperialism" of ascending symbolisms is ritually directed to conscious unifications of experience. The *white sap* that wells up out of the cut bark of the mudyi can mean milk (and so everything maternal and nourishing), semen (and all that is male and fertilizing), or, when focused on as beads, even children. The whiteness itself of the sap can be said to belong to the elemental whiteness that runs through the entire universe according to the central mystery of higher Ndembu initiations (evidently not referred to specifically in the nkang'a); this mystery tells of the "three rivers of God" that are said to stream unceasingly from Nzambi, the supreme being.[8] The rivers of white, red, and black weave through all things; each color is also an essential quality of the universe. White is purity, the most primordial spirituality, life itself, birth and rebirth, generosity, wisdom, and kindliness. Its life essence is evident in semen, milk, and cassava meal (the staple food in Ndembu diet); in their initiation Ndembu girls become able to generate this essence themselves in breast milk, and so participate directly in the godhead. In the coming-out dance of the nkang'a novice at the end of the ceremony, she appears before the men with white beads in her hair.

We find, then, that the mudyi symbol, outwardly simple, is inwardly amazingly complex. In a preliminary analysis, Turner has pointed to the existence of two poles of reference in such ritual symbols, the "orectic" (emotional and desire-laden) and the "ideological" (relating to social norms and institutions).[9] We have seen that the nkang'a invokes very basic feelings such as sexual desire and sex war (as with other peoples we have discussed, the Ndembu liken the procreative act to war).[10] The conflict between the mother of the novice and the nkang'a women is only partly a mock one, and the coming-out dance clearly appeals directly to the sexual desire of the men of the audience. In fact, the heightened sexual atmosphere of the initiation continues on through the night partying of the guests; casual liaisons in the bush, wild behavior, and brawls between rivals or jealous husbands punctuate the festivities.[11] As with the new year's festivities of the Ila, songs mocking the powerful and general rituals of reversal characterize this period. But the ideological pole of these symbols gives them an orientation toward social values. The norms of the culture deeply penetrate the organic desires, and the passions feed with their intensity the strength of the norms. From this point of view it is important to note how differing interpretations of the symbols anchor distinct social groupings and define them over against each other. The novice's new state, potential motherhood, is contrasted to the former immaturity she must "die" to; the separation of the novice from the mudyi tree and the older women is symbolized by the taboo on the girl's looking at the tree (it would make her go "mad"); women in general are contrasted to men and the nkang'a girl and women as a group to the girl's mother, etc. Within the liminal unity of the mudyi symbol elaborate structures are discovered, demonstrating anew the liminality of structure for the Ndembu.

A further consideration of the mudyi symbol has suggested to Turner that we may discover within any given ritual drama two kinds of symbols: "dominant" and what we may call here "subordinate" (Turner's word is "instrumental").[12] The dominant symbol in nkang'a is obviously the mudyi tree. The mudyi qualifies all the rest; that is to say, it gives all the other symbols a specific meaning and orientation. The other symbols, however, help define the amorphous nature of the dominant symbol by specifying the effect it has. We may say, the dominant symbol provides the orientation for the ceremony, while the subordinate symbols supply their own inner range of associations and give a context. Subordinate symbols thus define and extend the meaning of dominant ones, for each ritual symbol has its own depth and polysemous aura of meaning, and may for its part emerge in a latter part of the ritual cycle or in another ritual as a dominant symbol. Thus dominance is situational.

In an important later extension of these insights, Turner has pointed out that the simpler the symbol, the wider its "fan" of referents through both analogy and association.[13] The color white, for example, has an even wider range of meaning than the mudyi tree, which in turn is broader in meaning than the seclusion hut to which the novice is taken at the end of the first day. We see in this progression of complexity an increase in specificity, in which broad meanings are reduced and directed more precisely by the interplay between an increased number of symbolic elements. In the seclusion hut, the meaning of the mudyi posts as such is subordinated to the meaning of the hut as organic feminine space. And in the last stage of nkang'a, it is the girl herself who is the coordinated meaning of all the symbols. By this point hundreds of different simple ritual symbols have come together to generate this bride. She therefore is a complex, precise symbol as well as a very real human being. If we were to reverse the analysis at this point, and ask what "bride" means, we would have to consider each of the ritual elements that go to make up the force of this reality. We would discover, in short, a "reticulated network" of symbols arount her provided by the ritual context. What is true for the "bride" is true as well for every complex ritual symbol: each in the conclusion and abstraction of a hierarchy of meanings. Many simpler symbols combine together, the references of some canceling some of the other symbols, but also extending' them. The more complex the final symbol, the more its parts negate each other and produce an abstraction, a "sign" having only one specific meaning.[14] So Turner suggests; although, as we have seen, the "bride" who is the sum total of the nkang'a ceremony is far from being an abstraction! The nkang'a teaches that an abstraction can still have tremendous symbolic depth, if its parts retain an organic connection with the life-world of the ritual participants. The "felt significances" of the lesser symbols can enrich the final result without being negated by it; they remain to give an "affective glow," as Turner also notes.[15] They persist, in short, in the preconscious tacit awareness, just as Freud has shown so much of our symbolic experience does.

Turner's entire strategy is to recover those preconscious significances of ritual symbolism. His problem is one faced by almost every field anthropologist: how to make sense out of religious behavior when those he is concerned with do not consciously have the key themselves. The Ndembu, according to Turner, have very few grand myths to explain their multitude of rituals. How then to understand their rich ceremonial life? At first, Turner's answer was simply to reduce religious phenomena to social "ideology"—the recourse of most anthropologists. If the people do not really know why they are doing what they do, then the answer must lie in social forces of a latent sort, in the *functions* performed by the ritual. Turner's search for contexts, however, led him gradually to an appreciation of symbolic meaning itself. Each context of a ritual symbol is in effect an indigenous interpretation of it and of what it applies to (as we have already seen in earlier chapters). We might even add that every *complex* symbol is really itself a series of contexts, mutually modifying but frozen in time and presented to us in an instant, while in the course of a ritual cycle we can trace in time a similar series of modifying contexts played out around a *simple* symbol. Each ritual is as such a complex symbol spread out in time, and each complex symbol may be viewed as a condensed ritual, or as the static *simplification* of a ritual in a controlled direction.

The search for contexts is the necessary first recourse of any phenomenological investigator of ritual, although as we shall see everything depends on what we include in "context." Turner's method is ultimately very close to that enunciated by A. R. Radcliffe-Brown (a leader of functionalist anthropology). Three principles should govern the analysis of ritual, according to Radcliffe-Brown:

> (1) In explaining any given custom it is necessary to take into account the explanation given by the natives themselves . . . we cannot regard any hypothesis as to the meaning of a custom as being satisfactory unless it explains not only the custom but also the reasons that the natives give for following it. (2) . . . when the same or a similar custom is practised on different occasions it has the same or a similar meaning in all of them. . . . (3) . . . when different customs are practised together on one and the same occasion there is a common element in the customs.[16]

The first method Turner calls the "exegetical," which includes the folk etymologies given for the names of the items used in ritual by the participants. The second and third methods together he terms the "positional"; structuralist anthropology concentrates on such matters. He then adds another category, that of the "operational" meaning of the ritual. Under this category the analysis turns to the individuals handling the items, when, and with whom. This amounts to explicit inclusion of the social function of ritual in the analysis.

We cannot avoid what is often called the "hermeneutical circle" in such matters. Whatever is included at the start is also discovered as the "meaning" of the whole thing at the end. For example, Turner's deep exegesis of ritual symbols irresistibly recalls Freudian techniques for uncovering unconscious meanings. However, Turner eloquently argues that it is not the province of the anthropologist to apply Freudian categories and speculations; the anthropologist is oriented to social structure; the psychoanalyst toward psychological structure and sexuality.[17] Each has a different task to perform. Yet the historian of religions is not bound in the same way. He must be concerned with an "orectic" depth of symbolism that could well touch on such matters as sexuality and psychology, but which also extends beyond the "ideological" (Turner's term for "social") pole into properly religious intentionalities. One does not have to use psychoanalytic theories to recognize the importance of sexual categories in religious ritual or world view. Turner perhaps associates such categories too closely with Freudian speculation, excluding both from consideration despite the obvious importance of sexual themes in his material.

We need not invoke psychoanalytic concepts to understand the great importance of sexual imagery in ritual and the preconscious. Together with eating, which is also an important theme in ritual (and which is often associated with sexual intercourse in central Bantu cultures), sexuality intensely involves the body. It is a primary act, on one level purely physical, but at the same time, unlike eating, it *must* involve other human beings (and therefore society as such), and must therefore touch on norms and imply a sense of the cosmic order. Intense as it is, sexuality especially needs these associations if it is not to disrupt social and cosmic structures. At the same time sexuality necessarily involves all of the levels we have found to be important in ritual symbolism. The result is that its intensity gives passionate depth to norms and categories of the universe. The ascending symbolisms associated with it provide descending symbolisms with powerful girdering imagery. It is very common therefore to find sexuality used as a master symbol in ritual universes, which after all center themselves on the body and its world.

This last observation must be developed further: the spatial universe of the body is absolutely crucial for ritual. Religious meaning is mediated through the spaces ritual establishes for the body. We notice a peculiarity regarding Turner's descriptions of Ndembu religion; his analyses of ritual focus primarily on what we have called ascending symbolisms and their social referents. We gain as a result a vivid picture of the society and a clear sense of how the passions sustain that society. The discussions here are nothing short of brilliant. But there is no similarly clear picture of Ndembu cosmology, of how space is unified and articulated, of how the ritual establishes sacral regions in the universe or what the body *per se* has to do with this. As a result, specifically religious meaning as it englobes the whole of Ndembu life is not clear. Instead, we find a kaleidoscope of religious meanings varying with each ceremonial, a plethora of "dominant symbols," but lacking central coordination. The basic cosmology on which religious aspirations are based are therefore ironically clearer in the survey conducted by Smith and Dale on the related Ila, although the sophistication of their study is much less. Together, however, the two approaches permit us a very profound insight indeed into their common religious life.

It is evident that a very similar dispositional order exists among the Ndembu to that which we found among the Ila. Applying this to the nkang'a begins to reveal to us the elemental religious meaning of that initiation. According to a passing remark of Turner's informant, "the milk tree is where our ancestress slept when she was initiated. . . . One ancestress after another slept there down to our grandmother and our mother and ourselves the children. That is the place of our tribal custom (*muchidi*)."[18] The ritual is temporally a repetition of actions done *ab origine*. It exists outside of banal, commonplace time in the same way as the Ila rituals we have already discussed. The novice in entering into these actions joins in a history outside of her bodily history; she becomes all women who have done this before. Her body and its actions are transformed into a profound symbol. The same is true of the place itself where the ritual takes place. The milk tree is selected almost at random in the bush (of course it must meet certain criteria, such as small height and immaturity). It is certainly not the same milk tree under which other women down through time have been initiated. Yet, as the Ndembu informant's remark makes obvious, symbolically this tree with the space around it *is* the same tree that shaded the first Ndembu woman and all later Ndembu women. By lying down underneath it, the novice enters wholly symbolical space, an emphasis made even stronger by the location in the uninhabited bush. Like the bush itself, the rite is a continuation of primordial realities of space and time.

In the first part of the ritual, then, the elder women go spatially into the primordial era. They penetrate the wilderness, locate a mudyi sapling, clear an area around it and lay the novice wrapped in a blanket at its foot. For the entire day, despite the burning sun, the crawling and stinging insects, and other discomforts, the novice must lie motionless under the blanket, completely covered, in the position of a fetus. For the entire day the women dance around the sapling and the silent girl, droning their "instructional" songs in which it is said this is the place of the girl's "death," here also the place of her "rebirth." Naked, utterly still under her blanket-shroud, she dies into the mudyi symbolism so that its positive liminality will shape her anew. Her former self ends; even her own mother has no more claim to her, as we have seen. From "child" of former mother she herself is being made into a "mother" of future children. "The milk tree is the place of all mothers of the lineage [*ivumu*, literally "womb" or "stomach"]," we are told.[19] Generated in the shroud-womb of the primordial bush, the novice is then brought in the second phase to the seclusion hut, built (we are informed in passing) on the *boundary between bush and village*, out of the crossed supports of two mudyi posts. The hut, as details make clear, is both the novice herself and a further socialization (and humanization) of the "place" of the womb. The bridegroom's brother sits astride the top of the feminine hut, in a rite symbolizing the future sexual union itself.[20] As with the Ila, the Ndembu conceive of the hut as a feminine space, whose parts are anthropomorphically identified with the woman who occupies it. The identity of the hut-space with a cultivated (fertile) field is also made explicit with the hoeing of the ground before the erection of the hut.[21] In the third phase of the ritual, the novice ends her journey back from primordial time and space; leaving the semisocialized condition of the seclusion hut, she appears as the fully humanized yet still archetypal woman in her public dance in the village, and soon afterwards is borne off to her groom's hut. She recapitulates, in short, the history of humanity, and through this generates human space and time out of the primordial confusion: the bush, the fields, the village.

The process of transformation of the novice into a full human being, in short, conforms to primordial and cosmic intentionalities. But we may legitimately ask how it is that these transcendental orientations are embedded in the consciousness of the initiate; how is reality transformation and self-transformation made real and convincing? The problem is made even greater when we add that according to Turner no explicit mythical revelations are made. The mystery of the "rivers of God" is not disclosed, and even the spatial symbolism remains largely implied. All the novice knows is that she is undergoing a terrible emotional ordeal. To understand what is happening, we must deepen our discussion of ascending symbolisms and the preconscious disposition.

ASCENDING SYMBOLISMS, INITIATION, AND THE CENTERED SELF

Again and again we notice a coercive element in initiations all over the world. It is perhaps a universal trait.[22] It often verges on outright brainwashing, and yet produces the same subjective experience as religious conversion. The nkang'a novice is often treated brutally, and in general more as an object than a person. Yet this somehow creates enthusiastically adult Ndembu women. Boys too must undergo the same experience of seemingly arbitrary oppression and passivity before they become men. We must ask how such treatment produces such positive results.

Right at the start we might as well admit that none of this rough usage is necessary if the point of the rites is to convey knowledge, or even a convincing world view. The ritual merely involves the common elements of the Ndembu universe; in giving them an order and locating them in a cosmos, the rites would be convincing to Ndembu with no need for violence. Not even myths are needed to order such a familiar universe; ritual is sufficient. A young girl already familiar with Ndembu words and proverbs about white objects and breasts would find the ritual equation of breast milk to the underlying maternal principle of existence enlightening and convincing, for she would already know it tacitly.

Still, her treatment is harsh. Perhaps the point is not really the communication of specific information at all, but experiential upheaval itself, allowing the initiate to experience a *radical recentering* of experience around transcendental goals. Or, to put it another way, the religious reality disclosed in initiation only becomes part of the initiate, orienting the preconscious level into a characteristic disposition, when the previous preconscious dispositional ordering of experience is destroyed. Merely the presentation of ideas, however convincing those ideas may be, cannot have this effect on the organic level of consciousness.[23] For not just ideas are involved, but a whole orientation of the self. In childhood, the perceived world is known above all in terms of its effect on the self. According to the research of Piaget, a distinct and stable ego is the product of a long period of struggle, and is realized perhaps only by the eighth year, at least in the West. Initiation above all destroys this self-centered world of childhood, at least this is its primary intent. The adult produced by initiation is a person whose self and entire life is defined by a center outside himself or herself. This recentering is expressed through the acceptance of adult responsibilities and roles, within a transcendental order.

Initiation therefore generates a radical disorientation of the deep preconscious and the conscious ego world; it devalues the ego and the body and then reorients and centers the candidate on transcendental realities. This centering is made part of the inner disposition. Let us follow this process in nkang'a.

The disorientation of the girl initiate is begun immediately, in the first of the three phases of the ritual. She is removed from familiar surroundings and from those who support her familiar identity (her mother, etc.). Naked except for a loin cloth, she is forced to lie in a single position for long periods of time, wrapped in a stifling blanket (which covers the head as

well) in the hot sun, while the elder women of the nkang'a dance around her
singing sexually "instructive" songs. This *coercion of body postures* is most
significant. Not only do we build up and maintain a predictable world
through body action, but even more importantly, as long as we retain
control over our body, we have a way *into* the world under our *own*
control. The body is probably the most sacred bastion of the self-image. On
the self-image is built a world-image. Disturbing this body image, then,
affects the larger world of consciousness, and especially removing control
of the body from the ego deprives the latter of its chief assurance. Even
when the girl is permitted to move from the mudyi tree to the seclusion hut,
she is not allowed to will herself to walk, but she must be carried. She is
reduced to a passive object to be manipulated, an extension of other bodies
and other wills.

The same is evident in the invasion and take over of her physical self, her
body. Inside the seclusion hut, she is fed only by others, washed all over by
attendants, and shaved both on her head and on her pubes. Her sexual
organs are also manipulated; the instructress widens the girl's vagina with
her fingers, and various phallus-shaped objects are inserted into it to
accustom the girl to the coming wedding intercourse.[24] The novice's labia
are massaged and lengthened, and the sooty outer coat of certain mudyi
trees is rubbed over the vulva to blacken it; these operations are to heighten
her sexual attractiveness, as are the incisions made around the navel. Ash is
rubbed into the abdomenal incisions, to create raised cicatrices; men like to
caress these during intercourse. The effect of these bodily operations on the
girl is clearly to reduce her sense that she can voluntarily define who she is;
even the elementary and basic sense of ego-control over her body is taken
from her, and when it is later restored her body will be irrevocably different
and therefore so will her self-image. Scarifications and similarly
manipulative bodily operations are also common to male initiations
throughout Africa and beyond; often, as with the Ndembu boys, the body
is painted all over to transform the body image into something utterly
symbolic. The person is thus forced into a passive, recipient attitude to the
world. The ego is devalued along with its accustomed supports.
Preconsciously, this makes it impossible to judge the world from the
perspective of the self. One is not self-determined but other-determined.

The removal of the candidate to the bush at the start of the initiation
dramatically parallels the entry into confusion and psychic wilderness. The
spatial symbolism need not be conscious; the entire intent of the initiation
requires displacement from the girl's accustomed social environment.

To discover a stable *transcendental* center becomes for the candidate a
psychic necessity. Without such a center outside the self (the ego and the
body as autonomous centers no longer being viable), there can be no secure

sense of self at all, and the result would be complete disorganization of consciousness. There would be no *meaning* to life, no way to orient oneself. The definitions of identity ceaselessly provided by the instruction and the ritual are therefore decisive. The bodily operations and the songs all irresistably direct the novice to conceive of herself primarily as a woman, and sharing in woman's realities over against men. Men are made a complementary part of the psychic transcendental reality for which she is being shaped, part of the "other" that defines her as a person. But above all she is made aware of the centrality of the feminine in the universe. She is oriented around the mudyi symbol and all that is associated with it. The girl is forbidden to look directly at the mudyi, heightening her sense that it is crucial for her existence. It has power over her; if she looked at it, she is told, she would go mad: the source of her psychic disorganization but also her guiding beacon would then burst upon her with all its power unmitigated, and it would destroy her. It must be assimilated gradually, for the mudyi tree is the revelation of the universe. Clearly, it is one of the many forms of the Cosmic Tree symbol so commonly encountered in the history of religions. It presents a whole possibility of existence, and as mediated by the elder women who instruct her, the mudyi offers her the possibility of a defined self again. The symbolism is deep and rich; but above all, it signifies breast and womb potencies. Through these organs the novice is assimiliated to the first Ndembu ancestress. With her attention focused on these aspects of herself, a body image is restored to her in which her body is shown to be part of a cosmic elemental organism. The transformation is aided by the songs and instructions. She is taught that the society of women must be for her what the family and her mother once was. She is now a "woman," and not her mother's girl. The mock battle with the mother not only has specific meaning for the mother and the nkang'a instructresses, but also teaches the initiate that in the deepest sense she will never be able to "go home again" as a child. The multitude of meanings in ritual for the various participants in it is here vividly shown. The *action* is the unity, but the meanings are different for each person.

As the ceremony progresses, the girl begins to be allowed more control over herself; this coincides with an increasing clarity of the symbolic meaning of the initiation, and with this assimilation, a turning of the attention to the "Other" who confronts women: men. No doubt the increasing clarity of the meaning of the ceremonies does not signify a full grasp of the mudyi symbolisms. Perhaps only after assisting at later nkang'a initiations for other girls will she come to a full understanding of it. Initiation is a lifelong process. But the songs, treatments, instructions in sexual technique and in dance steps, the isolation with older women in the bush, and the intense interaction in the seclusion hut all convey the

meaning tacitly. The preliminary bewilderment begins to lift. Symbolically, she is another, organic and human form of the mudyi, just as the
seclusion hut is a cultural form. The mudyi as a forest tree is the wild
version of the symbolism, the hut/field is a domesticated form, and she
herself is their synthesis. As such, she can now appear before the guests in
her wedding dance. Now and at last she can be active, but only as the
symbol of cosmic femininity, as breasts and womb, and as bride. Soon
after, she is borne off to her groom.

At the moment of the dance, when she offers herself to the gaze of the
men, what is the condition of her consciousness? She now looks upon
herself in the context of the nkang'a initiation, with her attitudes entirely
transformed from what they had been before. All her perceptions now are
given a significance from the systematic reorganization of her universe and
from the key symbols at its center. Just as boys going through their
initiation come out seeing themselves and the world from a "man's"
perspective, so do girls come out as "women." Confronting the men for
whom she is intended as a woman, she knows her identity to be part of the
cosmic structure of things, and not just limited by her personality or ego. A
deep dispositional ordering has shaped her consciousness and even
preconsciousness, controling her self-identity and attitudes to the world
perhaps permanently. She accepts that there is a "rightness," a "necessity"
to her dance before the men, of an elemental and cosmic sort.

The coercive nature of the orientation, its seeming hostility to the ego, is
not accidental or superfluous. It is related to the very nature of
consciousness. The questing, contesting "imperialism" of global symbols
perhaps ultimately demands the ego as a coordinating center. But any
consciously organized structure is alien to the deeper world of desires and
feelings, at least to a certain degree. It is striking that there is no culture that
does not recognize the dangers that spontaneous passions pose to cultural
and spiritual norms. Every conscious order is apparently sensed
preconsciously to be arbitrary and externally imposed, even if in fact the
need for such order arises directly from the conflicting ascending
symbolisms themselves.

Thus there exists an experiential similarity between undergoing entirely
arbitrary brainwashing and mystical rebirth or religious conversion. To the
ascending symbols any order is arbitrary; because they desperately need
some coordination, however, the brainwashed victim can eagerly seize the
identity given him by his tormentors even if it requires his own total self-
condemnation. At least this affords a secure center from which to orient all
experience, and is constantly confirmed by everyone around him. It is
noteworthy that many of the intensely communal cults in the United States
and elsewhere also seek to reduce their candidates' self-confidence in the

same way (presenting, perhaps, their doctrines as "logical" when they are not, or accusing the candidate of absolute perversity), all the better to assure the completeness of the emotional conversion.

In the case of the nkang'a initiation, however, we do not have genuine brainwashing, for here the same world known to the candidate before conversion is returned to her afterwards, but enhanced and positively transformed. She has an absolutely necessary part to play in this world, and the values given to her experience consciously do not conflict with the preconscious understanding of it. Unlike brainwashing and artificial religious conversion, the initiatic consciousness does not conflict with the world known preconsciously. Instead, one confirms the other, and the preconscious is drawn into the Otherness of life instead of being pitted against it. There is, as a result, a unitary way of willing the world to be, a deep and coherent dispositional orientation, centering the ego willingly in a profounder reality it cannot wholly control.

Notes to Chapter 6

1. See Jean Piaget, *Plays, Dreams and Imitation in Childhood*, trans. by C. Gattegno and F.M. Hodgson (New York: W.W.Norton & Co., 1962); Heinz Werner and Bernard Kaplan, *Symbol Formation* (New York: John Wiley & Sons, 1963); and L.S. Vygotsky, *Thought and Speech* (Cambridge: M.I.T. Press and New York: John Wiley & Sons, 1962).

2. An interesting analysis of the sudden discovery of deductive symbolic thought by Helen Keller is given in Werner and Kaplan, *Symbol Formation*, pp. 110-12; Piaget in all his works is particularly interested in the triumph of this type of cognition, which in perfected form is "reversible thought": disciplined logical analysis.

3. See Audrey I. Richards, *Chisungu* (London: Faber & Faber, 1956), and Monica Wilson, *Rituals of Kinship among the Nyakyusa* (London: Oxford University Press for the International African Institute, 1957), and *Communal Rituals of the Nyakyusa* (London: Oxford University Press for the International African Institute, 1959), for some pioneering studies.

4. See, for what follows, Victor W. Turner, "Symbols in Ndembu Ritual," in *Closed Systems and Open Minds: The Limits of Naivety in the Social Sciences*, ed. Max Gluckman (Edinburgh: Oliver and Body, 1964), and reprinted in Turner, *The Forest of Symbols: Aspects of Ndembu Ritual* (Ithaca: Cornell University Press, 1967), pp. 19-47; also see the very detailed description of nkang'a in Turner, *The Drums of Affliction: A study of Religious Processes among the Ndembu of Zambia* (Oxford: Clarendon Press for the International African Institute, 1968), pp. 198-268.

5. Turner, *Forest of Symbols*, pp. 20f.

6. Ibid., p. 21.

7. Turner, *Drums of Affliction*, p. 220.

8. Turner, *Forest of Symbols*, pp. 59-62, esp. p. 68.

9. Ibid., p. 28 and following pages.

10. Ibid., p. 41.

11. Turner, *Drums of Affliction*, pp. 231-32.

12. Turner, *Forest of Symbols*, pp. 30ff.

13. Victor W. Turner, *Revelation and Divination in Ndembu Ritual* (Ithaca: Cornell University Press, 1975), pp. 160ff.

14. Ibid., pp. 162ff.

15. Ibid., p. 164.

16. A.R. Radcliffe-Brown, *The Andamanese Islanders* (New York: Free Press, 1922, 1964), pp. 234-35; the methods control Malinowski's studies, Durkheim's before him, and indeed are the natural expression of any phenomenologically oriented method.

17. See Turner, *Forest of Symbols*, pp. 32-47.

18. Ibid., p. 21.

19. Ibid.

20. Turner, *Drums of Affliction*, pp. 222-24.

21. Ibid., p. 222.

22. Nevertheless, the severity of initiation has been shown to vary in direct relationship with the social-cultural need to transform the novice from mother-attached child to cultural group-oriented adult. The stronger the child's attachments, the greater the severity, particularly if there is great on-going need for cooperative adult activity. This especially applies to male initiations, which tend in general to be more drastic than female ones. See, for a general review of anthropological research, Klaus-Friedrich Koch, "Sociogenic and Psychogenic Models in Anthropology: The Functions of Jalé Initiation," *Man* n.s. 9, no.3 (September 1974): 397-422.

23. It is important to emphasize this, in light of various attempts today to resurrect the theory that religion is really "pseudo-science."

24. Turner, *Drums of Affliction*, pp. 243-49. Note the long list of prohibitions controlling every movement of the initiate in highly artificial ways, pp. 243-44. Like an infant, she must be naked, can only whisper, must always look down and keep her fists pressed against her temples, must be utterly without will and obedient.

Chapter 7

Initiation and the Meaning of "Knowledge"

The study of initiation shows that ascending symbolism needs the integration of descending symbolisms, reflected in a dispositional ordering of experience. But some societies develop descending symbolisms, encapsulating systematic philosophical ideas, more than others. It is likely that the preference for complex, fully focused and worked-out systems of thought reflects a view that the universe is highly complex and even suffers self-contradiction, some aspects negating others. Most crucially, it may well be the case that such systems are the attempt to unify and control a world in which the important realities bearing directly on the fate of the individual are not accessible to the integrations of ascending symbolisms, that is, to sensory experience. The world known directly by the body is vulnerable to more distant forces and institutions, both cosmological and social. Descending systems of thought attempt to account for this more elaborate universe, and in the process frequently discount the bodily experience entirely. The world known personally becomes merely a shadow of more invisible but truer realms.

We might expect that such attitudes would be more common in societies that are well differentiated, with many different interdependent social groups to integrate together. Of course many outwardly simple societies produce astonishingly complex metaphysical systems. We need only mention the Australian aborigines, or the shamans of many Siberian and American Indian hunting peoples. But there does seem to be a general correlation between complexity of environment and of conscious thought. We notice, for example, that most Bantu cultures apparently lack elaborate systems of descending symbolisms, but they are also generally shifting cultivators with only semipermanent villages, and without rigid central authority (even in the case of many divine kingships). Many have arrived at their present locations only within the last few centuries. Cultures like those of the Ila and Ndembu have had too painful a history of decimating wars and migrations to have developed unified and elaborate philosophic systems. For cultures with such systems we must look to long-settled peoples, particularly those with centralized kingship or very strong secret societies, both of which assure the preservation and development of controlled, coherent and intricate systems. Here, in fact, the stress on "knowledge" and devaluation of sensory knowledge, might be expected to sustain a far more complex social and natural universe.

These conditions are met particularly well by a number of savanna cultures of west Africa. Here, in the rolling plains between the forests to the south and the Sahara to the north, agrarian societies have flourished for many thousands of years, developing great empires and highly sophisticated cultures. Their influence extends into the forested areas to the south, where kingdoms were established in ancient times in such localities as Benin and Ile-Ife in Nigeria.

The Bambara, a Mande people of Mali, provide an instance of the results of this history. The Mande have had one of the most glorious traditions of all the peoples of the western Sudan, and at one time the Bambara controlled an empire extending thousands of square miles over the savanna. Nevertheless, the Bambara appeared to the French authorities of the colonial period as a "typical African peasantry," without any drive and intellectually lazy, the only institutions that absorbed their interest being grotesquely ritualistic masked societies. Such was the judgment of the first major ethnologist to devote a full study to their religious life.[1] It remained for a later investigator, in a great stroke of luck, to discover that these "peasants" had a philosophy of the universe equal in complexity and profundity to the systems of Phythagoras or Plotinus, Aquinas, Spinoza, or Bergson. The Bambara, it now appears, have precisely the same assumptions as the Mbuti about qualities of sound, but they have worked out the details explicitly into a profound philosophy embracing all parts of a far more complex universe. This philosophy is communicated in stages to the initiate as he rises through the ranked masked societies.

The Bambara have an almost gnostic view of initiation. As did the Gnostics, they believe that the essence of transformation is the communication of saving knowledge. The doctrines that constitute this knowledge are taught in six stages, each of which is a separate initiation group or society. Those who have passed through all the stages are "new" beings, fully male, spiritually enlightened and endowed with the "Word," that is, possessing an immortal soul that bears the form of the universe and God himself. Yet despite this heavy stress on knowledge, when we look closely at the actual process of initiation itself we find the same psychological and spiritual transformations operating that we found in the Ndembu initiation of girls. Clearly, it is not knowledge that is the true core of initiatic transformation but the displacement of the self, by breaking down the body image, into a new transcendental universe in which the center is located outside the self.

We can show this by discussing briefly the sixth and last phase of induction into the sacred mysteries, the Kore society's initiation.[2] The boys are led from the village hooded and clothed in white anonymous gowns, and brought single-file to a sacred grove deep in the bush. They must enter the enclosure squatting, one by one, with arms outstretched as if blindly groping. Within, they are whipped with thorn branches and beaten with burning torches. This supposedly symbolizes the struggle needed to acquire truth. For us, it is more significant that this treatment renders the candidate a passive, frightened object of other people's arbitrary manipulation; the novice must witness his own complete vulnerability, and control returns to him slowly only to the degree that he conforms his body and feelings to the central dictate of others. Like embryonic beings, the candidates must cluster head down around a tree in the center of the grove; they must lie still for a long period under a blanket. Here we are strongly reminded of the same practices of the nkang'a; the effects intended are also similar. The tree, according to Bambara teachings, is the World Tree joining earth to sky; it is the source of regeneration, like the mythic tree in the beginning of time. From it the novices are born anew. *It* is their new center. Under the blanket they experience their "entombment" and also their gestation. As infantile beings the initiates must be fed and even dressed by the elders. The days that follow are devoted to the painful, laborious instruction in some 240 symbols that are suspended from the World Tree. These are common objects, such as pieces of cloth, a spoon, calabashes and carved figures; each is associated with a proverbial saying which alerts the initiate to the symbolic resonances of things. These symbols are merely the outward forms of the cosmic Word; wisdom consists in knowing the Word under all its varying outer forms. Deeper teachings are appended to this instruction. Even initiated youths do not attain to a full understanding of them until much later.

The heart of the esoteric teaching consists of the mysteries surrounding the Word. All of the universe is generated by the primal (and still continuing) vibrations that make up the Word. Out of this primal energy matter and finally form condensed. The vibrations marked out the cardinal points and up and down, in its oscillations. It produced from the center the seeds of all things, like the tree garlanded with symbols in the midst of the sacred grove. The esoteric names for these objects tap the primal "sounds" out of which they were created. Yet the world was not *known* until the vibrations doubled back on themselves in thought: thus arose consciousness, the "foundation of man." It established elemental order in the flux that preexisted.

The source of the structured universe, then, is *yo*, thought or will. It is the "spirit of nothing," the Bambara say, for in itself the will is utterly empty; it takes form in what it creates. Yo is the internal, ever silent word or voice

that "speaks" all that we know and see. It is said of yo, in an astonishing
Bambara saying, that it "comes from itself, is known by itself, departs out
of itself, from the nothingness that is itself."[3] All is yo, Bambara elders
believe, and all is essentially nothing. The entire universe is an emanation
from nothing (*fu*, "zero," "voidness").[4] Man is the image of yo. His own
speech repeats the first uttering forth of the world. Faro, the supreme being,
who rectifies the world by his commands, is the Primal Man or first form of
yo; mankind duplicates Faro in lesser form.

   For those who know, therefore, there is a silence at the core of the
universe. From it all things continually spring forth. In the face of the noise
of the material, social universe, the elders strive to return to the primal
silence. From it can come the purified Word anew, to banish all noise and
confusion. "Noise" dominates the everyday world. Dissension, strain, and
babbling fill the air. Initiates must join with their elders to restore the
perfect image of world harmony, participating with the cosmic yo and
joining with the thought of God, to produce a perfect universe.

   Since silence is the highest state, those who know do not speak, or rather,
speak seldom, and then pithily. Every action of such a person arises out of
stillness, and preserves the simplicity of truth. The Bambara elders of the
masked societies, and the aristocracy who dominate their highest levels, are
reserved, stoic, and decisive. They are always masters of their emotions and
their bodies. Others instinctively obey them.

   It is not easy to attain such a high state. It requires suffering. All "noise"
must be totally eliminated. Progression through the stages of cult is always
accompanied by painful ordeals. The initiate who flinches or cries out
demonstrates that his mind is more with banal and egoistic concerns than
with transcendental ones. The initiate must learn to transform noise into
the Word by confronting it with silence. Thus suffering (noise) becomes the
Word (serene harmony) when it is brought into contact with silence.
Flagellation is a favorite way of testing and demonstrating imperturbability. At funerals it is the custom to whip the corpse, whose absolute
immobility shows the final entry into silence. The dead have ascended the
last rung of initiation.

   Society reflects the cosmogonic hierarchy. The elder has the right to
control and direct the younger, and the aristocracy has the right to rule the
commoners and slaves. This hierarchy is generated by the Word as it
diffuses through society. The aristocracy, for example, observes decorum,
restraint, and order, thus embodying the Word. The masses on the other
hand are impulsive, confused, and noisy; they were made to obey the
aristocracy. All of this is verified by speech (through which the Word is
articulated in the world). Aristocratic speech is pure, while various
"impure" dialects are spoken by the commoners. In the same way women

are thought to be creatures that are by nature somewhat formless (even if more totally generative than men); they are garrulous and impulsive, lamenting loudly or rejoicing without restraint over every little thing, and their arguments split asunder polygamous households. The primordial formlessness that women embody in the world of society must be placed under the control of form and the Word, or the entire human cosmos will collapse. Women should be subject to men, especially to the older men who have risen through the initiatic ranks and as patriarchs rule their household.[5]

In Bambara culture, initiation is a fundamentally necessary institution of society. It clarifies the social distinctions and allocates them according to a single cosmic structure.[6] Those higher in wisdom are also those with more power to control the structures of society; children are responsible for very little, and accordingly their knowledge is small, while high priests and rulers rise to the final levels of initiation and are deeply shaped by the responsibilities that their position assigns to them to aid in the ongoing preservation of the universe.

To rephrase the matter briefly in the categories used to understand Ndembu initiation, the high initiate among the Bambara has oriented himself entirely to the transcendental source of existence. He is not self-centered but other-centered, even on the dispositional level. One can see by his demeanor that he enacts the cosmic will, not his own: he is quiet, unemotional, and without vacillation. His insight has transported him beyond the ordinary world of banal experience.

But although every initiate may strive for this state, the esotericism of the Bambara and their hierarchical social structure make it above all the attribute of the aristocracy. The stress on esoteric knowledge reflects and encourages a social and philosophical elitism. Among the Ila and Ndembu, all may experience transcendence more or less equally. Those most afflicted with illness in fact are more drawn into healing cultic initiations than others, and attain deeper transcendence, and chiefs also have a different fate. But among the Bambara, with the increasing emphasis on special secret knowledge, the universe is revealed as far more hierarchial in essence.

Thus we must expect that not every initiate knows the full systematic classifications we have outlined here from the French accounts. Those accounts in fact seem to suffer from their own form of elitism, traditional in French education: the philosophy of the esoteric mysteries is presented in systematic logical form which ignores or devalues social and metaphysical variation. But the important point for us to emphasize is the religious intention in all of this material: We see a longing for radical otherness that almost borders on world denial and which is certainly very idealistic.

Visible realities are merely the lowest rung of a wonderful spiritual pyramid of truth.

VARIETIES AND LEVELS IN ESOTERICISM

One result of the attempt to transform all the world into an explicitly conscious metaphoric system is in fact that henceforth a variety of interpretations is entirely admissible and even desirable. For this variety of significances is what makes metaphors. The case of the Dogon, also a Mande people and neighbors of the Bambara, vividly shows that the same culture can sustain several different descending systems of thought integrating the same ascending symbolism. Each such system rationalizes the same experiential world but from another angle, perhaps at the same time locating a social grouping within the world and serving as its distinctive viewpoint. The process of rendering the world into completely symbolic language may even end in explicit beliefs that any system is only one possible metaphor among many for ordering experience. We begin to get such a conclusion in the case of the Dogon.

The discovery that the Dogon have a rich esotericism preceded and encouraged the similar discovery concerning the Bambara. Both societies were investigated by the French ethnologist Marcel Griaule and his students. From the beginning their approach differed from the more usual anthropological method of devoting from six months to two years in the "field" (i.e., the community being studied). The French under Griaule instead studied a few cultures intensively, returning to the Dogon and their neighbors every year for decades. The research has not stopped even with Griaule's death in 1956. The reward for such unusually respectful and devoted study was the eventual revelation of a hidden world of knowledge entirely unsuspected by the first European ethnologists. These studies cast in an ironic light the large claims of the social functionalist studies of many other contemporary anthropologists, for they disclosed realms of wisdom that exist far behind the ordinary, everyday level of social interaction generally described. (Yet we cannot ignore that these "shallow" studies have forced us to a much deeper appreciation of the importance of religion in everyday life, something the "profound" studies have overlooked!)

The first reports on the religion of the Dogon showed a people apparently like many others in west Africa: the myths were brief and fragmentary, richer in clan legends than genuine creation myths, but the rituals were many and complex. The ceremonial life filled the days, apparently preserving poorly rationalized survivals from earlier cults. The masked societies lacked coordination with the cult of ancestors (*binu*), whose relations with the worship of nature spirits (*nommo*) governing fertility were unclear. The *nommo* were serpentine water spirits. There was also an active cult to the high god, Amma. Presiding over all of these cults were the priests of the earth, called *hogons*, who claimed to represent the most ancient custom. The claim was probably true, for the institution of the priest-chief of the earth, with characteristics very similar to those of the hogon, are common in west Africa among precisely the peoples who seem to preserve the most archaic forms of farming technology and religion, the Voltaic peoples.[7] The Dogon are on the northwestern periphery of the Voltaic area, and the cultural continuity is not surprising. Like the Voltaic priests of the earth, the hogon was chosen from the clan that claimed to be the aboriginal first settlers of the land; the ritual harmony they first achieved with the earth was continued for all later comers in their priest-chief, the hogon, who in fact was the embodiment of the first ancestor leader, Lêbé, who migrated thence. Each region had its own hogon. As the embodiment of the ancestral past, the hogon had authority over the *binu* cult to the ancestors, and as the priest of the earth the hogon had authority over the cult to the *nommo* water spirits. Uniting these spiritual powers of space and time, he submitted all to the cult of the high god, Amma, to whom he was the high priest. Endowed with such spiritual power, the hogon had political authority as well, presiding over the council of clan elders that governed each region.

The logic of the interrelationship between the cults may seem clear in this formulation, but this is because it is framed in the context of our earlier discussion of the Ila and other agriculturalists; to the ethnologists under Griaule it was hard to discern any overarching rationale for the profusion of ritual practices and cults. This was because in their first years of work few myths were available to structure the material. Those that were seemed unsatisfying. For example, in one of the best of the early works, *Les Âmes des Dogon*,[8] we are told that in the beginning Amma used to dwell among mankind, and they served him. One day Amma ordered a Muslim to bring him a drink of water, but the Muslim did not. Enraged, Amma left mankind forever. However, just before he ascended, a Dogon rushed to offer water himself, winning the blessings of God on his fields and instructions on how to communicate with him in the future. God gave the Dogon a sacred stone, *dugé*, which would serve as a shrine; from that time, the Dogon obtain sacred stones after lightning storms (the stones come down in the lightning and rain), which they place on earth mounds as shrines to Amma and the spirits. Thus the Dogon perception of the remoteness of the divine and also the meaning of cults aimed at overcoming the breach is explained by a myth of the "Fall" type. Such myths, telling of the separation of God from man as a result of some disobedience or stupidity of man in the beginning of time, are found not only in Africa but all over the world and are common especially among hunting peoples.

But in 1947 it suddenly and dramatically became apparent to the ethnologists that this was not the foundation myth of Dogon culture. Instead, the "Fall" tale was told to children (and apparently foreigners!) as an "infantile" myth. The actual cosmogony was related to Griaule by an old blind elder, who had been deputed from the council of elders to reveal secrets to the French anthropologist in return for the devotion and respect he had accorded them over the years.[9] In thirty-three conversations, the sage Ogotemmeli disclosed a complex and systematic world view that embraced within the same classifications all aspects of Dogon life, from farm tools to the cardinal directions. The parts of houses were revealed to be analogous to the basic species of plants, and these corresponded to a similar ordering of animals. The stars in the sky correlated with the types of grain, and to the knowledgeable Dogon the body as such represented in all its proportions, gestures, and even style of walking the harmony of the universe. The key to the universal structure was the cosmogony. To know it was to understand everything. Far from being weak in creation myths, the Dogon had a wealth of amazing detail in their cosmogony, which evidently could take a lifetime to learn with precision. In this myth, Amma never really withdrew from the earth, for Earth was his wife. He created her, and then in sexual union produced the living things of the world. The rain is the continued efflux of his fertilizing power, as are the sun's rays (conceived of by the Dogon as a very subtle fluid). But the full harmony of the divine order was prevented by a catastrophe which occurred at the beginning of time, which even today disturbs the perfection of the universe and which mankind must seek to overcome in partnership with God. This catastrophe was not the Fall, but a rebellion within the ranks of the primal divine beings God created. When God first united with Earth, their first-born reflected the chaos and uncertainty of all beginnings. It was Yurugu, the trickster, who sprang forth from Earth's womb, and tried to mate with his own mother. Even today, according to Griaule's first report, Trickster roams the wilderness in the form of the jackal. To purify the Earth of the jackal's polluting incest, the Nommo twin spirits were created, and they in turn helped shape and inspire the first eight human ancestors who continued their purifying work. Coming down from heaven in an ark containing the primal forms of all species of life, the ancestors sent out the animals to cleanse the earth. The purification also required the sacrifice of one of the Nommo serpent-beings, and also of Lébé, the oldest human and the priest to the serpent. With the remains of Lébé traced on the earth in the form of sacred *dugé* stones, the first fields were outlined; even today villages, compound areas and fields preserve this form, making of every human habitation and cultivated field an extension of purity into the pollution of the wilderness. Every ritual sacrifice is modeled as well on the primeval sacrifice of the first man, thus purifying the world anew, and especially consecrating every new field and enterprise. The task of humanity is to continue the purification and harmonization of the world that God began; for this reason all humans have the primal eight elements of the universe in their collar-bones. Each person images the universe. All existence is eightfold, according to Dogon esotericism; everything is also twinned, with a male and a female half. Although men have a female soul too, women retain more of the totality bestowed by the first Nommo demiurges. Men have to reacquire their divine androgeneity through ritual initiation; but then it becomes their conscious possession. Women therefore have great importance, although the Bambara attitude to them also can be found among Dogon men. The earth is feminine, and so is the village (which is said to have the form of a woman, or of a copulating couple); the house is also female. The harvesting of the most sacred variety of grain must be done only by naked women, with no men present.

It is quite impossible in this context to give a full account of the secret wisdom disclosed by Ogotemmeli to Griaule. Every detail of life is embraced by the esoteric system, which Ogotemmeli whispered to Griaule lest any women or children overhear. It is enough to say that it was not the final word on Dogon metaphysics. Griaule and his students continued their research and discovered that there was a deeper myth told initiates than the one given by Ogotemmeli. An interim report on their findings was published in 1954 in a symposium on African world views; it bore little resemblance to the earlier *Conversations with Ogotemmêli.*[10] One could even have supposed that each report dealt with a different people. Instead of a union of heaven and earth, we are told of the creation of the universe out of an infinitely small cosmic seed or cosmic egg. This seed was of the type known to the Dogon as *fonio (Digitaria),* the most sacred grain in their rituals. Within it in the beginning of time evolved the primal forms as if in a placenta. There were eight such forms, each a kind of vibration; as they developed inside the egg, the seventh vibration prematurely broke the "egg of the world" and its contents were hurled in all directions. The entire later history of the universe consists of the struggle of God to reunite all the elements again harmoniously. Man is in the image of the primal egg and, as we know, has the eight elements in his collarbones, four to each side. Each house, village, granary, and cultivated field is another replication of the cosmic unity in one area of existence after another. The first seed dwelt in the heavens, and we see it today in the pole star and the constellations that emanate away from it on all sides.

The major puzzle in this account was the reason for the premature breaking of the cosmic egg. Each of the vibrations was a nommo, we are told; the seventh nommo, a male, "for reasons which are obscure,"[11] refused to wait the normal period of gestation but in defiance of Amma broke forth bearing part of his placenta. He intended to make a world of his own with the placenta, to rival God. He committed incest with it. But Amma determined to purify the placenta and to make of it a good earth. This is the purpose of cultivation, to purify the polluted placental wilderness of the traces of Yurugu, the seventh nommo.

There is much more in the myth, including an account from a wholly different perspective of the ark.[12] We will have to forego further details, however, since it turned out that even this was not the deepest initiatic myth known to the Dogon. Evidently, Griaule and his students were being led slowly along the path that the Dogon candidates themselves had to traverse. The extraordinary sense of discovery and excitement that filled the first report of *Conversations with Ogotemmêli* was to be repeated at deeper and deeper levels.

In 1965, the first installment of a projected *magnum opus* appeared on Dogon myth, which gives yet another version of creation.[13] This work, of over 500 pages, merely concerns the first moments of creation; later stages presumably will be dealt with in future volumes. It is impossible to summarize even the most significant and exciting of the insights of this study. One can only list some of them briefly. The primal egg was really the primal Word, and this Word is identical with Amma, God. It developed from a primeval nothingness; within the infinitesimal point that was the Word there were two tendencies, one to expand, the other to contract. These two tendencies continue to control all existence, and are the "two eyes of Amma." Within the primal Word, they divide and redivide to form the eight elements, which in turn each produce eight forms to comprise the 256 "complete signs of the world," as the Dogon say, or "Amma invisible."[14] These are actual letters, which compose a complete script known only to the highest initiates. These supposedly illiterate sages do in fact have writing! The priests trace their words in the hidden foundations of altars as they are being built, in village and house foundations and on sanctuaries, to provide the true connection of the spiritual to the material world. The ignorant may think the visible sacrifices effect the link to the divine, but the wise know the reality of things is that they are veiled forms of the Word, which alone gives them life and being. A large part of the deepest initiation is instruction on how each of the letters materializes in stages in the various things of the world. Thus it is that if the primordial Word is Amma invisible, this material world is Amma visible, produced by the vibration of the divine energy into solid form.

In this deepest speculative system we discover a completely systematic and rational philosophy, which at the same time insists on the multiplicity of truth. What is told first in terms of the primal Word is therefore repeated in the same mythic narrative in terms of cosmic egg, the marriage of heaven and earth, and the separation of God from man. That is, the myths of the lower initiatic stages are taken up again in a more inclusive myth, and made to apply to later stages of the total creation. It is the word which became the egg, which eventually produced heaven and earth, etc. But the former myths are not simply repeated, they are also perfected. We learn that the trickster, for example, is not an evil being (neither is he a jackal, as Ogotemmeli perhaps purposely misinformed Griaule!). His true name is Ogo, and he is a culture-hero much like Prometheus. Amma needs Ogo's divisive actions in order to make a material universe; only in this way can full consciousness evolve, and the synthesis between material and spiritual arise, the goal of God. The trickster is really the hero of the creation myth, and the entire volume is named after him *le renard pâle*, the white fox. Only now is it fully explicable that Yurugu in the form of the fox is the patron of divination.

If the Word is the pattern of the universe, sacrifice is its dynamic. God purifies the earth of the excesses of Ogo by sacrificing the most perfect of the nommo, in whom are comprised all the others, his youngest "son." His blood drips down on the earth as purifying rain, reviving it with the fluid of divine life. All later sacrifices, including that of Lébé (reenacted by his present embodiment, the hogan), are modeled on that exemplary sacrifice; the entire cosmos is set in motion and continues in the cycle of life, through this process. From the sacrificed form of the divine is constructed the house, the village, the cultivated fields. Man himself is the duplication of this nommo who was sacrificed as an androgyne to be resurrected as a human couple; marriage is a divine perfection. Cultivation of the earth is not only a purification of it, it is a sacred mystery that repeats divine models. Man is a coworker with God in all the levels of life.

It is clear from this brief account that not only does initiation provide for the Dogon fundamental dispositional orderings of their everyday experience, bestowing a characteristic tonality and purpose to even the slightest aspects of daily life, but also that several different descending symbol systems can integrate a single "felt" world of ascending symbolisms. The actual world of empirical objects remains the same as one moves deeper into initiatic wisdom; the way they are perceived, however, changes radically. The Dogon organize the various levels of insight in a hierarchy of language: the initiates learn the "true" form of words, and each stage teaches a more refined and abstract language until one reaches the "purest" dialect of Dogon. In fact, each initiatic level does communicate a secret, "purer" language, a perhaps more archaic Dogon; initiates do not use slang or regional vocabularies. Yet all these languages describe the real world of Dogon experience.[15] They determine the realities of that world, and also make social stratification coincide with cultic vision. The elders preserve their authority, for they have gone deeper into wisdom than have the youth. Men have preeminence over women, for only men know the full secrets of the Word that displays itself in women, in their generativity and their arts of weaving and pottery. Certain regions and clans pride themselves on a purer, more archaic Dogon pronunciation than others, a claim that really asserts their deeper wisdom and intimacy with Amma. The higher levels of the cults have a prestige not shared with the lower cults. And the great cycle of rituals that enact the cosmogony, the Sigui, is the occasion once every seventy years when all the Dogon are ideally united as a single divine community.

It is striking to observe that as the levels of myth become more complex and articulated, their aim is simultaneously even more intensely to achieve unification of experience. This is evident, for example, in the various ways evil and the trickster are viewed. The more precise and systematic the thought, the further consciousness is forced to penetrate behind appearances, to reduce experience to an atomistic, abstract analysis, and finally to overcome multiplicity entirely by subsuming it under the One. How rudimentary the distinctions created by the myth of Amma and the scornful Muslim, when compared with the ordered and magnificent complexity of the deepest esotericism! We see here a thrust essential to descending symbolism, of ordering and thereby desubstantializing the world, a very different orientation from the ever more condensed, polysemous ascending symbolisms of concrete reality.

ESOTERICISM AND HISTORY

Even history is stratified in the various systems of symbolic integration. The tale of Amma and the Muslim serves the purpose of a polemical but essentially frivolous mockery, leaving the larger part of Dogon culture and religion unexplained. In contrast with the wisdom of Amma's Word, it is clear that the legend belongs to the folk level of culture. It deals with elementary distinctions that have been manipulated to serve one point and equally indifferently could serve another. Though topical, however, its basic drama belongs to a type of myth widely spread over all continents as the explanation of the distance between man and God. In many cultures, this myth of the Fall is made the ultimate explanation of life. Adventitious elements of merely topical interest are absent then. This is especially true of the most archaic hunting peoples; in Africa, the Mbuti have a similar myth. The next higher level of knowledge among the Dogon, which we may take to be the mythical world revealed by Ogotemmêli, is rich with dramatic action and appeals to an imaginative but still "external" understanding. Its fundamental drama of the marriage of heaven and earth is developed among archaic agriculturalists the world over, and is found from west to south Africa. At a deeper level of Dogon wisdom we discover the cosmic egg motif, which is found according to Hermann Baumann among megalithic cultures; these cultures often reveal complex social stratifications and elaborate myths integrating grain crop economies, meditations on the unity of life and death, and specialized priesthoods.[16] The innermost circle of Dogon thought, however, centers on motifs comparable only to the highest speculations of the later classical Mediterranean cultures, in the Graeco-Roman period. The mysteries of the cosmic Word or Logos, which interweave religious symbols and the elements of writing into a conception of the eons of Creation and which pivot on a mystique of redemptive divine sacrifice, are common to both culture-areas. There may even be a Muslim influence on the "script" with its 256 signs. It is hard to explain the coincidence of these ideas and their layering in the initiation ranks of the Dogon, but it is equally hard to avoid the conclusion that in these ranks there is a meditation on the accumulating historical experience of the Dogon. The contemplation of the most recent challenges and influences produced the most secret and profound levels of the initiatic societies. This would imply for the Dogon that the deepest initiatory revelations do not represent the most archaic ideas of the culture (as is commonly assumed), but the most recent innovations. The elders and priests, usually anathematized as the most conservative opponents of change, would in this interpretation actually be the mediums of the most harmonious and thought-through transformations, for they seek constantly to discover the spiritual meaning of new elements of culture and to integrate it into all they know. In this view it is the random and fragmentary change of particular elements of culture, which ordinary folk accept without much thought about its consistency with the rest of their culture, that produces cultural breakdown. The resistance of the elders is to disintegration, not to innovation as such, and they are the ones at the forefront of harmonious, more gradual change. As the most thoughtful members of their society, they are the most concerned with the *meaning* of changes others merely react to, or endure impatiently. They, in short, respond to new circumstances from a center in the transcendental structure they have internalized throughout a lifetime, while younger and less knowledgeable members of the culture, lacking a sense of the overall coherence of their universe, are less troubled by a purely personal, pragmatic approach to innovations.

It is important to add that there is growing evidence that some of the new religious movements in Africa today are directed by the most conscious leaders of traditional society. Sometimes we find that the generating force for these movements comes from the imperfectly integrated, more peripheral (or noninitiated) members of society—who may take refuge in explosions of ascending symbolisms, as in possession trance, violence or orgiastic behavior—while the orientation and philosophy of the movements come from former "pagan" priests or prophets, who interpret the trances and attempt new integrations of experience mingling tradition and modernity.[17]

NOTES TO CHAPTER 7

1. L. Tauxier, *La Religion Bambara* (Paris: Librairie Orientaliste Paul Geuthner, 1927).

2. Dominique Zahan, *Société d'initiation Bambara* (Paris: Mouton, 1960), Vol. 1, pp. 280-371.

3. Germaine Dieterlen, *Essai sur la religion Bambara* (Paris: Presse Universitaires de France, 1951), pp. 5f.

4. Ibid.; a more detailed treatment is Dominique Zahan, *La Dialectique du verbe chez les Bambara* (The Hague: Mouton, 1963).

5. Our discussion of the social and metaphysical correlates of "silence" is based on the work cited in the previous note, and on Dominique Zahan, "Ataraxie et silence chez les Bambara," *Zaire* 4, no. 5-6 (1960): 491-504.

6. It is significant, for example, that despite the egalitarian *communitas* of the Kore candidates, which will forever after make them comrades, they are also divided up during the initiation into eight ranks reflecting the ancient classes of Bambara society (and the eight modes of the "Word"): Priests, Famous Men, Nobles, Slaves, Warriors, Mercenaries, and Male and Female Commoners. The end of initiation abolishes this hieratic society. See Zahan, *Société d'initiation Bambara*. Communitas and hierarchy, liminality and structure, are again shown to be entirely compatible and indeed fused together indistinguishably.

7. On the antiquity of the Voltaic people and cults, see George P. Murdock, *Africa: Its Peoples and Their Culture History* (New York: McGraw-Hill Book Co., 1959), p. 78: "their culture probably reflects fairly closely what that of the Mande must have been like prior to their embarkation on a career of empire building and to the advent of Berbers and Arabs from the north." Also see Jürgen Zwernemann, *Die Erde in Vorstellungswelt und Kultpraktiken der sudanischen Völker* (Berlin: Dietrich Reimer, 1968), *passim*, and Robert Sutherland Rattray, *The Tribes of the Ashanti Hinterland* (Oxford: Clarendon Press, 1969, 1932), Vol. 1, pp. xii-xx, etc., among other authorities.

8. Germaine Dieterlen, *Les Âmes des Dogon*, Travaux et Mémoires de l'Institut d'Ethnologie (Paris: Institut d'Ethnologie, 1941), p. 240.

9. This account is from Marcel Griaule, *Conversations with Ogotemmêli* (London: Oxford University Press, 1965).

10. Marcel Griaule and Germaine Dieterlen, "The Dogon of the French Sudan," in *African Worlds*, ed. Daryll Forde (London: Oxford University Press for the International African Institute, 1954), pp. 83-110.

11. Ibid., p. 86.

12. "Ark" here translates the French *arche*; inexplicably both of the English translations so far cited mistakenly translate the term as "arch." The idea of the ark in which all things were contained in pairs is actually widespread in west Africa; cf. Marcel Griaule, "L'Arche du monde chez les populations nigeriennes," *Journal de la Société Africanistes* 18, no. 1 (1948): 117-28. Only an ideological repugnance for dealing with evidences of Judaic, North African and other "outside" historical influence can explain the general refusal to take note of such details.

13. Marcel Griaule and Germaine Dieterlen, *Le Renard pâle*, Travaux et Mémoires, 72 (Paris: Institut d'Ethnologie, 1965).

14. Ibid., pp. 64ff.

15. Cf. Geneviève Calame-Griaule, *Ethnologie et langage: La parole chez les Dogon* (Paris: Gallimard, 1966); this work, by the way, presents yet another Dogon cosmogony!

16. Hermann Baumann, *Das Doppelte Geschlecht* (Berlin: Dietrich Reimer, 1955), p. 377. However, the whole concept of "megalithic culture" is controversial, it must be admitted. Baumann's schemes must be taken with a grain of salt. The main point concerns the level of social and cultural complexity that accompanies these myths. Also see Charles H. Long, *Alpha: Myths of Creation* (New York: George Braziller, 1963).

17. This is notably the case with the Lugbara, where John Middleton has shown that several new religious movements were generated by non-Lugbara "prophets" and/or by female mediums (both peripheral to Lugbara culture), but were eventually oriented by Lugbara elders, prophets, and rainmakers into a constructive part of traditional culture. See John Middleton, "Prophets and Rainmakers: The Agent of Social Change among the Lugbara," in *The Translation of Culture*, ed. T.O. Beidelman (London: Tavistock Publications, 1971). Several other essays in the same volume, in particular one by the editor, suggest the same process elsewhere. Robin Horton has found that the strong emphasis on the supreme being in new schismatic forms of Christianity in west Africa may similarly be due more to the traditional recourse to God when intermediary figures fail to handle crisis than any special theistic emphasis in Christianity as such; he has pointed to a number of instances where the leaders of these new cults were the elders and leaders of the traditional religions. See his "African Conversion," *Africa* 41, no. 2 (April 1971): 104. I would like to suggest, in brief, that it is not any incapacity to adjust that may doom traditional African religions and cultures as a whole, but simply the lack of time for adjustment to the terrific novelty and pressure of the West and modernization. We may be sure that with the slower rate of change in former ages, a more constructive role was possible for traditional elites. In the case of one ancient non-African civilization, this has been documented at length: Paul Wheatley, *Pivot of the Four Quarters* (Chicago: Aldine, 1971), pp. 320f., shows that the first prerequisite for integration of novelty and innovation in ancient China was the amplification and elaboration of the ethical and cosmological systems at the cult centers. Out of these cult centers grew the first cities. The priests and aristocrats sanctioned socio-political and administrative innovations making urbanized culture possible. We may go further, and suggest that the modern belief that innovators generally stand outside the main-line institutions merely reflects the unprecedented rate of cultural breakdown and reformation of the past few centuries in the West; the belief has no particular validity for other ages in the West, or for other cultures.

Chapter 8

World Out of Joint: Millenary Cults and the Conflict of Experience and Knowledge

It is an evidence of the crisis that the West and modern technology have forced on African cultures that the elders of these cultures are viewed with impatient contempt by many of their own youth; there is no time for integrations. In such circumstances, the response to change is often dictated by the imperatives of ascending symbolisms, not descending symbolisms, by emotional conflict and not systematic and dispassionate unifications. The anguish experienced by Africans at this disintegration of transcendental structure is not foreign to the West either, for we too have been torn again and again out of tentative integrations by the sheer rapidity of cultural change. We speak of the "generation gap" between young and old, and the "future shock" of the change from decade to decade, even though we at least are thoroughly shaped by the very culture that causes the changes. Nevertheless, communal cults and even millenary movements spread among us, and many of the peripheral members of our society turn to trance states, drugs, and other methods of freeing ascending symbolisms from rational descending symbolisms or social institutions.

For us, too, then, the result is revitalization movements that affirm psychic discontinuity and are reflected in social divisiveness. We should not be surprised at the greater intensity of such movements in Africa. There we find that the traditional logic of initiation ceremonies or rites of reversal may be imitated, but out of this direct union of man with divine, a new order is generated that is often strictly separated from the old one, even though the old one may go on, embodied in other people in society. Possession, violent revolt, rites of reversal and orgiastic behavior may occur, and the claim may be made that the old age and its oppressive social institutions have been abolished. A new age is dawning, actualized in the holy community.

The parallelisms with new year's ceremonies are many and striking. We find the same ritual humiliations, the same atmosphere of emotional freedom (and sometimes orgiastic release), the same equalizing *communitas* that we have already discussed. The parallels are not really surprising, since these movements proclaim the death of old time and the birth of new time, just as the new year does, but now everything is extended to cultural history. Like new year's festivals, their purpose is the creation of sanctified community, the renovation of the cosmic order; unlike those traditional festivals the new community is marked off from the old and those who still preserve it. The holy fellowship does not include all of the social groups that existed together preceding the renovation. Instead, with the establishment of the cult community a sharp "we-they" dualism generally comes into play: the lingering groups from the old age are identified with the evil anticosmic powers that the cult fights.

There is in these groups, then, a split in consciousness quite unlike the traditional awareness. In traditional cults the social order and the spiritual order are ultimately harmonized, and the ascending symbolisms released by the rites of reversal are drawn into a reaffirmation of the social and cosmic orders. In the new movements, however, the social order is first totally rejected as it stands, and then out of this only certain elements are reintegrated into the sanctified community. Other social values are given strongly negative meaning. Society stands against society. Since the members of the new community come from the society they condemn and experience in themselves the overthrow of values, we can see in this situation a cultic elaboration of an unhealed split in consciousness. A conflict in reality sensed on the preconscious, dispositional level is reified and institutionalized and discovered to lie in the cosmic order itself. Rites of reversal, therefore, do not cease after a week or so, as in traditional new year's ceremonies, but are continued in the new community as the expression of a new, permanent order of things over against the lingering institutions of the old age.

In brief, millenary cults are attempts at the permanent extension of new year's cults in a universe suffering a radical split at the heart of things. There are three forms that these movements generally take, depending on their attitude to the cosmos and to the society that mediates the cosmos. The three are revolutionary militaristic movements, like the famed Mau-Mau; movements stressing altered states of consciousness per se; and movements creating new elaborately structured holy communities of their own.[1]

All of these communities seek "freedom," but freedom is a complex and difficult condition to attain, and it can be variously understood. Certainly the social identities anchored by inauthentic descending symbolisms must be overthrown, but what constitutes authenticity is not so easy to determine. The militantly revolutionary groups offer a vivid instance. They too teach impulsive revolt against social constraints and against inauthentic ego-identities located in evil cosmic structures. Like the other groups they wish to abolish history and offer a new communal identity in which the ego is subordinated to an authentic reality beyond itself. But these revolutionary groups commonly insist on strong internal social hierarchies, often more rigid than the societies they reject. Like other millenary groups, it may be precisely the *dis*orderly "injustice" in society they wish to abolish. The self-identity is merged with the group (and so all are equally involved in *communitas*), especially when confronting the enemy. Within the group, however, the leaders are generally obeyed slavishly; there are distinctions in the ranks of fighters; and often the militaristic group does not claim to join all tribes or cultures together; rather, it is quite particularistic. Freedom here means absolute submission to authentic order and authority, and is expressed through violent destruction of all that would stand in its way: the "old order."

The revolutionary militaristic group may be seen as an intensified form of *witch-finding movements*, differing mainly in extending the wished-for purge from the periphery to the center of power. Witch-finding movements have been reported on from all parts of sub-Saharan Africa, and there is some evidence that they are at least semitraditional ways of dealing with general social breakdown. They have apparently occurred from quite early times. The evil that afflicts a society (famine, epidemic, social dissension, etc.) is in this movement blamed on specific individuals and so removed from the general society. By killing or neutralizing disruptors of the divine order, all negative liminality is eliminated and no fundamental restructuring of society or the cosmos is needed. Witch-finding panics can grip an entire region; all work then comes to a stop, and the entire population gathers to witness or participate in the ordeals of suspected witches.[2] Sacrificial rites of a piacular sort predominate. It is impossible not to think of close parallels in European and general world history when one reads accounts of the African movements. The "show trials" of the Soviet purges, the Nazi persecution of Jews in the 1930s and 1940s, the public hanging of "spies" in Iraq in the last decade, and even the public *auto-da-fé* executions of the Inquisition in early modern Spain, as well as the obviously similar witch-trials of late medieval European culture, all come to mind. Very recently we have seen the same atmosphere pervade the public accusations and trials of "Madame Ch'ing and her gang" in China. In the case of the African movements, a general relaxation and exuberance spreads over the country as the diviners go from village to village locating and punishing the witches. Beer parties, festival dancing, and similar expressions of released passions end the panics. Impulse life and social-cosmic norms are reunited. Witches, on the other hand, are believed to live permanently in unrestrained impulse gratification. In witch-finding movements ascending symbolic structures flow into the cosmic normative order and reinforce that order; impulses are finally submitted to the coherence of descending symbolic structure, and those persons who supposedly cannot do this are expelled.

But for revolutionary movements, the evil in the universe and in society has grown too great. The social structure that permits such disorder must be abolished not reaffirmed, and this implies a major cosmic upheaval. Sacrifice is not merely of individuals but of entire societies. These movements often employ an "end of days" terminology and anticipate the establishment of a utopia of mythic dimensions. It is particularly interesting that very often these movements express their repudiation of the normative order and its spiritual underpining by inverting witch symbolisms. They break the fundamental taboos sustaining the divine order, and exalt the life of the passions. It is as if they have decided to take the part of the very witches that the traditional witch-finding movements exorcise.

The rejection of the taboos of the normative order, however, only means that other norms constrain revolutionary participants. Initiation into these societies often uses death and rebirth symbolisms. The freedom of impulse gratification may ironically require iron discipline as well as the license to kill, plunder, and rape; the new norms still connect the group with transcendental sources of power. All of this comes out quite clearly, for example, in the initiatory ordeals of the Mau Mau. Initiates were required to violate the fundamental norms of Kikuyu culture (in some cases they had to murder tribal collaborators with the Europeans, or more often to have sexual relations with the corpses of animals). Such things only Kikuyu witches did. Yet the ordeal generated a feeling of absolute release from former restrains and of new birth, as one autobiographical account demonstrates:

> My emotions during the ceremony had been a mixture of fear and elation. Afterwards (while hiding outside) in the maize I felt exalted with a new spirit of power and strength. All my previous life seemed empty and meaningless. Even my education, of which I was so proud, appeared trivial beside this splendid and terrible force that had been given me. I had been born again and I sensed once more the opportunity and adventure that I had had on the first day my mother started teaching me to read and write. The other three (companions) in the maize were all silent and were clearly undergoing the same spiritual rebirth as myself.[3]

The initiate was now "other" and bound to "otherness." Henceforth his behavior, however violent, would express his essential spiritual passivity before the new reality which filled the *cultus* and unified its members, a passivity similar to the traditional initiates in the male societies of Kikuyu warriors (here "manhood" was shown in battle), or to the acceptance by the nkang'a girl of her "womanliness."

When the evil and oppressive structures of the cosmos cannot be repelled by violent revolutionary action, the view of the universe grows more pessimistic, and refuge is taken in more or less separatist cults. But this is not a merely political response. Many millenary movements of a nonmilitant sort arise in situations where political revolution might be feasible or even occurring. The decision to choose one or another option is above all a moral and spiritual one, expressing more or less optimism about the spiritual nature of man, society, and the cosmos. If the ills of life are not the result of external forces, but are found in the very nature of man and the universe, then movements arise to transform that nature.

There are two general types of these movements: those emphasizing ecstatic states and personal salvation, and those developing new holy communities and rediscovering the sacrality of structure. They emphasize one or another of the two transcendental intentionalities, in short. In them we find the most extreme examples of what these intentionalities imply for ascending symbolisms and descending symbolisms.

As early as 1948, B.G.M. Sundkler in an already classic study of millenary movements grouped these cults in the south African context into two main types conforming very well to our distinctions: the "Zionist" and "Ethiopian" churches.[4] It is interesting that both movements, while Christian, make marked use of explicitly Jewish symbolisms and practices, referring to the Old Testament (the Jewish Scriptures) in its own right and not as subsumed in the 'New.' This has scandalized and embarrassed Christian commentators greatly, and most have put down such symbolisms to merely political protest or to an indigenous misunderstanding of spirituality.[5] But these practices (which have been remarked on in millenary movements from all over the world) have positive spiritual significance. The classical Jewish perspective permits an integration of everyday life, family structure, and the normative structures of the universe into transcendental freedom. This fundamental emphasis is in harmony with traditional African attitudes and spirituality, however strictly a particular movement may teach the burning of traditional shrines and "medicines." But even with this basic emphasis in common, African millenary movements can differ in the degree to which *primordial* intentionalities or *structural* intentionalities are stressed. Within "neopagan," "Hebraic," "Christian," or "Muslim" groups the same polarization can be detected. Some groups within each of these categories make a radical break with the historical past and its main institutions, and assert the overwhelming reemergence of primordial time; these movements characteristically are oriented by sharp "we-they" dichotomies, are hostile to banal common-sense logic, and insist instead on the importance of ecstatic visions and possession trance. Rejecting the authority of ordinary social institutions, they generally submit instead to charismatic leaders who embody the "otherness" members seek. So great is their insistence on subjective states they often extend their repudiation of traditional "medicines" to all medical care, preferring to seek spiritual healing. But those groups developing the structural intentionality insist on some form of historical continuity and depth, are more rational about medicine, and are less insistent on ecstatic salvational experiences but emphasize sanctified community. In south Africa the primordial longing is best represented by the Zionist groups, whose entire goal is to reexperience the pristine "Zion" of ancient days through ecstatic visions, egalitarian community harmony, and even a messianic abolition of present history. These groups are characteristically formed and led by charismatic leaders who are able to share their own intensity with others, but the passionate attitude to the spirit and suspicion of hierarchical structure also tends to generate many schisms and to keep groups small. Ethiopian groups, however, exemplify the longing for transcendental structure in their emotional restraint and love of ritual pageantry and hierarchies. Their link to authentic Christianity is through group participation in the ancient forms of worship. Authority is held by the wise, not the ecstatic.

The sermons of Zionist churches tend to be poetic, evocative, and highly emotional, directed to stirring up the congregation to ecstatic states.[6] The prayers are "free prayers," improvised simultaneously in a bedlam of sound, intense, and usually quite simple though some can achieve complex effects depending on the speaker. In some Zionist groups the sermon tends to be superseded by testimonies of personal experiences on the part of the members of the congregation.[7] The service, in short, may be characterized as emotional and turbulent and is loose in form. The themes of the sermons and prayers, as of the visions that come to the elders, stress the presence of primordial spirits and of the end of days. Personal difficulties are especially stressed in prayers.

Ethiopian services give a different impression. They have their emotional moments, but they are quieter, more structured and elaborate. The prayers often follow written forms, some of European derivation. Sermons are the center of the service, and the Bible is more emphasized than in most Zionist services. Testimonies may occur in Ethiopian churches on occasion, the result, according to Sundkler, of Zionist influences.[8] Speaking with tongues, rolling on the floor or shaking and shouting in ecstatic seizures, are atypical, however; quite the opposite from Zionist groups. Sermons and prayers stress the holy community's link to authentic revelation, rather than the "healing" themes or personal dilemmas central to Zionist groups. The path of holiness however can include stirring singing, joyous "shouting" of praise to God, and similarly emotional worship. Elaborate vestments and ritual add rich and solemn color to services.

The "Ethiopian" church (Sundkler uses the term fairly loosely) may or may not trace itself explicitly back to Ethiopia, but it does stress historical continuity. If the Zionist churches show the strong influence of "ascending symbolisms" and the primacy of the impulses, the Ethiopians stress "descending symbolisms," order, hierarchy, and norms. Personal salvation is less stressed than is the continuance of the divine order. Spiritual growth tends to be viewed more as a process of gradual refinement as one rises through the sacred ranks of the church, rather than the sudden ecstatic enlightenment of the Zionist churches. Neither is there such a sharp split between the saved and the damned as in Zionist groups, notwithstanding the antithesis in both these groups between themselves and Europeans.

Neither of these groups advocates pure sensual expression or total freedom beyond norms. Chaotic impulses are in fact identified with witches (which these cults protect their members against) and with the alien Europeans. It is interesting that for many African cultures undergoing violent change during the colonial period the Europeans, like the witches, were viewed with a certain envy for the supposed freedom of their sensual life and desires. They could do anything and were not bound by the cultural inhibitions and sanctions that restricted African village life. (One might compare this to the European stereotype of the "naturalness" of Africans.) The witch-finding movements sought to free people from the threat and temptation of impulsive demonic freedom and despair, but Europeans could not be so easily controlled. On this level, Western culture was even more demonic a threat than witches: Europeans seemed to signal the triumph of primordial chaos. The impression the Lugbara first had of Europeans makes this quite clear:

> They were cannibals (as all Europeans even today are thought to be, except those well known to Lugbara as individuals), they would disappear underground, and they walked on their heads and could cover vast distances in a day by this means. As soon as they were noticed they began to walk on their legs, and if attacked they would vanish into the ground and come up some distance away; they would then walk away on their heads. I have heard it said that this is still the way in which Europeans behave in their own country on the other side of Lake Albert.[9]

It is evident from this account that acquaintance with the Lugbara has had commendably civilizing influence on the Europeans, for in proximity to them the European relinquishes his savage ways.

But there have been too many Europeans, and they have too much raw power, so that as John Middleton shows, the coming of the Europeans seemed to bring with it a return to the chaos of the beginning of time. Lugbaraland had to be generated anew. Cultic attempts at creation of a more harmonious world swept the land from the 1880s on, the most prominent of which was perhaps the Yakan water cult. This centered on the final return of the dead. The spirits hovered over and dwelt in those who drank holy water and joined the new cultic community; many would react to the presence of the dead by going into possession trance during ceremonies. Orgiastic meetings were held in the bush: in this cosmic new year's celebration the village was no longer a sanctified space. Not only the living and the dead, but also the young and old, and men and women joined together in fused equality, just as in the primordial age. The white man would be overthrown, but so would all other things that participated in false history: traditional shrine objects, filled granaries, everything that suggested the old life of everyday alienation and egoistic strife and failure, were destroyed. Only with this grand sacrifice would all evil be swept away and a new cosmic order begin. The sacrificial imagery of the new year, here as in other cults of millenial renewal, dominates everything.

The simple dichotomies of such groups suggest a rather desperate attempt to control the chaos of impulse and to institute some order in sensory experience. They demonstrate graphically what happens when descending symbolic structures are stripped from individuals, and the coordinating ideas of a culture are destroyed. Reorganization must begin with simple oppositions such as "we-they," divine-demonic, saved-damned, etc; perhaps a privileged space should be built at first (a cultic center, or sectarian community) in which organized structures and descending symbolic systems can again flourish. In these separated sacred communities, the restorative logic of the new year may take an entire generation or more to work itself out, but each cult begins sooner or later to develop rationalized institutional and philosophical structures. Structure again proves itself central to all meaningful existence. The Yakan water cult, for example, has been gradually transformed into a thoroughly Lugbara institution, as rainmakers and prophets have adapted it to traditional values. The women may continue to experience the nearness of the dead in ecstatic seizures, but their testimony is interpreted to the cult members by the prophets who preside over the ceremonies, and with the passing of time these spirit communications have stressed more and more the upholding of traditional values.[10]

In the case of a number of new cults, the need of their religious leaders to reconcile their new experiences with traditional views still persuasive to themselves and others has often produced remarkable intellectual syntheses.[11] However poetical these symbolic unifications are, their development signifies the impending synthesis of the entire universe of experience into the religion. Ecstasy begins to give way to a degree to integration, a process Max Weber has described as the "routinization of charisma."[12] It is not, as we can see from our discussion, primarily a sociological process at all, but a cosmological one, involving the reintegration of ascending symbolisms into the unified religious focus provided by descending symbolic systems. The world of everyday experience is in this way restored to full meaning. The "salvation" that is wrought is not in the first instance of the person, but more profoundly, is of the world as a whole.

NOTES TO CHAPTER 8

1. See especially Bryan R. Wilson, *Magic and the Millennium* (New York: Harper & Row, 1973), and Kenelm Burridge, *Mambu* (New York: Harper & Row, 1960); also useful are Victor Turner, *The Ritual Process* (Chicago: Aldine, 1969), and Mary Douglas, *Natural Symbols* (New York: Pantheon Press, 1970).

2. Reports of witch-finding movements have come from all parts of Africa in recent decades. See Audrey I. Richards, "A Modern Movement of Witch-Finders," *Africa* 8 (1935): 448-61; M.G. Marwick, "Another Anti-Witchcraft Movement in East Central Africa," *Africa* 20 (1950): 100-12; and Barbara E. Ward, "Some Observations on Religious Cults in Ashanti," *Africa* 26 (1956): 47-61, for some representative articles. Of particular interest are the discussions by Mary Douglas, "Witch Beliefs in Central Africa," *Africa* 37, no. 1 (January 1967): 72-80, and Jan Vansina, "The Bushong Poison Ordeal," in *Man in Africa*, ed. Phyllis Kaberry and Mary Douglas (London: Tavistock, 1969). For an interesting discussion of some European parallels, see H.R. Trevor-Roper, *The Crisis of the Seventeenth Century: Religion, the Reformation and Social Change* (New York: Harper & Row, 1968), chapters 1-4; and Adolph Leschnitzer, *The Magic Background of Anti-Semitism* (New York: International Universities Press, 1956).

3. Josiah Mwangi Kariuki, *"Mau Mau Detainee* (London: Oxford University Press, 1963), p. 27, as quoted by Benjamin Ray, *African Religions* (Englewood Cliffs, N.J.: Prentice-Hall, 1976), p. 170.

4. B.G.M. Sundkler, *Bantu Prophets in South Africa* (London: Lutterworth Press, 1948).

5. H.W. Turner, "A Typology for African Religious Movements," *Journal of Religion in Africa* 1, no. 1 (1967): 1-34, divides "Hebraist" groups into ecstatic or prophetic antiidolatry groups ("Israelite"), whose loose structure makes them promising for missionary efforts, and the "Judaistic" groups stressing rite, festival, and community holiness rather than mere ecstasy; these groups resist missionary efforts and are criticised harshly as "legalistic detours from a fuller Christian faith" (Turner, p. 9). Hostility to Judaism is blatant in this study. The frequent millenary use of Jewish symbolisms in other regions of the world was probably first noticed by Vittorio Lanternari. *The Religions of the Oppressed*, trans. L. Sergio (New York: Alfred A. Knopf, 1963), pp. 36-43, 239, 245, 252-54.

6. Cf. Gerhardus C. Oosthuizen, *The Theology of a South African Messiah* (Leiden: E. J. Brill, 1967), on the sermons, prayers, etc. of Isaiah Shembe, a Zulu "Messiah."

7. Sundkler, *Bantu Prophets*, 2d ed. (London: Oxford University Press, 1961), p. 191. The best and most detailed description of a Zionist service is by J.P. Kiernan, "The Work of Zion: An Analysis of an African Zionist Ritual," *Africa* 46, no. 4 (1976): 340-56. Also Oosthuizen, *The Theology*.

8. Sundkler, *Bantu Prophets*, p. 192.

9. John Middleton, "The Yakan or Allah Water Cult among the Lugbara," *Journal of the Royal Anthropological Institute* 93 (1963): 80-108.

10. See note 17 of Chapter 7.

11. A striking instance has been well described by a number of researchers: the Bwiti cult of Gabon. The cult has integrated Christian and traditional metaphors into an extraordinarily rich fabric; we may be sure that similarly sophisticated study would disclose the same kind of process in many other cults. See, for a few of the studies on the Bwiti, James W. Fernandez,

"Symbolic Consensus in a Fang Reformative Cult," *American Anthropologist* 67, no. 4 (1965): 902-29; *idem*, "Unbelievably Subtle Words: Representation and Integration in the Sermons of an African Reformative Cult," *History of Religions*, 6, no. 1 (1966): 43-69; and Stanislaw Swiderski, "Le Bwiti, société d'initiation chez les Apindji au Gabon," *Anthropos* 60, no. 5-6 (1965): 541-76; *idem*, "Le symbolisme du poteau central au Gabon," *Mitteilungen der Anthropologischen Gesellschaft in Wien* 100 (1970): 299-315; *idem*, "Notes sur le Ndeya Kanga, secte syncrétique du Bouiti au Gabon," *Anthropos* 66, no. 1-2 (1971): 81-119, and *idem*, "Remarques sur la philosophie religieuse des sectes syncrétiques au Gabon," *Canadian Journal of African Studies* 8, no. 1 (1974): 43-53.

12. See Max Weber, *The Theory of Social and Economic Organization*, trans. A.M. Henderson and Talcott Parsons (Glencoe, Ill.: Free Press, 1947), pp. 363-91; a detailed application of this to new religious movements in Africa and elsewhere is in Wilson, *Magic and the Millennium*.

Chapter 9

Conclusion: The Unification of Symbolisms in Ritual

We tend to romanticize localized religions and societies; they are "primitive"—without the privileges but also without the burdens of culture, spontaneously natural. Of course this is not true, no matter how often we call them *Naturvölkern* (nature-peoples) or sentimentally contrast them with our own alienated state. There is a curious tendency to indulge in such fantasies particularly (it seems) among anthropologists of Marxist persuasions.[1] German ethnology is also still permeated with these nostalgias.

But there exists also in localized societies a gap between the world known on the preconscious level through ascending symbolic unifications and the world known in clear consciousness. The African does not live in seamless organic unity with his universe. No doubt Western man has far more of a split between the sensory world of the body and the speculative world of "scientific reality." But the split exists among the Dogon and Ndembu as well, as their recourse precisely to painful and multiple initiations shows. The same is indicated by the new year's festivals and even more drastically by those 'frozen' new year's festivals, millenary movements.

Mere existence always resists schematization. Although on the preconscious level "hot" and "cold," "male" and "female," "light" and "dark" all do elaborate a somewhat predictable world, the principle for the organization of these perceptions is not inherent in them and must finally come from outside. The organizing principle for the child is the self, the center that coordinates all "light," "dark," and other symbols. Yet this center is itself fragile and ultimately fails to unify experience; there is too much "otherness" to life for the ego to control it all. Only a genuinely transcendental center organizes the preconscious disposition and sensory symbols in a secure order. Religion aligns the passions with the consciously known structures of the universe.

The role of the personal self in these integrations is crucial. Religious crises are also social crises. Social institutions, sustained even if transcended in esoteric initiations (as in the case of the Dogon), are defended more desperately in witch-finding panics, revolutionary movements, and millenary cults. The reason for this coincidence of social and religious factors, it may be suggested, lies in the nature of personal identity.

The Levels of Experience: The Basic Forms of Thought:

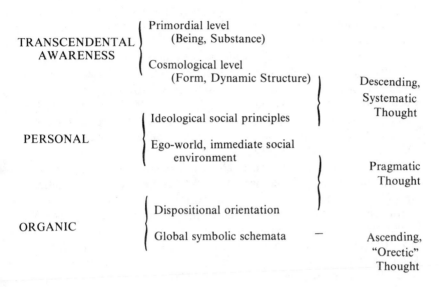

The Three Awarenesses Linked by Religion and Ritual

Figure 2

Religion fuses together three levels of awareness: the preconscious level, the personal level, and the transcendental level. The personal level is the pivotal link between the other two and is oriented above all by the ego. The ego permits a socialization of preconscious ascending symbolisms and gives them a dispositional ordering of a preliminary sort, centered on itself. But the ego itself depends on the assimilation of social rules and the accommodation to other persons. So it is limited by the very structures that give rise to it. The ego is therefore fundamentally unable to control all of its experience. Left to itself, it must make use of pragmatic, rational thought to move through its social world effectively. Social ideology is a break on pragmatic egoism but not a sufficient break. Without anchoring social principles in the universe itself, society remains vulnerable to egoistic manipulation, the unchecked scramble to power of competing egos, and arbitrary despotism. In most African societies, unchecked, impulsive egoism is equated to witchcraft. There is then a need even on the social level to discover transcendental realities that are beyond the reach and manipulation of any ego but instead condition both egos and society in general. Religious awareness is based therefore not merely on the Freudian or Jungian conflicts of the competing bodily-based experiences (the "imperialistic" ascending symbolisms), nor even on the sociological functions of inter-human behavior, but arises out of the need to weave all of these together with the rational concerns of the ego into a unity with the ultimate sources of reality. Religion guides the contact with not only preconscious symbols and orientations but also divine beings and norms known directly to the ego-self as constraining it. *Both* the preconscious and the transcendental realms are "other" to the ego, the first giving an acute sense of reality (ascending symbols), the second a sense of divine order (descending symbols). Working together, they place the ego-self securely in a holy universe.

Many aspects of consciousness coexist in religion. The body, the ego, and ultimate being are all brought together. So are the dispositional preconscious, social ideology, and cosmic law. The first series of relationships (bodily senses and passions, the identity, and primordial being) tend to be most emphasized in religions of salvation, the second series (disposition, moral ideology, cosmic order) in religions of structure. The differing emphasis has far-reaching implications that cannot be pursued here, but in both we see the action of the three levels of awareness (preconscious, personal, and transcendental).

Every religion is built up from the personal unification of ascending and descending symbolisms. The form of religious action that most directly and effectively engages these symbolisms is ritual. Ritual demands the body and the senses, requires the ego and establishes community with others (thereby reflecting ideology as well), and is oriented to transcendental goals. As initiation most typically shows, the prototypical "action" that engages all levels of awareness and both types of symbolisms is the process of centering: transforming the focus of life from the ego-self to the Other. All ritual perpetuates this orientation, and sediments it in the preconscious disposition.

Since religion requires the integration of three levels of awareness, it may be pointed out that all theories are too one-sided which define religion as merely "expression" or "application," as really prelogical or "proto-scientific," or even as simple sociological projection or psychological creation. Quite apart from other factors, the phenomenon of "centering" as the crucial component in religion renders all these views inadequate. Scientific thought, for example, cares nothing for "centering," for it refuses to claim to capture reality or to compel belief. It is indifferent to the need to conform human action to reality. Instead, it cultivates methodological agnosticism.[2]

But there is an area in religion that seems especially close to science, at least to many observers: magic. We shall now turn to such matters as divination, possession, trance, and witchcraft to find out if they are indeed merely pragmatic and bereft of spiritual insight.

NOTES TO CHAPTER 9

1. For recent evidences of this romanticism, see Claude Lévi-Strauss, *Tristes Tropiques*, trans. John Russell (New York: Atheneum, 1964), or Stanley Diamond, *In Search of the Primitive; A Critique of Civilization* (New Brunswick, N.J.: Transaction Books, 1974).

2. The idea that religion is really a pseudo-science, soon to be outdated by Western advances, used to be common in philosophical and anthropological circles, but has more recently been criticized as simply another expression of Western cultural imperialism. Ironically, the theory still survives unself-consciously in Communist countries, with strong impact on Soviet and Chinese treatment of subject cultures. In the free West, Claude Lévi-Strauss clearly espouses the theory; see *The Savage Mind* (Chicago: University of Chicago Press, 1966), pp. 221, 228, and in relation to Africa it has been argued by Robin Horton: see his "Ritual Man in Africa," *Africa* 34, no. 2 (April 1964): 85-103, and "African Traditional Thought and Western Science," *Africa* 37, nos. 1&2 (January, April 1967): 50-71, 155-87; also see R. Horton and Ruth Finnegan, ed., *Modes of Thought* (London: Faber & Faber, 1973).

PART FOUR

RITUAL ENCOUNTERS OF
SELF AND OTHER

Chapter 10

The Experience of Possession Trance

It is often said, even by experienced field workers in anthropology, that localized religions are "single option" spiritualities, providing very little personal choice of life possibilities and tending to promote one path and cultural-spiritual character to the exclusion of others.[1] There is of course a difference between localized cultures and our own in the variety of options provided to their members. But anyone familiar with the intensely personal world of most localized cultures well knows that individual personality is not annihilated in social unity; very strong characters, of remarkable diversity, maintain themselves and flourish.

Perhaps the greatest school for character is adversity. There is certainly enough of that in most localized cultures. Illness and death afflict more people earlier in life than in our own culture; there can be no turning away from the reality of mortality and failure.

Quite aside from the specific medical ideologies that are appealed to in a particular culture, we may distinguish three general ways of meeting suffering and healing it. Each in fact is a distinct way of responding to the otherness of life and of defining the place of the self in relation to that otherness. Almost every culture permits the choice of any of the three, or several in combination. They are witchcraft, possession trance and mediumship, and divination. The key religious element in each is the way the self is centered in realities beyond its control. In this chapter we shall discuss possession trance phenomena, reserving the others for later treatment.

SOME SOCIOLOGICAL AND PSYCHOLOGICAL APPROACHES TO POSSESSION TRANCE

On any given day there are probably many hundreds or more likely thousands of people all over Africa experiencing possession. Some of these do so as part of the climax of public ceremonies—as we have seen, rainmakers, chiefs, and even divine kings might demonstrate the approval of the spirits of their installation or everyday performance in this way. Others might become possessed inside a dark hut, crouched under the sloping roof or perhaps twisting on the floor, as part of healing rituals. Some mediums might fling themselves about wildly, slashing with a sword at bystanders with a violence that may in fact end in bloodshed; others might quiver quietly and mutely in one place, head drooping.

Among the Alur, a Nilotic people of northwestern Uganda and eastern Zaire, for example, possession generally is part of rituals lasting at times throughout entire nights of drumming, dancing, and violent exertions. The value of such sessions as sheer entertainment should not be ignored in societies largely restricted to face-to-face encounters and the monotonous uniformity of everyday life. Aidan Southall tells of children running off toward the sound of drums and clanging bells when these signals of a possession seance broke the quiet twilight atmosphere of an Alur village. When Southall himself entered the hut of the ceremony, he found in the flickering illumination of the fire that it was crowded with people, the middle-aged diviners sitting at ease on chairs at the far end of the room, and eight or ten women gathered around. Two women were kneeling, shaking violently; the electric contagion of their trance affected spectators so that the babies some women carried had to be taken from them lest they be dropped.

> One woman began to be very violently taken, jumping about the floor on her knees and approaching the fire, her whole torso shaking, her shoulders flexed forward and shuddering, her head lolling madly round and round and side to side as if head and neck were a ball on a piece of string.[2]

Soon another woman was as violently seized, and the spectators were kept busy preventing the two of them from jumping into the fire in their random movements. One of the mediums seemed to be pushed by her spirit against the other, and the two of them grappled fiercely together, kneeling still on the floor. Eventually, one of them was propelled "as if (by) some sudden inner force" right out the door, and she rolled about the pounded earth ground of the compound under the stars, trembling uncontrollably. The seance might continue in this fashion, with dancing and oracular pronouncements, throughout the night and into the next day. Such visitations by God and/or his spirits heal the sick, it is said.

Alur mediums are chosen by the *Jok* spirits through the experience of illness or suffering. No one consciously wishes to become a medium, and the selection is often resisted, but it is impossible to avoid.

Among the Fon of Dahomey and the related Nago and Yoruba cultures of Dahomey and Nigeria, possession is very different. There the individual *seems* to be almost entirely subordinated to the communal aspects of cult. While sickness or bad luck may be a sign of election (as determined by diviners), a person may also dedicate a member of his family to a demigod in gratitude for some great stroke of fortune, or a family may try to continue their traditional allegiance to a demigod by promising it one of their children as a future medium. Women afflicted by sterility may promise a demigod the child they hope to bear. Within these cultures individual preferences, failures, or suffering may not be so decisive. Fon and Yoruba demigods have very stereotyped characteristics, and these are always imitated by their mediums. They do not seem, in short, to act out their own desires. Ogun (Yoruba) or Gun (Fon), demigod of iron and of all who use it (warriors, hunters, blacksmiths), is coarse and even dangerous; entranced mediums are physical and obscene. Shango (Yoruba) or Hevioso (Fon), who controls the thunder and rain, makes his mediums jolly and forceful, and enables them to do remarkable magical feats like piercing their tongues with iron staffs without leaving scars or releasing people tied with ropes. The possessed mediums of Orishala, on the other hand, demonstrate the serenity and wisdom of the creator as they walk tranquilly about in white robes, speaking with dignity to the audience. Some demigods are extremely violent, others cynical, others yet again lustful or motherly. Yet the selection of a medium for one or another demigod is often quite arbitrary. Among the Fon (unlike the Yoruba), a medium can have only one demigod, so that he or she is in the most literal way fated to embody (while in trance) only one character mode. So strongly stereotyped is the behavior of a medium that those possessed by Shango even as far off as Haiti loll back and cross their legs in the same way.

Yet however predictable the behavior when under trance, the experience of possession itself is a frightening one. There are vivid descriptions from the Fon and Yoruba, too, of the terrorized expression that passes over the face of the medium as he or she struggles against "going under" (as we might put it). Almost everywhere the loss of ego-control so decisive for possession is viewed as a little death. The soul often is said to "battle" with the spirits; genuine agony and fear is often felt by the neophyte, and he or she may waste away to little more than skin and bones while resisting the "call." The possession initiation ceremony itself may be structured like funeral rituals, as we shall describe later. Despite this, there is no shortage of mediums, and we even read of entire villages amongst the Yoruba in which the majority of people are mediums.

In fact, possession trance states are apparently more common among sub-Saharan African cultures than anywhere else.[4] We must of course distinguish mediumistic states from shamanism, which flourishes among Siberian peoples and throughout American Indian cultures.[5] In Shamanism, the crucial trait is the continuing clear consciousness of the shaman: his ego-self remains alert and exerts control, even though he finds himself able to soar to the highest heavens or sink down to the bottom of the ocean on spiritual missions. He can journey in trance far off to the land of the dead to retrieve newly dead spirits and restore them to their bodies, or he can do battle with evil spirits or other malevolent shamans who are harming his people. Possession trance is also very common in the Mediterranean area, in European and Western cultures, and in south and east Asia, although in these cases it is often interpreted as demonic possession requiring exorcism (even so this is not always the case, as instances of pentecostal sects, or mystics possessed of angelic voices, etc. witness).[6]

A number of recent studies have tried to understand the psychological and sociological aspects of possession trance by examining it on a comparative basis. I.M. Lewis has noted that possession is often sought by those groups in a society that are oppressed, such as the poorer classes (in highly differentiated, class societies) and women.[7] Drawing on a wide range of monographs that present the same argument in terms of specific cults, Lewis suggests that the weak try to achieve in trance the power and respect they lack in their ordinary social roles. In trance they can act out their desires without reproach (since the demigods, spirits, or ancestors are "really" responsible), and coerce others into paying attention to them and catering to them. Generally, Lewis believes, peripheral members of society are possessed by "peripheral" powers. Since the mediums have little personal investment in the normative institutions, neither do their spirits, which are arbitrary, violent, or selfish. At the same time, more "central" members of society might also seek or accept possession trance, but in such cases the spiritual forces are more central to the cosmos. Kings or prophets are possessed by the culture-hero ancestor, or even God himself. When leaders submit to possession, this implies that they feel insufficient to decide the crucial issues of society themselves, or that the people demand legitimation of the leader's authority through the gods, for no "merely human" ego can control existence.[8] In such societies, the entire cosmos is felt to be oppressive to normal self-awareness.

Mary Douglas has offered another theory, based on body image and ego-boundaries.[9] She contrasts the case of the Nilotic Nuer (where a strong sense of personal responsibility and ego autonomy is inculcated in children and adults) with that of their ethnic and cultural kin, the Dinka (the Dinka have a more diffuse social structure and a more diffuse ego-identity as well). For the proud Nuer, possession trance threatens self-mastery and is therefore strongly resisted. It is regarded as punishment for one's sins, an *invasion* by obviously unsympathetic spirits that must be exorcised through various expiations. Against Douglas, however, is evidence indicating that the Dinka view possession in much the same way Nuer do.[10]

The proposed correlation between body image and social ideology may be too Durkheimian, and may ignore the multi-layered distinctions between organic, personal, ideological, and cosmic levels that we have tried to outline earlier, but it remains suggestive. The correlation, however, may work in precisely the opposite way from Douglas's theory. According to Lenora Greenbaum, who has made an extensive comparative statistical study of African cultures and possession incidence, it is not "social diffuseness" but "social rigidity" that leads to the pursuit of altered states of consciousness in Africa.[11] Possession trance is most common in societies with slaves, two or more free classes, and dense populations over 100,000— i.e., possessing "fixed internal social distinctions."[12] In such societies, ego identity is fixed in terms of social role, and this role is often lifelong. Escape into a more authentic self-expression can come only through the temporary if regularized experience of possession trance. At the same time (supporting Greenbaum's thesis although not mentioned by her), the social diversity and density so striking in these societies might give everyone the daily experience of other life possibilities. The "intersubjectivity" of our entire knowledge of the world has been richly demonstrated by phenomenologists; even when briefly meeting another person, we instantaneously "take up the world" through the other person and our interaction with our acquaintance is also an internal conversation. For persons locked into unsatisfying identities, the constant experience of the possibility of other life options in the course of daily social intercourse might well lead to a willingness to permit other more powerful egos to take oneself over. This is especially likely for the weak and powerless whose egos lack full control of their own fate anyway. We must recognize the effect of "relative deprivation" as a very important factor.[13]

There is a major difficulty in Greenbaum's thesis, which Erika Bourguignon recognizes but cannot resolve, and that is that possession trance is very frequent in Brazil and the United States (e.g., the charismatic movements, meditation cults, etc.), but these are not societies with "fixed internal social distinctions," nor "rigidity." Their social mobility is exceptional in cross-cultural perspective. However, when we take into account "relative deprivation," the effect of constant contact with diverse life options, the difficulty seems lessened. This is especially true when we add that social differences in power and experience are quite marked in these societies, despite their mobility. And in addition, the very rapidity of social change in them reduces the stabilizing authority of normative institutions and of the egos they imply and sustain. Social role identities are sensed to be arbitrary, externally imposed, heteronomous, at the same time as the immensity of these societies conveys to some the sense of helplessness to control one's own social identity and destiny.

In a very recent publication, Erika Bourguignon has called attention to an important comparative study that helps shed light on another aspect of this fundamental problem of the self-concept.[14] The study, by H. Barry, I.L. Child, and M.K. Bacon, shows a strong correlation between economic base of the society and attitudes to the individual's role in society, as exemplified in child-rearing methods. Without forgetting that every culture permits a variety of personalities and attitudes, we can nevertheless use the study to help explain why possession trance is very rare among small hunting-and-gathering band cultures, like the Mbuti Pygmies, and why when trance states are cultivated by hunters and fishers, as they are among the Bushmen, Siberian and American Indian peoples, these states preserve ego lucidity and a sense of self-control and mastery. Shamans typically view their spirits as "helpers," not absolute masters, and after trances they generally can recall all their experiences. The egos of possessed mediums are so eclipsed, however, that they commonly are unaware of all their behavior while in trance and are not responsible for it.

The study finds that children are raised to be compliant in societies where there is a constant need to conserve and care for food over long periods of time (as in herding and agricultural societies), while in societies where loss of food can easily be made up over a short term period (as in hunting and fishing), children are instead raised for "assertion." The long-term requirements of herders and farmers requires routine and social coordination on a large scale. Deviation, innovation, or experimentation would risk a food supply whose loss could not be made up for a long time. Adults must be cooperative, dutiful, and obedient to their seniors and leaders. Children are taught these virtues from a young age. Hunters and fishers, however, have smaller groups in which each person is more able to sustain himself; the catch need not be stored for long periods, risks are short term. Socialization in these groups is therefore toward self-reliance, independence and initiative. Interestingly, whatever the society there are sex differences: girls have generally greater pressures toward compliance, while boys are more often trained to self-assertion.[15]

As Bourguignon remarks, we can expect to find possession trance in the types of societies that emphasize compliance (and, we should add, among the social groups such as women and the poor where such pressures are greatest). On the other hand, societies that emphasize assertion are likely to have nontrance possession beliefs current (such as explaining illness as possession by spirits, or, we might add, divination through observing possessed external omens).[16] In compliance-oriented societies, the behavior that is proper in relating to other persons would naturally be extended even more powerfully to spiritual beings. "The individual enhances his power and his status by total abdication and self-effacement before the spirits."[17]

For our purposes, "compliance" and "assertion" must be specified to relate to the ego-self. It is this level that is most directly taught in child-rearing, but in possession trance the preconscious self actually asserts itself, taking the part of the divine order against its own ego-self (which dutifully retires). We can see in the various attitudes to trance, therefore, an even more detailed typology of societies than is suggested in the foregoing remarks. The gradient not only applies to whole societies but as well to groups within societies, whose view of the ego identity differs according to their specific fates. In effect, even in the same culture there can be different "universes," often associated with different social groups. In those "protest" communities that devalue completely the ego level of experience and the institutions that are extensions of it, such as the hippie subculture, trance can be expected to be nonstereotyped (whether lucid or not). Here, just as Douglas suggests, there are the least rigid social and cosmic boundaries, and only a vague distinction between self and external reality. Formless, acosmic states are often sought, and the preconscious self is not viewed as a structured entity. Some groups, however, even among counterculture cults, and also among shamans, some yogins and devotional mystics, devalue immediate social and cosmic structures without devaluing the ego or the cosmos *per se*: lucid trance reveals the hidden springs of existence. Here the ego is not self-sufficient; it must accept nonpragmatic, nonrational realities on their own terms, but these preconsciously known worlds do not demand the disintegration of the ego. Trance is moderately stereotyped. Yet more subservience to extrinsic social definitions of the self is indicated in full-fledged possession trance: the ego is completely identified with social role, but this role does not permit full contact with reality. Here we would expect the experience of oppressive social hierarchies and more elaborate cosmologies, as well as the most stereotyped trance behavior, for particular "others" are the controlling powers in personal experience. A perhaps less optimistic world is that in which the self feels utterly constricted by the social and cosmic boundaries, and no visionary escape of the ego is possible (or perhaps desirable), so that possession *beliefs* do not flow over to full trance possession. Ordinary people even in shamanistic, devotional, or mystical societies often fit here: the ego is still strong and able to deal satisfactorily with reality, even if this reality is ultimately controlled by "others" and is rationally (egoistically) opaque.

There are varities of possession trance, which continue the modulations of self and universe, as Sheila S. Walker has suggested in a stimulating analysis.[18] She finds three types, "predominantly cultural," "cultural and psychological" equally, and "predominantly psychological." Walker's categories are an attempt to deal with the phenomenon of possession trance on precisely the same cosmological level that concerns us. The first category, "predominantly cultural," describes cultures in which cosmos and society are unified. The cosmological intentionality (the ultimate sense of reality) can be enacted through acceptance of social institutions and roles, even if it is assumed that insignificant egos cannot internalize the whole system. The possessing agents are "powerful nature deities concerned with the functioning of the universe and the life of the whole community."[19] The possession ritual usually consists of the reenactment of scenes from the lives of the gods or primal ancestors. These great spirits are often thought to come from a great distance to possess their votaries, either from the celestial heights, distant mountains, or primordial times. In this way they graphically express the insignificance of human affairs, and their own generalized, universal, or ultimate structural nature. The medium is typically chosen by criteria that have little to do personally with him or her, as in the case of the Fon. Often the social group has an ongoing link to that spirit, appointing a medium to it in each generation. As a result of such methods of selection, the depth of trance is often slight, and a long and rigorous training may be needed to develop trance abilities and stereotyped behavior. In any case, trance behavior is highly stereotyped.

The second category, "mixed cultural and psychological," develops a deliberate rapport between the medium's personality and the main traits of the spirit. Both need each other; the trance is therefore deeper, and projection of personal desires in trance behavior is evident. Mediumistic behavior is naturally less stereotyped as a result; training is shorter, and the spirits are generally closer to everyday life (minor spirits or ancestors). The cults typically stress healing of individual problems and illnesses. Most African cults would fall into this category. Mediums are usually "called" by personal difficulties and are not chosen by others arbitrarily. Grand mythic structures are not danced out in possession, but the spirits respond directly to individual problems. Here, in short, trance does not so intensively mediate cosmic structures.

The third type of trance is the most pathological, uncontrolled, and violent. Here we usually have to do with disorganized communities (perhaps in the process of radical change) where the cosmological structures and controls are weak or confused.[20] Here there are no checks on ascending symbolisms; the descending symbolic unifications are very faint or entirely absent. Although the ego gives way in trance, the self is possessed by personal desires, embodied in acosmic spirits who may lack any name or who might be actual people known to the medium, rather than by well-defined moral figures.

We should add to these three categories a fourth: possession cults verging on witchcraft. These can be found in many African societies, including the highly structured ones. In short, there need not be an "objective" disorganization of the cosmos; all that is needed is a personal perception of the inadequacy or hostility of the cosmic structures. Here belong the tales of zombies, bewitched and even formerly dead persons who are slaves of demonic witches or sorcerers. Witchcraft also belongs to this category, for it too is a kind of possession, as we shall see when we discuss it. Often, in any case, we encounter tales of persons forced against their will, while still retaining mental lucidity, to do horrible things. Such tales are also well known in the West; the strong good-evil and spirit-flesh dichotomies of the West, along with the beliefs in an awesomely powerful Satanic kingdom, have often produced among the discontent an anticosmic, satanic revulsion, which may be repudiated by the lucid "good" self, but enacted none the less by the demon that possesses it. Veritable epidemics of such hysteria accompanied the end of the Middle Ages and the first transformations of modernism. These nightmares of power and impotence are not found only in the European culture, however, but also in Chinese and Japanese religions, and among Siberians, American Indians, in Malaysia, and in Africa.[22]

Power indeed lies at the core of possession ideology. The essential trait that all the theories we have reviewed hold in common is *heteronomy:* personal powerlessness to define the authentic self. Possession is therefore common and institutionalized most readily in societies where the ego-self is felt to be imposed from outside on the individual. This is true for hierarchical societies with "social rigidity" in an obvious way, but also for societies like our own in constant change, so that all identities are felt to be transitional, "merely" institutional, and perhaps part of a vast, alienating uncontrollable society and cosmos. Yet possession trance is not merely a protest against imposed identity and oppressive power: It also ironically affirms these realities on an ultimate level, for the transcendental spirit that "possesses" one also submerges the impotent self.

The really basic question is, what *kind* of possession is it—positive or negative, integrating or disintegrating? We apply here our dichotomy of positive and negative liminality. Just as liminality is positive when it builds up the divine order, and negative when it disrupts it, so too is possession positive (and cultically institutionalized) when it aids in the integration of the individual (and his society and universe) and negative when it causes disintegration and fundamental psychic and cosmic conflict. The problem for society is how to control and direct the experience of the radically Other into channels supportive of the social and cosmic order. Negativity and even pathology result from the inability of the social order to integrate these experiences into its own normative context. The problem is therefore both social and psychological, and the basic common denominator is the religious intentionality. Tendencies that might drive a person mad in one culture might well be conceived of as expressive of the transcendental realms in another and so not mad at all; in the latter cultures there are ways provided to normalize and give positive spiritual value to the experiences. But as we have also seen, a culture might create these trance experiences in its normal members, if it believes them congruous with primordial realities and the obligations of society. (It is even possible that possession trance practice in some societies may drive unbalanced individuals into full insanity; we cannot make any definitive statement about whether possession practices are healthy or unhealthy from the psychological point of view.)

One of the chief ways in which a culture transforms the threatening otherness of trance and of possession agents into positive cult is through *naming*. By naming an afflicting spirit, it is spatially, socially, and cosmically located in the divine order. Cognitive and spiritual control is gained, raising the spirit from the preconscious to the conscious level. Naming is often the first step in turning a spirit possession (shown in sickness or misfortune) from negative to positive liminality. Diviners are eager to thus "cosmicize" the unknown afflicting agents, after which commonly they are sacrificed to and a social and normative, ongoing relationship is established between them and the former victim. As long as the spirit can be brought into the social network of mutual recognition and obligation, it is positive and supportive in nature. The most horrifying aspect of negative possession, however, is that it is ultimately "irrational," mysterious, arbitrary and thus utterly disintegrative.

Along these lines, an interesting recent study of ancestor cults has shown that there are two basic kinds of such cults, lineal and bilateral.[23] The lineal cults to ancestors identified with the clan, its property and fertility, emphasize the positive liminality of these spirits. Such ancestors seldom afflict (or possess) their descendants and have their best interests at heart. The spirits serve instead as normative models for the living. But bilateral cults, to ancestors not of the dominant lineage and so not directly associated with the clan and its interests, often center on allaying the potentially disruptive and negative impact of the spirits. These spirits afflict people regardless of the clan's norms, throw people into trance, cause disease and death, and must be propitiated. Every effort is made to bring them into obligatory networks, such as a regularized cult. The lineal cult participates in the general integration of the divine order and the group, but the cult to spirits peripheral to the community signifies disorder, chaos, and evil.

Amongst the Nyoro, to give an instance of the importance of cosmicizing and naming, the most positive possession spirits are those closest to the social group, the most negative and dangerous those from alien sources.

The latter are hard to control, and those they possess suffer wasting disease, madness, and even death:

> The more "outside" a ghost is, the more dangerous it can be. Thus unrelated ghosts . . . may be among the most dangerous of all. The ghosts of former domestic slaves, of blood partners (who are by definition of separate clans), and of wandering *unnamed* ghosts are among the most difficult to deal with.[24]

The Tonga of Zambia (dwelling just to the south of the Ila) have very similar beliefs:

> When the living cease to remember the mizimu [ancestral spirits] and no longer call upon them by name, they become nameless spirits wandering at large, who now work only for evil. "They have become like ghosts." Over these the living have no control, for in forgetting the names they have lost the means of summoning or propitiating the spirits.[25]

These spirits cause illness, only occasionally throwing people into literal trance. But a fascinating, emphatically possession trance kind of cult directed to the naming and domestication of foreign spirits is widespread throughout east, central and southern Africa.[26] Surprisingly similar cults of affliction are in Ghana, in West Africa.[27]

The Nyoro of Uganda, for example, distinguish between "white" and "black" possessing spirits. The first are the beneficient mythic culture-heroes, the Chwezi, who are represented as intruders into the country who long ago brought culture with them, warred with the aboriginal inhabitants and subdued them, and passed on after establishing order. The Chwezi, in short, represent alienness transformed into the entirely positive and benevolent. But the "black" spirits are more recent chaotic invaders from foreign cultures (including Arabs, neighbors to the north and elsewhere). In recent years, these dangerous spirits have been multiplying:

> Those powers which are directly or indirectly associated with Europeans are especially striking. These include such spirits as "Europeanness" (not, it should be noted, individual Europeans), "aeroplanes," and—peculiar perhaps to Bunyoro—a remarkable spirit called "Empolandi," or "Polishness." This last grew from the fact that during the last world war several hundred expatriate Poles spent some years in a large camp in northern Bunyoro. So large a number of white persons all in one place was something new, and more than a little ominous, to Nyoro, and the phenomenon was readily enough assimilated to the traditional mediumistic cult.[28]

Those afflicted with such spirits act, in trance, as they conceive Europeans to act, demanding rich foods, exaggerated respect, dressing in White Man's clothes and uniforms, using their language (i.e., speaking gibberish), drinking tea at tables covered with flowers and a white tablecloth, etc. Among the Ndembu and Luvale of Zambia, and the Chokwe and

Ovimbundu of Angola, "the afflicting agents are said to be the spirits of living Europeans that fly about at night 'troubling Africans'."[29] These spirits are suspiciously like witches, who also fly, especially at night, belong to the bush and remote places, and cause tuberculosis and death. But unlike witches, opposition can become self-identification. Then these spirits offer guidance into their own cultures. The African need not always be closed out of the secrets of the White Man's power. Naming the affliction shows the way to cultural and spiritual assimilation of it.

With the increased trauma of change and oppression in the past century, cults of affliction appear to have spread among peoples that never had them before and even threaten to oust ancestral cults and witchcraft beliefs among some cultures.[30] Many of the new religions may be derived from such possession cults. Among the Lozi of Zambia, for example, an entire religion has been developed from European spirit affliction, the Twelve Society.[31] This cult was founded by a man who had been a Seventh-Day Adventist and who had failed miserably in urban Westernized society. Believing he was possessed by a "European," he ran off to the bush and in a visionary experience met a spirit who aided him in overcoming his alien nightmare. He was able to cure others similarly ill, and appointed the first twelve he healed as his "apostles" (following his spirit's directions and in conformity to Christian imagery). The treatment consists of emulating the excessive cleanliness of the Europeans, wearing white and spotless clothes (recalling traditional Lozi ideas of "whiteness" in the process), bathing, eating European food in cultic settings, and giving up all witchcraft charms. Members "witness" to their cures in church by going into trance.

THE EXPERIENCE OF POSSESSION

The sense of disorientation and confusion afflicting the founder of the Twelve Society is not very different from what the initiate goes through in traditional initiations. To achieve transcendence of the self, one must first break through the categories of the ego reality. The peculiarity of possession cults, however, is that this experience of ego disorientation is not a once-and-for-all thing, but is institutionalized and repeated. If initiation is "re-symboling," the trancer undergoes again and again this re-symboling, in which ego autonomy is lost, and the cultural and cultic expectations and symbols shape the ecstasy "in the manner of a hypnotic command from an overpowering will."[32] The effect of these symbols is directly on the primary processes of thought, shaping the ascending symbolisms directly.

Autobiographical accounts of possession trance are rare; detailed and analytical ones rarer still. But we can follow step by step the process of trance in the remarkable account by Maya Deren of her own trance seizure, in the course of her study of the voodoo cults of Haiti.[33] The very name of the cult indicates its close kinship to the religions and possession cults of Dahomey, Nigeria, and Ghana. Particularly striking is the effect of environment on the repatterning of inner consciousness, to make it ready for trance.

The atmosphere of the ceremonies is permeated with what we might call a "dispositional expectancy" of contacting awesomely transcendental realities. The *loa*, the spirits who possess their "mounts," may not say anything of immediate consequence, but their very remoteness fills the roofed court with a sense of divinity. That the mediums retain no consciousness of their actions while in possession is merely evidence that the loa are utterly unlike man. This unlikeness the "mount" himself experiences at the moment of seizure: "Never have I seen the face of such anguish, ordeal and blind terror as at the moment when the loa comes."[34] Therefore, Deren insists, there is no personal (i.e., egoistic) benefit in these seizures: it drains the devotees' money and time in ceremonies, and occasionally the loa do physical harm to their serviteurs. This is a side to possession we need to remember, since so many studies try to show that possession is egoistically self-serving. Yet, clearly, possession serves deeper, dispositional yearnings.

"By destroying his own pattern of character, he opens the way for the voices, the visions."[35] Deren shows how this transcendental destruction of the devotee's character is accomplished. The role of music in it is fundamental. Invariably at the ceremonies there is a bass drum (the *maman*, or "mother"); its heavy beat often coincides with the deeper rhythms of the brain, and comes to "capture" them. The smaller drums embroider the beat. The dancer's concentration on these rhythms soon crowds out all other sensations. Crucial to this physical-psychic meditation is the effect of the sudden "breaks," or syncopated pauses or changes in beat:

> When the maman "breaks", the dancers "break" with it; that is, they interrupt the small, tight repetitious movements and take long, relaxed steps, in time to the "breaking." . . . since [the beat's] cumulative tension is also the cumulative concentration which brings the loa into the head, the drummer then becomes, to some degree, arbiter of the loa's arrival; for, by withholding the respite of the "break", which interrupts this concentration, he can "bring in the loa" to the head of a serviteur. When the drummer is particularly gifted and acute, he can also use the break in precisely the inverse fashion. He can permit the tension to build to just the level where the "break" serves not to release the tension but to climax it in a galvanizing shock—the first enormous blow of the "break"—which abruptly empties the head and leaves one without any center around which to stabilize. . . . The person cringes with each large beat, as if the drum mallet descended on his very skull; he richochets about the peristyle, clutching blindly

at the arms which are extended to support him, pirouettes wildly on one leg, recaptures balance for a brief moment, only to be hurtled forward again by another great blow on the drum.[36]

Time seems to move more slowly as the ultimate moment of possession nears. Objects drift apart and their general significance fades; the subject becomes unable to grasp the connecting links between sensations, and his attention locks onto particulars. The dancing reflects this: the steps in time to the music falter, and the feet seem rooted to the ground, having lost the necessary connection between beat and action. The dancer stumbles in stupefaction from one place to another, until at last the foot remains too long in one place, and the waning control of the ego collapses completely. The face relaxes and falls forward or backward; the body trembles; and, in a shocking sweep, the loa ascends.

The external aids to trance induction are important. The beat becomes a focus, and then finally a replacement, for the ego's will. As the rhythm is internalized, it becomes the coordinating center—and when even this is taken away in the "break," nothing is left. One becomes the plaything of the drummer, entirely submitted to the arbitrary, external order he creates, tossing about under his beat. The center is now psychically entirely outside the self.

Deren was taken unawares by the power of the music and dance. More probable is that a deeper, dispositional part of herself had already learned by the long study and frequent attendance at sessions, to identify with the dissociated, loa-governed mediums. One evening, watching the dancing and no doubt longing as a professional dancer to join in, she began to feel a "strange, subtle thinning out of consciousness . . . the warning auras of possession."[37] The feeling, especially the "heaviness" of her limbs, disturbed her, and she left the enclosure. Nevertheless, something in her drew her back, and she decided to pit herself against the music and the loa. Clearly, an inner capitulation had already begun; when a possessed medium approached her to receive her salute to the loa, the effect of the music and the awesome impact of the spirit almost carried her off. A bystander, seeing the dazed look on her face, brought her back by digging his nail into her palm, and she completed the ceremonial greeting:

> The sharp, sudden pain restores me. . . . As I step forward for my salutation I concentrate on the memory of that pain, almost as one might finger an amulet at moments of crisis. It serves me well. The contact of the left hand with the loa produces only a momentary shock, which passes rapidly, like an electric current.[38]

These remarks are fascinating. Evidently Deren already needed external stimuli to provide a center for the self. As we say, she tried to "pull herself together." Yet her attitude remains curiously ambivalent. Despite claiming that she wished to resist the loa, she "challenged" them further by actually entering the dance floor and joining in. The quick, gay beat soon tired her, but she pushed herself to her limit, finally getting a second wind at the very point when her ego entirely conceded priority to the beat: her inner self suddenly doubled, and time slowed. All tiredness miraculously gone, she could observe herself as if from a vast distance. Her body was no longer her own, but another's. She watched every detail of it, following in slow motion the movements of her skirt or the graceful sweep of her hand moving to the beat. (This doubling of the self, accompanied by a disintegration of the connecting links that help make up the sense of time, is an important phenomenon; it is reported from many cultures, including cases of exorcism in the West and in "speaking in tongues." It would seem to be a stage in many if not all possession experiences; for some seizures, this is as far as trance goes. We have mentioned the occurance of "lucid trance" before; it is especially common in shamanism and apparently signifies a strong personal and cultural sense of the "self" as ego. Only doubling of the self is permitted, but not its obliteration. In Haiti and Africa, however, trance must eclipse the self to be authentic.)

Enraptured by the peculiar spectator vision of herself, it is only when Deren turns

> to say, "Look! See how lovely that is!" and see[s] that the others are removed to a distance, withdrawn to a circle which is already watching, that I realize, like a shaft of terror struck through me, that it is no longer myself whom I watch. Yet it *is* myself, for as that terror strikes, we two are made one again, joined by and upon the point of the left leg which is as if rooted to earth. Now there is only terror. "This is it!" Resting upon that leg I feel a strange numbness enter it from the earth itself and mount, within the very marrow of the bone, as slowly and richly as sap might mount the trunk of a tree . . . a white darkness, its whiteness a glory and its darkness, terror.[39]

With a desperate effort, she wrenched her leg loose and kept dancing, clinging to the beat that guided her. But again the split in the self came, "except that now the vision of the one who watches flickers, the lids flutter, the gaps between moments of sight growing greater, wider."[40] Whole moments disappeared, and she found herself facing directions she had no consciousness of turning to; the blows of the drum pounded her, catapulting her across space. Staggering from point to point, the drums and singing drowning out any other sensation inside her head, she at last found that she was unable to uproot her leg from the ground:

> There is nothing anywhere except this. There is no way out. The white darkness moves up the veins of my leg like a swift tide rising, rising; is a great force which I cannot sustain or contain, which, surely, will burst my skin. It is too much, too bright, too white for me; this is its darkness. "Mercy!" I scream within me. I hear it echoed by the voices, shrill and unearthly: "Erzulie!" [the feminine spirit of

love, who is taking her over]. The bright darkness floods up through my body, reaches my head, engulfs me. I am sucked down and exploded upward at once. That is all.[41]

She first became conscious again after a timeless void, and slowly emerged like a deep-sea diver from great depths, or as if rising from the abysmal darkness of "an infinitely deep-down, sunken well."[42] (The association of light, upward direction, and consciousness is an interestingly universal one in world religions.)[43] Only after some moments did the world of things appear, at first without any meanings attached to them. It is extremely important that things and meanings are *not* simultaneous, but distinctly separate in the first few moments of awareness. A spatial/temporal world must be reconstructed on the grid of the senses, and only then does an awareness of the body and the ego-self arise. Deren remarks in wonder on the preliminary clarity of things, existing outside relationship:

> How purely form it is, without, for the moment, the shadow of meaning. I see everything all at once, without the delays of succession, and each detail is equal and equally lucid, before the sense of relative importance imposes the emphasis of eyes, the obscurity of nostril which is a face.[44]

This condition not only reminds us of the ideal of nirvana or Zen satori; more pointedly, it is identical with well-known symptoms of schizo-phrenia.[45] In such a world, there is no ego, no world; thought remains impossible and a terrifying idiocy threatens to triumph.

It would be impossible to find a more eloquent evidence of that loss of descending symbolic unity and focus that possession trance actually signifies. All the more important, therefore, is the training of the medium to a *standard behavior* in trance; bodily action and a genuine alter ego are defined and elaborated in the course of the induction, to replace the lost coherence of the ego-world. Possession is not mere "self-expression," Deren insists, and she cites the constant attributes of particular loa, no matter who the "mounts" (mediums) may be. Erzulie, for example, is always supple, lively, voluptuous and flirtatious in her dance, even if her "mount" is an ancient, arthritically crippled woman whose astonishing exertions in trance leave her in critical condition for days afterward.[46] Ghede, a terrifying king and clown, is shown in photographs taken six months apart, in different localities and with different 'mounts' (one a woman, the other a man), to have precisely the same posture and demeanor: seated haughtily, wearing glasses, and smoking a cigarette, right leg casually crossed over left and hands in lap.[47]

Deren concludes from such proofs that the loa are real. In any case it is evident that it is impossible to talk of mere ego gratification here. The same is probably true of the majority of all possession cults. Much deeper realities are involved. In fact, we get much closer to the inner truth of possession trance when we take seriously the evident inner readiness of the individual, so deep as to be dispositional, to overwhelm, crush, and erase the ego-self. Mediums experience a tremendous release at the drastic, total takeover of the spirits. Perhaps they have resisted the 'call' for a long time and suffered agonies on this account. But at the moment of decision and full possession, all questions are resolved. A radically "other" reality has taken over. There need be no more hesitancies or doubts; one's life is no longer one's own. The wild exultation of the release commonly is expressed in extremely violent behavior in new mediums. They must be trained for some time, and have numerous seizures by the spirit, before intelligible speech and regularized action develops. It is interesting to read that occasionally new mediums have to be prevented from hurting themselves in their passionate exertions. Another indication of the felt ego-repudiation and sense of personal impotence can be seen in the reports of mediums going into trance whenever crises or emergencies develop. An automobile accident, village on fire, battle or earthquake might produce many possession seizures. This is the close equivalent of the "daze" that most people feel in the midst of catastrophe. The individual thinks that everything is "unreal," or that "this is not really happening to me." An automatism may carry them through the disaster; afterwards there may be no memory of what they did. The trained medium has simply ingrained the underlying attitudes deep into the dispositional level of the preconscious self. Existence is capitulation.

Yet to understand possession cults, I think, we must go even deeper than this. There is a very positive aspect to the trances. They do not after all produce schizophrenic individuals but on the contrary are regarded in their cultures as genuinely healing experiences. Ego and alter ego are well bounded even in the disposition; and many mediums appear to be well integrated persons in everyday life (although some, the less organized ones, may indeed exhibit psychiatric difficulties). It is striking how often one encounters in descriptions of seizures the feeling of euphoria that the medium feels after coming out of trance. Margaret J. Field, in her monograph on possession cults in Ghana, says that this peaceful euphoria is so characteristic it is even used specifically as an important part of healing rituals in coastal areas. A person afflicted with bad luck or illness will be brought under possession, following which his sense of peace, reconciliation, and happiness will assure him of a new life.[48] She also writes that the pentacostal groups in Ghana explicitly compare this euphoria with "the afflatus of the Holy Ghost of the early Christians."[49]

It may seem irrelevant to mention in this connection the gaiety that often sweeps through a nation on the declaration of war, or the peaceful exhilaration that people feel upon participating in a historical event. But neither of these is so different. There is a deep longing in us all to be swept away by *ultimate* experiences and *definitive* being. Submitting ourselves to an authoritarian leader who reveals to us our irrefutable destiny, falling in love, or experiencing religious conversion, we are flooded with a sense that (just as Maya Deren exclaimed at the point of ecstatic seizure), "This is it!" No more petty improvisation is necessary. We are lifted up into the transcendental plane of existence, in which all flows necessarily into actualization with no responsibility from us any more. The ego is eclipsed. All of life is now focussed and given a necessary order.

It may seem that our sociologically founded earlier conclusion that the feeling of ego heteronomy, and the longing for an authentic self, are the essential traits in possession trance conflicts with this view that possession exposes the medium (and the audience!) to radical otherness. But these conclusions are not opposed. Possession trance cults reveal to devotees the ultimate powers ruling their private or cultural universe, and these powers take over responsibility for their lives. From this "spiritual" stance one can regard the ego-self without agitation as merely peripheral, given over to everyday banality, to insignificance, failure, and death. The reality contacted directly in trance will go on in any case. By being erased into that reality, one can at least be sure one has truly lived, dwelt in power and true being beyond all relative structures.

There is only one last paradox to deal with, and that is that the role of possession trance cults for society in general can be precisely the opposite from its role for the individual medium. Just as possession assures the medium of the immediate experience of overwhelming otherness, although controlled through training to produce stereotyped behavior, so for the nonpossessed the medium serves to *deflect* otherness. The hierarchies and imposed identities that the medium breaks through remain protective and necessary for others and for the medium as well when not in ecstasy. Fragmenting otherness into various spirits, which afflict particular people only at particular places and times, permits the entire divine order to exist in security. Mediums are lightning rods. A precisely similar role can be seen in the cult of saints and tales of exemplary martyrdom, etc., in the Middle Ages. The saints, whose exaggerated piety and worldly indifference grew superhuman in the retelling, came to be the center of healing cults, prayers for fertility and rain, and succour in war; that is, to be appealed to to support the general everyday course of things that they supposedly had turned their backs on. The myth of the hero has always served to preserve nonheroic realities. Aidan Southall comments on the possession cults and festivals of the Alur:

> The great communal festivals devoted to *Jok* [God, Spirit] are normally occasions of joy and thanksgiving, but it is rejoicing that the people have been spared and that normal good fortune in health and harvest has been vouchsafed.

There is no wish for a closer personal approach to or visitation from *Jok,* whose coming to the individual seems always to take the form of sickness or other misfortune. It is consistent that most diseases are seen as manifestations of *Jok* and therefore natural that his visitations are greatly feared. Yet celebration and rejoicing to receive him are the only answer to his coming. The only hope is to receive him fully and with gladness, so that he may, as it were, pass through and out "into the grass" where he can again be externalized in his shrine and dealt with at a safer distance in prayer and sacrifice.[50]

CONCLUSION

The radical transcendence of the spirits poses a problem: How is the extreme psychic disorganization that marks their coming translated into coherent trance behavior? Here we see the most striking instance of the power of ritual, for the answer is that the medium learns through ritual to develop specific traits and to mediate the spirit in the most "transparent" fashion.

Sheila Walker has as we have seen characterized possession trance cults on the basis of the degree of cosmological and cultural imprint on ecstatic behavior. The more the medium integrates the entire cosmological order into the trance, the more the trance serves the general normative, social, and spiritual orders, the more it is ritually controlled and the fewer its pathological aspects. Ritual remains true to itself, in demonstrating in this most striking way its integrative orientation.

The Fon show these points most clearly, for their possession cults are perhaps the most cosmologically oriented of any African religion. We have seen that membership in the cult to a *vodu* (Fon spirit or demi-god) is often quite arbitrary; personal psychological predispositions would seem almost irrelevant. But we must not forget the general Fon attitude to the spirits, which makes every Fon receptive to the possibility of their actualization. As in every other intensely mediumistic religion in Africa, Fon begin attending seances as children and even play at being possessed. They like to dance the various vodu dances they see at cult centers. In Haiti and elsewhere in Central America the social conditioning has continued in the traditional way, with children learning to refer to themselves in the third person, splitting part of themselves off from the rest.[51] So possession is a psychological possibility for quite ordinary and normal adult Fon. Nevertheless, the actual initiation is a drastic one. Its harsh training is in place of the long sickness and psychic disorganization of the afflicted that serves the same purpose in other religions' more individual, psychological-ly oriented cults. The cause of the sickness, in those cases, is known immediately to the afflicted person as a supernatural, and the diagnosis of the diviner helps inculcate the "set" that later possession behavior will play out. The very illness of the medium-candidate forces him or her to concentrate constantly on the spirit seeking to take over.

However, the Fon develop all this very systematically. The candidate, who is so far perfectly normal in many cases (although his candidacy may be launched by his unexpected seizure while watching a vodu ceremony), is taken into seclusion. Surprisingly soon after this, he appears publically in full possession, whirling about at a terrific speed and falling rigid on the ground, "killed" by the spirit. He is now "dead," and is carried away in a shroud. A week or two later, in another public dance, he is "resurrected" as the fully possessed medium. This is a very tense ceremony for the relatives and friends who attend it, for it is really possible that the "resurrection" of the corpse will not occur, and he will lie there truly dead. There follows after this sometimes two or more years of private instruction of the medium, who is secluded in the cult center, before he is permitted to return to everyday life. But it is said that when he returns, he is completely disoriented in ordinary affairs: he needs to be taught ordinary Fon again like a child, needs to be guided about, and never responds to his old name.[52]

Clearly, drastic experiences are induced in the candidate. There is good evidence that hallucinogenic drugs and a special diet are administered to the initiate, to reduce him to a state of hypnotic suggestibility and utter passivity.[53] He is also kept in deep fear of the magical powers of the cult elders and spirits. The result is that through constant practice of vodu possession behavior, coupled with unremitting psychological pressure and disorganization, the medium truly comes to have two distinct ego-centers. Possession is made dispositional, by being ritually imposed directly on the orectic, ascending symbolic level of consciousness. Henceforth, whenever the medium hears the drum rhythms that announce the coming of "his" or "her" vodu, he or she will go immediately into trance.

In this way, the fully initiated medium can live a perfectly ordinary life from day to day, working in the fields, fulfilling family responsibilities, marrying and having children, without in any way experiencing disruptive seizures—but when the drum rhythms on festival days or at shows announce the "coming down" of the vodu, the ordinary social personality melts away, to be replaced by divinity.

Yet the more the possession trance is raised by ritual to normative, focused behavior, the more it integrates all levels of the self; Herskovits and others have frequently remarked that Fon possession trance is often shallow, with the medium aware of his or her behavior.[54] And mediums in their ordinary life are very sane and balanced people, for the most part. In short, the ritualization of their trance serves to integrate them very well into their world, assigning a role and a place to the various egos that jostle for possession of the body and submitting all to a deeper, more universal dispositional order. Through ritual, possession cults enable radical otherness to flow into the human sphere in a positive way, building up the universe and integrating the individual into it, rather than tearing it down and destroying the individual. Ritual causes power to serve order.

NOTES TO CHAPTER 10

1. Such views might be found repeated in several of the essays in *Modes of Thought*, eds. Robin Horton and Ruth Finnegan (London: Faber & Faber, 1973), for example. It has also been much in evidence in "culture and personality" studies; an early instance is Erik Erikson's celebrated *Childhood and Society* (New York: W.W. Norton & Co., 1950). Such views are now rejected. Anthony Wallace, for example, found that only 37 percent of Tuscarora Indians conformed to their "modal personality structure." See A. Wallace, *Culture and Personality*, 2d ed. (New York: Random House, 1970), p. 153.

2. Aidan Southall, "Spirit Possession and Mediumship among the Alur," in *Spirit Mediumship and Society in Africa*, eds. John Beattie and John Middleton (New York: Africana Publishing Corp., 1969), p. 234.

3. E. Pierre Verger, "Trance and Convention in Nago-Yoruba Spirit Mediumship," in ibid., p. 54; much of the above description of Fon-Yoruba cult is from this essay, but also see our later discussion of Fon religion.

4. Erika Bourguignon, Introduction to her edited *Religion, Altered States of Consciousness and Social Change* (Columbus: Ohio State University Press, 1973), pp. 18 & 21.

5. Following Bourguignon, ibid., and Mircea Eliade, *Shamanism: Archaic Techniques of Ecstasy* (New York: Pantheon Books, 1964).

6. Bourguignon ignores these instances of positive possession, as does T.K. Oesterreich, *Possession: Demoniacal and Other* (New York: University Books, 1966, 1930), in his survey. Only Oesterreich's anti-Semitism and ignorance of Judaism leads him to trace demonic possession back to Judaism (see ibid., pp. 3ff., 170-72, 206-10), when in fact it was a general Hellenistic attitude ultimately going back to Egyptian and Mesopotamian antiquity, which Rabbinic Judaism generally rejected firmly. Very few cases of possession are mentioned in the Talmud, and these generally relate to non-Jewish individuals and environments.

7. I.M. Lewis, *Ecstatic Religion* (Baltimore: Penguin Books, 1971).

8. Ibid., pp. 133ff. Lewis's use of the term "shamanism" is too loose, of course.

9. Mary Douglas, *Natural Symbols* (New York: Pantheon, 1970), pp. 75-77, 86-95.

10. Cf. the summary of Dinka views in Benjamin Ray, *African Religions* (Englewood Cliffs, N.J.: Prentice-Hall, 1976), pp. 65-68.

11. Cf. Lenora Greenbaum, "Societal Correlates of Possession Trance in Sub-Saharan Africa," in Bourguignon, ed., *Religion*.

12. Ibid., and also the next essay by Greenbaum in the same work, "Possession Trance in Sub-Saharan Africa: A Descriptive Analysis of Fourteen Societies."

13. This is the valuable implication of the otherwise exaggerated essay on female rivalries by Peter J. Wilson, "Status Antiquity and Possession Trance," *Man* 2 (1967): 366-78.

14. Cf. Erika Bourguignon, *Possession* (San Francisco: Chandler & Sharp Publishers, 1976), pp. 47-48, citing H. Barry, III, I.L. Child, and M.K. Bacon, "Relations of Child Training to Subsistence Economy," in *Cross-Cultural Approaches*: Readings in Comparative Research, ed. C.S. Ford (New Haven: HRAF Press, 1967), originally published in *American Anthropologist* 61 (1959): 51-63.

15. H. Barry, III, M.K. Bacon, and I.L. Child, "A Cross-Cultural Study of Some Sex Differences in Socialization," *Journal of Abnormal and Social Psychology* 55 (1957): 327-32.

16. Bourguignon, *Possession*, p. 47.

17. Ibid., p. 48.

18. Sheila S. Walker, *Ceremonial Spirit Possession in Africa and Afro-America: Forms, Meanings and Functional Significance for Individuals and Social Groups* (Leiden: E. J. Brill, 1972), pp. 152-57.

19. Ibid., p. 155.

20. Ibid., p. 154.

21. Ibid., p. 157.

22. Oesterreich, *Possession, Demoniacal and Other*, sufficiently demonstrates this, although Bourguignon, *Possession*, p. 6, unaccountably claims demonically compulsive, lucid possession exists only in the West.

23. William H. Newell, "Good and Bad Ancestors," in *Ancestors*, ed. W. H. Newell; World Anthropology Series (The Hague: Mouton, 1976), pp. 17-29.

24. J.H.M. Beattie, "The Ghost Cult in Bunyoro," Ethnology 3, no. 2 (1964): 149 (my italics).

25. Elizabeth Colson, "Ancestral Spirits and Social Structure among the Plateau Tonga," in *Reader in Comparative Religion*, ed. William A. Lessa and Evon Z. Vogt (New York: Harper & Row, 1965), p. 438. This search for the names of alien, foreign spirits so as to tame their demonic nature strongly recalls the Medieval Christian conviction that knowledge of Hebrew (not really Latin!) enables magicians to call upon demons by their true names and to master them; the conviction was of a piece with anti-Semitism, in short. The Jews, on the other hand, often preserved in Hebrew script in their magical literature the garbled Latin, Babylonian, Egyptian, Greek and other "true" names of the evil spirits! Of course in both religions the authentically Hebrew names of spirits also reflected the belief that Hebrew was the original language of God and the authentic speech of the spirits.

26. Beatrix Heintze, *Besessenheits-Phänomene in Mittleren Bantu-Gebiet* (Weisbaden: Franz Steiner, 1970), Karte 4, p. 180; pp. 254-55, etc.

27. Cf. Margaret Field, *Religion and Medicine of the Ga People* (London: Oxford University Press, 1937); David Tait, *The Konkomba of Northern Ghana*, ed. J. Goody (London: Oxford University Press, 1961), pp. 224-25; and V. L. Grottanelli; "Gods and Morality in Nzema Polytheism," *Ethnology* 8, no. 4 (October 1969): 392-93.

28. John Beattie, *Bunyoro: An African Kingdom* (New York: Holt, Rinehart and Winston, 1960), p. 78. The generic nature of the spirits' names is significant. It is European culture that afflicts the Nyoro, not particularly individual Europeans.

29. Victor W. Turner, *The Drums of Affliction* (Oxford: Clarendon Press, 1968), pp. 119f., also 127, 130, 293, 301-302, and 330.

30. Barrie Reynolds, *Magic, Divination and Witchcraft among the Barotse of Northern Rhodesia* (Berkeley: University of California Press, 1963), p. 64; also Heintze, *Besessenheits-Phänomene*, pp. 254-56.

31. Reynolds, *Magic*, pp. 133-36.

32. Odd Nordland, "Shamanism as an Experiencing of 'the Unreal,' " in *Studies in Shamanism*, ed. Carl-Martin Edsman (Stockholm: Almquist and Wiksell, 1967), p. 177. This is an excellent essay.

33. Maya Deren, *Divine Horsemen: Voodoo Gods of Haiti* (New York: Chelsea House, 1970), pp. 247-62.

34. Ibid., p. 249.

35. Nordland, "Shamanism as an Experiencing," p. 176.

36. Ibid., pp. 241-42.

37. Ibid., p. 253.

38. Ibid., pp. 254-55.

39. Ibid., pp. 258-59.

40. Ibid., p. 259.

41. Ibid., p. 260.

42. Ibid., p. 261.

43. Cf. Mircea Eliade, *The Two and the One*, trans. J. M. Cohen (New York: Harper & Row, 1965), pp. 19-77.

44. Deren, *Divine Horsemen*, p. 261.

45. For striking case histories and a profound analysis, see Maurice Merleau-Ponty, *The Phenomenology of Perception*, trans. Colin Smith (New York: Humanities Press, 1962), pp. 111-13 (which, to be sure, concerns a brain-damaged person), 281-91, etc.

46. Deren, *Divine Horsemen*, pp. 230-31.

47. Ibid., Plates 22 and 23, facing p. 247.

48. Margaret J. Field, *Search for Security* (New York: W. W. Norton & Co., 1960), pp. 57, 77f.

49. Ibid., p. 78.

50. Southall, "Spirit Possession and Mediumship among the Alur," p. 255.

51. Erika Bourguignon, "The Self, the Behavioral Environment, and the Theory of Spirit Possession," in *Context and Meaning in Cultural Enthropology*, ed. Melford E. Spiro (New York: Free Press, 1965), p. 48.

52. See Melville J. Herskovits, *Dahomey: An Ancient West African Kingdom* (New York: Augustin, 1938), Vol. II, pp. 178-79; Geoffrey Parrinder, *West African Religion*, 2d ed. (London: Epworth Press, 1961), pp. 81-94; Pierre Verger, *Notes sur le culte des Orisa et Vodun*, Mèmoires de l'Institut Francais d'Afrique Noire, 51 (Dakar: I.F.A.N., 1957), pp. 95-108, etc.; Roger Brand, "Initiation et consecration de deux voduno dans les cultes vodu," *Journal de la Societé des Africanistes* 44, no. 1 (1974): 71-91.

53. See the account by Verger in the previous note, esp. pp. 72f. and 96, and especially Peter T. Furst, *Hallucinogens and Culture* (San Francisco: Chandler and Sharp, 1976), pp. 39-43 and the descriptions of similar American Indian practices on pp. 140-44. On the use of fear by cult priests, see Parrinder, *West African Religion*, pp. 86-88, and Herskovits, *Dahomey*, Vol. II, pp. 184-86.

54. Cf. Herskovits, *Dahomey*, Vol. II, p. 199.

Chapter 11

Divination and Transcendental Wisdom

Among the Fon of Dahomey, there are several kinds of divination. They differ so much between them that we must suspect not only different histories behind them, but also different religious intentionalities and roles. By looking at the Fon, we can discover some essential characteristics in divination systems in general.

On the most ordinary, everyday level, any Fon can get tentative answers to questions he may have by casting kola nuts, analyzing the entrails of fowls sacrificed to a vodu spirit, or even spinning eggs.[1] The underlying assumption here seems to be that the spirits invoked, or the minor spirits nearby, will *indwell* the nuts, the eggs, or the chicken and leave a "sign." Family heads often use these methods, but everyone knows that they are too banal and episodic to be reliable. Just because anyone can use them, they can be influenced too easily. More awesome and "objective" are the *mediumistic* divinations of the spirit-shrines, in the course of which the great vodu enter into and possess their priests and announce their will. As we have just seen in the previous discussion of possession, the relationship between the vodu demigods and their mediums is necessarily passionate and ecstatic. The mediums often structure their initiations like marriage ceremonies, for they are vodusi, "mates of the god." It is said that a man's chief desire is for his vodu, and this desire leads to divinity; in other words, the path to revelation is through overwhelming power and desire. Shrines to the vodu fill the land, and anyone who ignores them will suffer (or will find a near relative suffering) sickness, constant bad luck, psychosis, or death. Yet in all of this cultic activity, it is hard to find any intellectual uniformity. The vodu not only vary from locality to locality; they include also spirits and demigods that at one end are really ancestral spirits or even animated medicines, at another genuine nature spirits with power over the weather, fertility, and the whole of life. Even more confusingly, the myths of particular cults vary from place to place, and the version of the *total* Fon religion, and of the various roles of the vodu in it, differs considerably from one cult to another. The only divination system which presents a uniform and all-embracing vision of Fon religion is the highest system of all, *Fa*, which teaches *wisdom*.

To give a very brief idea of the variety of interpretations that is apparently endemic to the culture, we might mention that while Mawu-Lisa is generally accepted as the supreme being of the Fon, the myths of various vodu cults suggest that this is an androgenous being, or two separate beings of opposite sex (Mawu female, Lisa male); twins borne of Nanabukulu, a mother-goddess; or another name for her; or instead the offspring of the parents of Gbade (another divine figure).[2] Each of the major pantheons (Sky, Earth, and Thunder-Sea) has its own version of the cosmogony, in which the general agreement is slanted to place their own major vodu in a central role. Thus the Thunder pantheon (devoted to Hevioso or Xevioso, similar to the Yoruba Shango) identifies its chief vodu with the Sky and Mawu-Lisa, and one Hevioso priest insisted to Herskovits that Mawu-Lisa was really Sogbo, the mother goddess and creator of all; her husband-son, Agbe (sometimes equated with Hevioso), rules the world.[3] The reader will perhaps agree that in all these group and individual explanations there is no single unified descending symbolic system, despite several attempts to create one. But all vodu priests agree that the Fa priests are the systematic philosophers for them all.[4]

Herskovits suggests that the various vodu were originally associated with specific clans (*sibs*) as their legendary founding ancestors or divine guardians. Knowledgeable Fon even say that each vodu was first revealed to an individual family, whose members became its hereditary high priests.[5] With the increasing integration of Fon culture (particularly with its political unification under increasingly autocratic kings, and the development of cities), the vodu began to inspire nonclan members, creating a general cult. Practically every extended family came to include relatives who belonged to cults to all the major pantheons. Each individual, however, could only be a devotee of one pantheon and the "wife" (medium) of only one vodu in that pantheon.[6]

By the reign of King Agaja (1708-1740), the real founder of the Fon Empire, the cults to the vodu were the chief means of divination, and often families would rally around the oracles of their vodu and resist the central government. According to present traditions, the spirits invoked in divination were especially the *gbo*, ghosts; these ghosts explained death and illness through witch accusations, creating dissension even in local groups. The king "hated this gbo because it permitted too many alliances against him," according to a Fon informant.[7] So the king actually outlawed gbo divination and brought in Fa divination (perhaps from the Yoruba); Fa divination does not utilize possession states.

We can see in the relation between the passionate, trance-oriented gbo and vodu divination and the highly intellectual Fa system the differing consequences of an emphasis on ascending symbolic experience or an emphasis on descending symbolic unifications. The oracular cults were part of a socially and cosmologically centrifugal diversity, one family over against another, and even one individual against others (in witchcraft accusations). The logic of passionate desire even led to alliances against central authority. The Fa system, on the other hand, is an entirely conscious, rational attempt to order the whole of reality into one vast classification system. On this basis everything in life can be explained. Its logic is that of centralization and rational control, and it is easy to understand why the king favored it and established it as the highest level of divination in the land under the direct control of his chief court diviner. This man would preside over the training and examination of other Fa diviners. Nor are we surprised to learn that under such continuing support through the generations, the Fa system developed a number of yet more esoteric levels of interpretation, some known only to the court diviner.[8]

Henceforth, the only way to the vodu was through Fa. The free expression of power and being, in the vodu cults, was in this way given an overall coherence and framework. Although afflictions were caused by the "heat" of the vodu, one could only learn which vodu were striving to communicate with oneself through resorting to the "cool" Fa diviner. He disclosed the hidden fate that even controlled the vodu. Fa is not a vodu, but above them. He is the personified wisdom of Mawu-Lisa, or the messenger of God. In the brief summary of Herskovits:

> It is Mawu as parent of the other gods, who gave them their power. It is Mawu who, according to the diviners of Destiny, holds the formulas for the creation of man and matter. It is Mawu who sent the art of divination to earth so that man might know how to appease the anger and thwart the ill intentions of the reigning pantheon heads, Mawu's children. It is Mawu who gave her favorite son, the trickster Legba, to man to help him circumvent Fate. Most important of all, it is Mawu who, though she divided her kingdom among her children, the other Great Gods, and gave each autonomous rule over his own domain, has yet withheld from all of them the knowledge of how to create, so that the ultimate destiny of the universe is still in her hands.[9]

Fa divination, in other words, is ultimate wisdom, while the vodu merely embody arbitrary passion and power. But the wisdom dwells at the very sources of reality, beyond passion and power. It controls the vodu.

Something of this is indicated by the role of Legba, the grotesque trickster whose gamboling, ugly figure is very often carved in statues at shrines. He is especially marked out by his huge erect phallus. He is the troublemaker of the cosmos, stirring up trouble wantonly at times so that people will sacrifice to the vodu for help, but he is also the power who can free the afflicted from the coercion of the vodu. He is not subject to the laws of this lower world, yet, significantly, he is the companion of Fa, and access to Fa can only be gained after preliminary sacrifice to Legba. He is even said to be another aspect of Fa.[10] Thus it would hardly do to call him the Fon satan, as some Westeners have. For all his brutal and phallic activities, Legba embodies freedom ultimately subordinate to the divine order and Mawu. It is as if, beyond the immediate human world of personal spirits, structured personality must dissolve completely in an experience approaching chaos. Here dwells Legba, inhabitant of the wilderness. But on the further side of this experience of the seemingly demonic stands Fa, the "Voice" of Mawu, the embodiment of the elemental laws deeper than personality. If, as we shall see, sacrifice deeply shapes the inner structures of divination, Legba clearly embodies the principle of transformation at its heart, the transformation that leads to enhanced order and harmony (Fa) at the end. What seems to personal identity as "evil" as it gazes from "this side" into the divine is disclosed on the hither side as a first step into a larger cosmic harmony.

The trauma of possession, which as we have seen also is a frightening one, is from this perspective merely a lower stage in a transformation which should lead to integrated consciousness again, with fully restored systematic structures directing clear consciousness.

Fa itself does not disappoint our expectations. It is an astonishingly profound philosophy. Its priests are not *vodusi*, "mates of the demigods," but *bokono*, "repellers (of danger)," or *babalawo* (the Yoruba term), "father of mysteries."[11] Fa "is the unity of life: he is the interior voice of Se (the impersonal Universal Spirit), and the exterior voice which reveals the truth to those who consult it."[12] The Fa system is built up through the interaction of 256 signs, each of which controls an elemental part of reality.[13] Each element is itself, however, the product of a series of binary impulses (represented by open or closed cowrie shells, whole or broken lines, odd or even numbers, plus or minus, or male or female). Together they generate the entire world, including the vodu. He who understands and controls the signs controls even the vodu. In Fa myths the vodu are represented as coming to Fa to understand their own problems and get out of scrapes. Just as the vodu did in the beginning of time, so do humans now. That is, human beings are lesser versions of the vodu and can transcend themselves only through wisdom, not passion. When they do so, they repeat primordial enactments of reality.

The Fa signs constitute a vast community of their own; the first sixteen are said to be the mothers of all of the rest, but their own interrelations are as abstract and elaborate as any Kabbalistic system of *sephirot*, Hermetic systems of aeons, or Western theological system. The first two signs are the parents of the other fourteen that follow; the first is Mawu (the Mother, East, Day, Light, Head and Thought—resident in the earth), and the second is Lisa (the Father, West, Night, Moon, Flesh, Land of the Dead, Passion, and Air or Heaven). The next two signs are twins of opposite sex, one Water, the other Fire. They together comprise the four cardinal points, the four primal colors, the seasons, times of day, and so on. The other signs are similarly interpreted. All of the signs, and even more the gods and material things woven by them, emanate out of Se, primal impersonal spirit.

To each sign proverbs and myths illustrative of its basic meaning are appended. Every Fa diviner knows some of these sayings, but only the greatest know as many as six hundred verses for each sign. Many travel about from place to place to sit at the feet of great diviners and learn their store of wisdom; one is never finished with the study of Fa. The totality of the knowledge contained in it is the sum of Fon life, systematized and illuminated by the ultimate structures of existence. The Fa corpus is an encyclopedia of Fon myth, for example. The myths of the various vodu are associated with the signs that govern the spirits. But the basic meaning of Fa is already present in the myth that is illustrative of the first Fa sign. It tells that in the beginning of time, Eyes and Head, elder and younger sons of Se, were set a riddle by their father that would determine their nature for all times.[14] Se put two gifts before them: one calabash wrapped in silk and filled with wonderful food, the other filled with gold and silver but covered with a soiled cloth. Eyes chose the beautiful gift, and joyously ate the food inside; Head chose the other, but found only black sand within. Nevertheless, certain that there was more to the matter, he dug down in it, and found wealth. Soon his improvident brother was dependent on him to survive. And so Se decreed that Head would henceforth be the "elder" of Eyes on a spiritual level, although in terms of nature Eyes was the first-born. The reader will perhaps not be surprised to learn that here, in the commentaries on Fa, we can find one of the major sources for the Br'er Rabbit and Br'er Fox stories told so widely in the American South.

The training of a *bokono* takes many years, and traditionally even included study abroad at Ifa centers in Yoruba-land and elsewhere.[15] Fa is a universal, international wisdom that also embraces history, medicine, technology and psychology. Many of the greater bokono had extensive quarters in their compounds for lodging the sick and mentally disturbed who needed their constant attention. It is evident therefore that the bokono had no time for ecstatic indulgences. In fact, he was supposed to be the very embodiment of "coolness" and "freshness," (Fa means both of these concepts); he must be above anxiety, passion, and egoistic desire. The bokono cultivates tranquility, quite unlike the vodusi; if he ever becomes angry or does an unethical act, the forces he has engaged through his powerful meditative serenity will turn on him and destroy him. He must be the very personification of equilibrium, for this is what it is his task to bring to his patients and society. Whenever anyone's life is troubled by unknown and uncontrollable forces; whenever sickness, bad luck, sterility or psychosis threaten, the Fa bokono must be consulted to discover the hidden forces at work so that they can be propitiated and brought into harmony with the victim. Fa must also be consulted before any regular ceremony or feast. For this reason the Fa system and cult is the central pivot of Fon life. Everyone, from slave to king, makes use of it at all crucial points in his life.

It is interesting to observe the relationship between Fa and the vodu. The Fon festivals, and even more the personal problems that arise in life, are governed most immediately by the vodu. When they are angry (which occurs very often), they afflict people and demand sacrifices. They personify, as we have seen, arbitrary power and passion. But before one can know which vodu is weighing on one's soul, Fa must be consulted. Thus wisdom heals what primal passion disturbs. Fa offers a transcendental perspective, from which the vodu seem merely petty and even in a way nonsubstantial. The very highest levels of Fa esotericism have nothing to say about the vodu; instead, they analyze the primary cosmic elements themselves, and one level is devoted to astrology. Fa, in short, works a depersonalization of the Fon cosmos. Many Fa priests in fact tend to look down upon the vodu cults. The vodu, they say, are the very essence of the desires of their devotees, which some bokono consider to mean that "the vodu are only a creation of man."[16] The vodu are not interested in truth, and neither are their followers. Truth demands impartiality and renunciation. The Fa tales often tell of the willful vodu in the beginning of time getting into foolish scrapes, and even the most powerful of them finally had no alternative than to come to the "weak" Fa. In some of these myths Fa is pictured as an amorphous being, without arms or legs, unable to move or stand up by himself. Yet no one can outwit him.

The greatest fault, in the ethics implied in Fa philosophy, is excessive self-will. Fa is not a method for changing one's fate but for coming to terms with it and thus mitigating its worst features. A wise man knows his ingrained failings (what Fa considers his "destiny") and avoids subjecting himself to otherwise inevitable pitfalls. One must learn to accept one's own limits. Vodu possession, on the other hand, can be seen as an experience of breaking out of those limits.

Thus we come to the irony that possession trance begins in passionate and even self-centered desire but ends in obliterating personality in the immediacy of the experience of transcendental power, while Fa divination wisdom begins by depersonalizing everything (even the individual is a compound of many Fa elemental signs) and ends by restoring the person to himself and his own limits. The vodu offer the way of nonconscious transcendence and contact with primordial being; Fa offers fully conscious transcendence and integration into cosmic structure.

I have gone on at such length about the Fon systems of divination not only because of their great fascination as such, but also because they are particularly clear forms of the basic types of divination. These may be categorized as "possession" and "wisdom" types, with perhaps an intermediary third form, "intuitive" divination.

The main point about these categories is that they are determined by the *indigenous theory* of the divination, not the emotional state of the diviner. In particular, when viewed in this light the reading of omens and the movements of sacred animals or objects generally conforms to possession ideology, for these external objects are believed to express directly a spirit's will. The vehicle is "possessed" by a divine being. That is why the chicken falls to the north when slaughtered, let us say, rather than to the south or east. It is, perhaps, the hand of God. Even in terms of oracular possession, we often find reference in the literature to mediums "acting out" possession. They are not (on some occasions) actually possessed, or they may be only slightly possessed. Yet the important thing is the enduring meaning that is given their pronouncements, not the transient, variable emotions or feelings that accompany them. (Recent studies of altered states of consciousness have shown that native theories actually strongly affect the way physiological states are interpreted, even determining their final course. That is, the same state that might be interpreted as mere dizziness in one culture, might be obvious evidence of possession by a god, or impending mystical transformation, in another—and as a result the experience itself will develop in different directions.)[17] There are, as a result, all sorts of conditions that might be considered divinatory spirit possession, including behavior of things external to any human.

In possession divination, whatever agent is chosen by the divine is already liminal. The kola nuts used by many west African peoples are commonly said to come from the first trees; or to be given by the spirits; or even to be the transformed, sacrificed body of a primal being. The medium demonstrates his "election" by peculiar behavior; or he may be from a family hereditarily set apart for the spirits; or he may show his calling by a striking run of bad luck, sickness, or depression. In any case, by embodying in themselves the energies working in the present, the agents disclose a direction to events hidden to the banal consciousness, to which man should conform himself. This form of divination implies the personality of the spiritual realm. Personal agents of the divine are the intermediaries to man; often there is a hierarchial spiritual bureaucracy of a kind down which messages are passed to this world. Humans, having the weakest form of personality, can only humbly receive these messages and respond with sacrificial propitiation or other accommodation. The possessing spirits may not be awesome (they are often close ancestors among the Bantu peoples, for example), but their will cannot be questioned. The universe of oracular pronouncements is generally one of personal power and conflict, and requires obedience to arbitrary wills.

Wisdom divination is very different. In it, the personality of the human clients, and even of the spirits and gods, are all subordinated to a profounder cosmic order. Systematic descending symbolisms unify the whole of experience, and a dispassionate attitude to life is inculcated. Often, as in the Fon case, this type of divination ends in the affirmation of the direct control of the supreme being over every aspect of life, for the classificatory system is his hidden plan for the universe and flows directly from him. There is, in any case, a positive resistance to violent trance states or personal passions. The diviner must preserve his equanimity and inner poise. Many forms of wisdom divination in Africa reduce all things to atomistic impersonal elements, which in their regular interaction produce the variable passing show of the senses. To stay at the level of the mere perceptions and desires, however, is to miss the profound reasons for things. The resemblances to early Western science and to the Enlightenment philosophical contempt for religious enthusiasm are many.[18]

Occasionally there may be encountered in central and southern Africa an extraordinary form of divination, neither fully possession or wisdom in type, which perhaps should be characterized as a third form, "insight" or "intuitive" divination. It does, however, share essential attributes of both possession and wisdom divinations, and a closer analysis shows it to have a structure that can be interpreted culturally in either way. It is tempting to claim for this apparently more elementary form of divination a deeper antiquity than the other two forms or even to see it as the source of the others, but we can only confirm that its priority is typological, not necessarily historical. In insight divination, the specialists claim the ability to determine intuitively and without explicit possession or the application of esoteric sciences the identity and problems of the clients who come to them and, while in the same heightened spiritually alert state, to discover the cause of the troubles. Often they achieve great fame for their ability to locate lost articles or to find thieves and witches. A common preliminary test of these diviners is for the client to demand that the diviner relate details of the frequently arduous journey to him that would seem quite impossible for him to know. Some of these specialists proceed by asking questions or making statements to which the client must indicate either brief assent or dissent; the scepticism of clients precludes this from becoming an obvious guessing game. The often remarkable penetration of the diviners seems the result of a heightened consciousness that perceives and integrates small clues in their environment, ranging from nonverbal reactions of clients to their responses to questions to an awareness we might call extrasensory. These diviners are often reported to be highly intelligent and to have a thorough knowledge of social interactions and of human character. It can be readily understood how easy it would be for this sort of divination to pass over to elaborately structured classification schemes characteristic of wisdom divination, or how on the other hand it might extend the heightened state of consciousness necessary to this mantic activity to a theory of possession.[19]

LIMINALITY AND SOCIAL STRUCTURE IN DIVINATION

Surveying the African instances, it becomes evident that the form of divination that is most common in folk usage is the possession or agent type (in which omen animals, divinatory instruments, or mediums are possessed by a demigod or spirit and are involuntarily agents of a higher will). Knowledge of deeper levels and a more inclusive classification of phenomena is usually reserved for an elite who more likely follow the wisdom form and center divination on the supreme being, beyond the gods and spirits.

This is certainly clear enough among the Fon. In a similar fashion the mediums of the Aro Chuku shrine of the Igbo of Nigeria exercised nominal and sometimes actual political power over most of the Igbo, including lesser oracular shrines, largely because of its accepted supremacy in a religious hierarchy: Chuku, God, spoke through the Aro Chuku shrine, while lesser agents of Chuku spoke through mediums at other shrines. The deeper wisdom and primordiality claimed by Aro Chuku priests have recently been supported by the discovery there of a sacred script of hieroglyphics preserved by the priests perhaps from the late second millenium B.C., when it was possibly conveyed to them by Cretan traders.[20] The Lugbara of Uganda/Zaire believe, too, that the greatest diviners are inspired by God, Adro, directly; lesser, merely locally known diviners who are more vulnerable to error are indwelt by the Adroanzi, the "children of God," who include the ghostly dead.[21]

Varieties of possession divination, involving mediums and such agents as chickens, are very common in central and southern Africa; ancestral and local spirits communicate their will in this way to their kin groups and village inhabitants. But there also exists an 'international' divination system having great similarities from Zaire and Angola to South Africa, and those who have mastered it have high prestige in their societies. It seems to have had its source in the ancient court circles of Monomotapa (or Zimbabwe) and southern Zaire empires. It is a form of wisdom in which reality is broken down into as many as 205 elements, each of which is represented by a bone, a piece of wood, or some other object in a winnowing basket. To answer a query, the contents of the basket are shaken (after the proper invocations), and the pattern of symbols at the top of the basket are analyzed. The possible number of interrelationships between 200, or more commonly 100, symbols is obviously enormous, and the training in the use of the basket and its contents is long and arduous, often involving travel to study at the feet of famous sages from other tribes. Among the Ngombe of Zambia it is said that a novice diviner must first kill a near relative before the basket will divine properly; everywhere it is agreed that the sacrifice of some form of life, usually a chicken, is needed for the bones to become animated. But the life that then fills the bones is integrated into a universal classification, one that embraces the entire cosmos and which some diviners speak of as the "Word" of God.[22] It has been remarked of basket divination in the context of one culture:

> The art is so perfect that bone-throwers can find any amount of satisfaction in practising it. Consider that, in fact, all the elements of Native life are represented by the objects contained in the basket of the divinatory bones. It is a résumé of all their social order, of all their institutions, and the bones, when they fall, provide them with instantaneous photographs of all that can happen to them. This system is so elaborate that I do not hesitate to say that, together with their folklore, their *lobola* customs, and their burial rites, it is the most intelligent product of their psychic life.[23]

Victor Turner has written that its practice is in effect a 'cybernetic' system, into which the specificities of social interaction in a particular village and kin-group are fed, together with the precise problem (sickness, barrenness, etc.), and an answer attuned to the anxieties and cognitive-emotional realities of the clients is produced. A true healing very often is thereby brought about.[24]

We have found in the instances discussed a suggestive correlation between spiritual hierarchies and social hierarchies and practices in which a prestigious, impersonal elite wisdom contrasts to a common, ecstatic worship of intermediary agents.[25] In a phenomenological sense this social structuring of divination types has a remarkable similarity to another pattern also widely found in African cultures. That is the tendency to associate greater wisdom and deeper access to reality and even to the supreme being to diviners located *further away* from the local village and to think of local diviners as mediums to regional spirits, of a lower level, more immersed in the merely human condition and subject to kin ancestors and demigods. Local mediums are less awesome or fenced about with prohibitions, may work in daily life intimately with their neighbors, and generally have no special dress. On the other hand, the greatest authority is given to diviners who have traveled into far-off cultures to learn wisdom; unlike local oracles, these practitioners make use of complex methods requiring long training. Often their training is associated with royal courts. These specialists may well be an important vehicle for culture contact and innovation, though their role in culture change has generally been ignored.[26] But the profound motivation of their quest is to discover the deeper levels of existence and to articulate these levels in a systematic unification of understanding. For this very reason, their wisdom is often esoteric and multilayered and has an initiatic structure. The home realities are insufficient.[27]

One may suggest that these phenomenological and social correlations combine to help explain a remarkable tendency in wisdom divination to be centered in royal courts, or at least to take its rise there. We have seen that the Fon kings instituted Fa divination in their nation specifically to control local mediumistic cults. They established a hierarchical control in which the chief royal diviner possessed the most elaborate esoteric knowledge and supervised the training of all Fa priests. These priests, in turn, governed the recourse to the schismatic vodu on the part of the ordinary people, even determining which vodu were to be worshipped, what the details of ritual propitiation were to be like, and so on. Thus, the tendency we have discovered in wisdom divination to undermine the personal and immediate social realities that confront the diviner and client is controlled and directed to the upbuilding of a hierarchical cosmos and state. The two, cosmos and state, are closely integrated. Allegiance to the king and the universe are joined. The chief Fa priest and former court diviner, in fact, complained to Bernard Maupoil that with the destruction of the Fon kingdom by the French the control of Fa and certification of diviners had lapsed. As a result, entire levels of interpretation had disappeared, and self-seeking and amoral Fa priests had arisen who used their knowledge for power, demanded high prices from clients, and even stooped to sorcery.[28] Divination began to be used for selfish and passionate purposes by persons seeking to escape the consequences of the chaotic collapse of traditional society.

As long as a society remains near the subsistence level and relatively undifferentiated, the wisdom that is handed down through the generations requires the patronage of a centralized, enduring government, or of an organized secret society able to subsidize training and enforce uniformity. Without this the system loses its esoteric dynamic and becomes part of folk practice. An instance of this appears to be the *hakata* dice method of divination prevalent even today in central and southern Africa. This involves the casting of four dice, symbolically related to each other as male and female, elders and children, thus affording a symbolic representation of everyday social interaction. The Ila know of this method of divining, but say it came to them from the Lozi peoples; its use occurs all the way to the eastern coast, where it has been described as used by the Pedi and Thonga by Henri Junod.[29] But it is most common in Rhodesia, among the Sotho and Venda and particularly the Shona peoples, all of whom have inherited much of their culture from the ancient Zimbabwe kingdom that used to exist in the area. That kingdom was evidently an active participant in international trade in the Indian Ocean. The similarities between the dots on the dice, especially in the forms that have been discovered in connection with Zimbabwe culture, and the signs used in the extraordinarily elaborate divinations of Madagascar and Fon-Yoruba culture, suggest that the dice are another version of the Persian-Arab divinatory system that pervaded the Muslim world in past centuries and influenced African cultures.[30] In any case, authorities seem to agree that the hakata dice system had its source in court circles in the ancient Zimbabwe kingdom.[31] Now, however, it is used everywhere by the common people, and has little prestige. The meanings associated with the various throws are fairly simple, probably little like the interpretations that formerly existed. Apparently more than four dice were formerly used.

The basket divination that we have just found to exist among many of the same cultures, and especially in Zambia, Angola, and southern Zaire, seems instead to have had its source in the great southern Zaire kingdoms. As it is more complicated, it still requires long training and retains more prestige than the hakata dice.

On the folk level, it may be supposed, the distinctions we have found between the two varieties of divination tend to merge, especially as long as the explanatory wisdom can be ignored by ordinary folk so that they can use both themselves. When the client comes to a diviner, whether or not it is a medium or a "sage," the priest still seems to be just another personal intermediary to higher powers. No doubt the choice of a medium or a wisdom diviner implies some distinct view of the self and reality, but on this level the two are not always easy to differentiate, even for diviners themselves. We read, for example, that among the Shona, the *hombahomba* diviner first cast his hakata dice twice "and then becomes possessed; he may now discard his *hakata* and divine through his spirit."[32]

In any case, both types of divination induce a similar sense of the other-centered nature of life. In wisdom one gives conscious assent to the transcendental structures that pervade all reality and which as a totality directly point to the supreme being who is their source. Thus we often find that wisdom divination and rites involving destiny souls in effect constitute a direct cult to the Supreme Being ignored by ethnographers.[33] In possession, however, the sources of reality are acknowledged through the overthrow of consciousness. Precisely the passionate and personal nature of this experience often leads to a belief that intermediary spirits or demigods are involved. These lesser spirits are the ones more involved in the immediacies of everyday life and society. However, in east Africa the widespread prophetic cults directly contact the supreme being.[34] Another possession cult directed to the supreme being is the Mwari cult of the Matopo Hills in Rhodesia, in which a medium is possessed by Mwari, but diviner priests interpret her words in accordance with wisdom for the petitioners.[35] As has been well said in specific reference to a people of Chad:

Everything proceeds as if the Mundang divinatory system is able to make use either of a constituted knowledge or an ecstatic technique to mark the difference, the gap: the Other Word. This Other Word, that of *Maseng* [God], that of the *mozumri* [spirits], is what is in itself irreducible to all manifestations of experience.[36]

The pervasive ideology of both possession and wisdom divination, in short, is sacrificial. One of the most pervasive features and accompaniments to divination of any sort is explicit sacrifice. Occasionally, the act of divination is a sacrifice as such: The verdict is read from the entrails of the victim (as notably among the Nilotics and others of east Africa),[37] or from the movements of a sacrificed fowl (or even the fact of its death, as in Congolese poison ordeals), or from the bones and blood of sacrificed victims (as in central African basket divination, where the bones themselves come from victims, and the blood of a final sacrifice must animate a novice diviner's basket). All Fa sessions end in directions for the proper sacrifices to offer the vodu, and often Fa must begin with a sacrifice to Legba. All of these rituals enact spiritual transformations in which one offers one's existence up to the essential structures or powers governing one's life, to order to receive it back renewed and conformed to the divine order. As George K. Park concluded from a sociological perspective over a decade ago, divination shifts attention from the personal and idiosyncratic to the deeper, normative, and impersonal causes that affect life. In doing so it recreates social (and cosmic) order, rediscovering it in the midst of all change.[38]

NOTES TO CHAPTER 11

1. Melville J. Herskovits, *Dahomey: An Ancient West African Kingdom* (New York: Augustin, 1938), Vol. II, p. 202, 209.

2. Ibid., Vol. II, pp. 101-105, etc.

3. Ibid., Vol. II, pp. 150.

4. Ibid., Vol. II, pp. 213-17, etc.

5. Ibid., Vol. II, pp. 169, 178.

6. Ibid., Vol. II, p. 185 n. 4.

7. Ibid., Vol. II, pp. 208-209.

8. The entire system is detailed in Bernard Maupoil, *La Géomancie à l'ancienne Côte des Esclaves*; Travaux et Mémoires, XLII (Paris: Institut d'Ethnologie, 1943).

9. Melville J. and Francis S. Herskovits, *An Outline of Dahomean Religion*, Memoires of the American Anthropological Association, 41 (1933), p. 12.

10. Cf. Maupoil, *La Géomancie*, pp. 76-84, 177f., 190ff., 352, etc.; most works on Fon religion discuss Legba at some length, as do studies of Yoruba religion (where Eshu-Elegba is equivalent).

11. Maupoil, *La Géomancie,* pp. 112ff., also 60ff.

12. Ibid., p. 62.

13. The whole of Maupoil deals with this. Also see Rene Trautman, *La divination à la Côte des Esclaves et à Madagascar;* Mémoires de l'Institut Francaise d'Afrique Noire, I (Paris: I.F.A.N., 1939), William Bascom, *Ifa Divination* (Bloomington: Indiana University Press, 1969), Wande Abimbola, *Ifa Divination Poetry* (New York: Nok Press, 1977).

14. Maupoil, *La Géomancie,* p. 434.

15. Ibid., p. 128. Some Fon legends derive the system from Ile-Ife, the sacred city of the Yoruba, others suggest an origin in Mecca, the sacred city of Muslims. In fact, Fa does show ancient Mediterranean and Near Eastern influences.

16. Ibid., pp. 263-64.

17. See the important study by Arnold M. Ludwig, "Altered States of Consciousness," in *Trance and Possession States,* ed. Raymond Prince; Proceedings, Second Annual Conference, R.M. Bucke Memorial Society, 4-6 March 1966 (Montreal: R.M. Bucke Memorial Society, 1968).

18. For many Renaissance scientists, the universe was woven of elementary "syllables" in literally Kabbalistic, mathematical fashion. See, for some striking examples, Frances Yates, *Giordiano Bruno and the Hermetic Tradition* (Chicago: University of Chicago Press, 1964). The nineteenth-century logician John Venn has described even Sir Francis Bacon's approach to science as a "mathematical view of the universe, in its extremest form. . . . We find the universe all broken up, partitioned, and duly labelled in every direction; so that, enormously great as is the possible number of combinations which these elements can produce, they are nevertheless *finite* in number, and will therefore yield up their secrets to plodding patience when it is supplied with proper rules." As Martin Gardner adds, "Science, to pursue the metaphor, is one stupendous task of cryptanalysis." See Gardner's "Mathematical Games," *Scientific American* 227, no. 5 (November 1972): 118. What is especially striking to us, however, is that this cryptanalysis is oriented to prediction, and is therefore in every way identical in itself to the principles behind Fa divination.

19. G. van der Leeuw, *Religion in Essence and Manifestation,* trans. J.E. Turner (New York: Harper & Row, 1963), Vol. II, p. 379, distinguishes between two types of divination, one "calm and almost scientific," and the other "more ecstatic." Plato is cited as the source of this contrast between "Oionistic" and "Mantic" phases of divination (see *Phaedrus,* 244; Plato's *Timaeus,* 72, could also have been added). The problem with this approach, however, is that it emphasizes the problematical emotions, and confuses the issue of agency: *who* acts. Our own approach stresses instead the cognitive aspects of divination, and is concerned with the meanings applied by indigenous participants. For example, the Zulu diviner consulted by M. Kohler, *The Izangoma Diviners* (Pretoria: 1941), pp. 28 and 60, affirmed that for him there are three basic types of divination: by the spirits (*imilozi*), i.e., "possession"; by the use of "bones" classifying reality, i.e., "wisdom"; and divination of "the head," in which the diviner intuits the answer while conversing with the clients, i.e., "insight." But the ambiguity of this third type of divination often leads to its being grouped with one of the other two: in the accounts in Rev. Henry Callaway, *The Religious System of the Amazulu: Izinyanga Zokubula, or Divination, As Existing Among the Amazulu, In Their Own Words* (London: Trübner, 1884), *passim,* insight divination is generally explained as possession in a non-ecstatic way by the ancestral spirits. According to Michael Gelfand, the Shona recognize two basic types of diviners, the *nganga* and the *mushoperi* or *hombahomba;* see *idem, Shona Religion, With Special Reference to the McKorekore* (Cape Town: Juta & Co., 1962), pp. 106ff. The nganga uses *hakata* dice (the four dice in their 16 variations and further combinations of relative positions, etc., symbolize all the stages of life and all social roles of both sexes—a popularized form of wisdom divination), or is possessed by *shave* spirits, while the most prestigious hombahomba diviners are more intuitive. They can even tell spontaneously the names of strangers who come to them for advice, it is said. But they also make use of hakata dice. Gelfand tells of one session in which a hombahomba used dice: "He casts them twice and then becomes possessed. He starts by telling the delegation from where they have come, the name of the deceased, and what kind of person he was. Then he proceeds

to relate the cause of death" (ibid., p. 110). Here we find a curious mixture of both "wisdom" and "possession" techniques to produce "insight."

20. Kathleen Hau, "The Ancient Writing of Southern Nigeria," *Bulletin, Institut francaise de'Afrique noire* 29, serie B, no. 1-2 (1967): 150-78. On the social role of the Aro Chuku shrine, see Simon Ottenberg, "Ibo Oracles and Intergroup Relations," *South-Western Journal of Anthropology* 14, no. 2 (1958); 294-317.

21. John Middleton, "Oracles and Divination among the Lugbara," in *Man in Africa*, eds. Mary Douglas and Phyllis M. Kaberry (London: Tavistock Publications, 1969), pp. 264, 269, etc.

22. Most detailed studies of particular cultures in this vast area make mention of "basket divination"; for an overview, see Barrie Reynolds, *Magic, Divination and Witchcraft Among the Barotse of Northern Rhodesia;* Robin Series III (Berkeley: University of California Press, 1963), pp. 100ff., and the detailed treatment in Victor Turner, *Ndembu Divination: Its Symbolism and Techniques*; Rhodes-Livingstone Paper 31 (Manchester: Manchester University Press, 1961); the Thonga of South Africa have a clearly traditional emphasis on the "Word" conveyed by the divinatory bones, according to Rev. Henri Junod, *The Life of a South African Tribe*, 2d ed. (London: Macmillan Co., 1927), Vol. II, pp. 385, 541 and 570; on the last-named page, we read the following significant statement: "But the *Bula*, the Word, is not generally looked on as being the utterance of the ancestor-gods. The bones are, in a certain sense, *superior to the gods* whose intentions they disclose. The *Bula* is the revelation of a more or less impersonal power, independent of the gods" (italics are Junod's). The diviners, in fact, appeal directly to Tilo, the "impersonal" High God: Junod, pp. 429-31.

23. Ibid., p. 521.

24. Ibid., p. 18.

25. A social patterning of identical type can be found among more differentiated cultures. Contrasting the folk shamanic mediums to the priestly Brahmans, David G. Mandelbaum has shown the same traits in Indian village societies in his "Introduction: Process and Structure in South Asian Religion," in *Religion in South Asia*, ed. Edward B. Harper (Seattle: University of Washington Press, 1964), esp. pp. 8ff., where the literate Brahmanic tradition equates to the wisdom divination discussed here. In China, Confucian mandarins made use of the *I Ching* (a classic of wisdom divination) while recourse to mediums was characteristic of folk religion. But the cosmic classifications of the *I Ching* controlled gods as well as men, subordinating both to a deeper impersonal process. Confucian scholars could even be agnostic or contemptuous of the popular cults of gods and spirits, exorcisms and possessions, while daily consulting the *I Ching*. On social aspects of these beliefs, see C.K. Yang, *Religion in Chinese Society* (Berkeley: University of California Press, 1961), pp. 48-56, 134-37, 142-43, 244-77. And in Judaism we find the same basic dynamic not only in the Talmudic pursuit of wisdom and distrust of possession, but also in the later development of the highly intellectual bent of Kabbalah; both served to devalue the less controlled, passionate cults of the folk religions surrounding the Jews in exile. A similar orientation probably also influenced the development of Christian theology, Pythagoreanism or even of astrology in the Hellenistic world.

26. But see Reynolds, *Magic, Divination*, p. 99.

27. Witches also know the lands of outer darkness. Margaret Field has an illuminating note on this in her *Religion and Medicine among the Ga People* (London: Oxford University Press, 1937), pp. 124f.: "Taylor has said that every tribe believes its barbaric neighbors to be more deeply steeped in darkly wonderful magic than it is itself. This is profoundly true of the Ga when thinking of either medicines or witchcraft. A Ga will tell you that the worst witches are the Fanti, the Fanti will refer you to the Nzima and the Nzima send you still further, till you conclude that the worst witchcraft recedes like the end of the rainbow. In medical practice, also, the more time a physician is known to have spent in Dahomey and the more medicines he can exhibit from there, the better equipped he is considered, and to have been as far afield as the Northern Territories is the equivalent of having studied in Vienna."

28. Maupoil, *La Géomancie*, pp. xi-xii, 148, 159-63, etc.

29. See Smith and Dale, *The Ila-Speaking Peoples of Northern Rhodesia* (London:

Macmillan and Co., 1920), Vol. I, p. 272; H.A. Junod, "La divination au moyen de tablettes d'ivoire chez les Pedis," *Bulletin de sociètè du Neuchatel de Geographie* 34 (1925): 35-56, and *idem, The Life of a South African Tribe*, Vol. II, pp. 603-08; for a general description, see also A. Winifred Hoernlé, "Magic and Medicine," in *The Bantu-Speaking Tribes of South Africa*, ed. I. Schapera (London: George Routledge and Sons, 1937), pp. 237-39.

30. See Trautman, *La divination*; very significant in this connection is not only the manner of patterning dots, their binary male-female oppositions, and so on, but also the importance of multiples of four, and especially the importance of the number of sixteen, in all the systems. See, on the use of sixteen, the Venda evidence, Hugh A. Stayt, *The BaVenda* (London: Oxford University Press, 1931), pp. 286-90. As in the Fa system, each sign has its name and proverb, recited as a greeting to it when it appears in a session.

31. See evidence in ibid., and also in Hoernle, "Magic and Medicine," p. 291. The dice were apparently also related to elaborate divining bowls in Zimbabwe.

32. Michael Gelfand, *Shona Religion*, p. 109; also see *idem, An African's Religion: The Spirit of Nyajena—Case History of a Karanga People* (Cape Town: Juta & Co., 1966), p. 44.

33. An interesting example is the Nupe, who make clear that their *eba* (very similar to the Yoruba *Ifa* and Fon *Fa*) divination is *nya Soko*, "of God." When all the signs are built up in a session, the diviner says, "Good, God is there." See S.F. Nadel, *Nupe Religion* (London: Oxford University Press, 1954), p. 54. Among Mande peoples, divination explicitly interprets the "Word" of God, also as among so many other west African peoples the trickster helps convey this "Word." Also see Junod's remarks in footnote 22, above, on the Thonga. For some other references, see Forde, ed., African Worlds, pp. 7f. (Lele), 46 (Abaluyia), 88f. (Dogon), 159 (Shilluk), 171f. (Ruanda), 215 and 228 (Fon), also note p. 197 (Ashanti)—in other words, seven out of nine fairly randomly selected societies demonstrate the direct linkage of divination and destiny to the supreme being.

34. In some cases, a Jewish influence on east African prophetism is obvious, as in the case of the Meru, where associated with the prophetic cult are myths very similar to the Biblical account of Creation and Fall, Exodus from Egypt and even the "seven Noahite commandments." No Muslim or Christian myths are evident. See B. Bernardi, *The Mugwe: A Failing Prophet* (London: Oxford University Press, 1959), 52-58, 126, 136, 140, etc.

35. See M.L. Daniel, *The God of the Matopo Hills* (The Hague: Mouton, 1970).

36. Alfred Adler and Andras Zempleni, *Le Baton de l'aveugle: Divination, maladie et pouvoir chez les Maundang du Tchad* (Paris: Hermann, 1972), p. 178; this excellent study was called to my attention by J. David Spero. Translation mine.

37. A vivid description of such divination is in Elizabeth Marshall Thomas, *Warrior Herdsmen* (New York: Alfred A. Knopf, 1965), pp. 138-44 and Plate XIII (on the Dodoth).

38. George K. Park, "Divination and Its Social contexts," *Journal of the Royal Anthropological Institute* 93, no. 2 (July-December 1963): 195-209. The socially conservative thrust of divination, however, obtains only in generally stable societies, and even then primarily in wisdom divination. In unstable situations of oppressive rule or alienating change, possession divination can give rise to full-fledged millenary upheavals; the sensory universe and ascending symbolisms assert themselves apart from the social structure. Wisdom divination, too, offers a passive but profound protest against agonizing personal suffering, as we have seen. When more differentiated social structures develop, and role specialization permits the permanent separation of wisdom structures from the state government, the inner tendency of this form of divination serves as an aid to individualized protest against the entire society. Astrology during the Graeco-Roman period offers a particularly celebrated instance of this: see F.H. Cramer, *Astrology in Roman Law and Politics*, Memoires of the American Philosophical Society 37 (Philadelphia: American Philosophical Society, 1954), and the first volume of A.J. Festugière, *La révélation d'Hermès Trismégiste*, 4 vols. (Paris: 1944-54). The *I Ching* also moved from an early center at the Shang Dynasty courts to later mandarin and eremitic circles, and is part of the counter-culture in this country. Traditional Western astrology in the modern West offers another interesting example of the same dynamic: through this "wisdom" divination a clear protest against both the institutions and the ideology

("science") of the general culture is registered. The leap to a profounder transcendental reality is especially noticeable among working-class women and "hippies," who affirm through astrology contact with a vast, elemental context of personal value outside of and invisible to the ordinary society. For devotees, the Zodiac and natal sign provide a spiritual kin-network of universal dimensions, giving an immediate fellowship with strangers (in a world of strangers), and offering a community more lawful and reliable than troubled personal ties. The self is thus freed from immediate personal pressures. (I am indebted to discussions with Ms. Francis Butler of the Department of Anthropology, Allegheny College, for this reference to contemporary astrology.)

Chapter 12

Witchcraft

In the context of African religions, unquestionably the most influential work on witchcraft practices and ideology is the 1937 classic by E. E. Evans-Pritchard, *Witchcraft, Oracles and Magic among the Azande*.[1] This work has not only inspired most of the current theories about African witchcraft, but it has also shaped to a considerable degree the terms of the current debate over the relationship between Western science and African religion.[2] The reason is simple: Evans-Pritchard regarded Zande divination and witchcraft as magical attempts to deal with the philosophical and social problem of causation. As such, any religious aspects of these practices were derivative or irrelevant.

Witchcraft, according to Evans-Pritchard, operates according to a strict logic. It assumes a world in which power is manipulated according to basic rules, and which is mystically accessible to magicians. This power is neutral. The *mangu* witchcraft-substance that exists in the body of both witches and witchdoctors, for example, is used by the former for evil, by the latter for good. *Benge*, the medicine used in poison ordeals, simply responds truthfully to any question put to it, regardless of the intent. Assuming such forms of power, events which otherwise would be put down to mere chance are revealed as comprehensible and lawful. There is no mere chance, for the Zande. For example, the Zande store their grain in granaries elevated above the ground on wooden posts. These posts are infested with termites. Everyone understands that termites weaken the posts, and eventually the granary will collapse. But why, let us say, did it collapse just when my son was sitting under it? That is a question that is not explained by talking of termites. There was a certain particularity to such a blow, a purpose that remains to be discovered. Termites always bore in wood, but granaries do not always fall. Humans, however, act purposefully and particularly. My son's death was therefore a result of witchcraft, someone's evil purpose.

It is possible to find out the guilty person. If the poison oracle consistently answers "yes" when supplied with my envious neighbor's name, there can be no question about it (the oracle is so structured it generally answers positively 50 percent of the time, negatively the rest).

Evans-Pritchard insists that no personality is involved in the medicines. In peculiar contradiction to his highly sophisticated analysis of symbolic language and religious metaphor in Nuer culture, he argues that despite the fact that the medicines of the Azande are *constantly addressed as persons*, they have no physical arms, hands, or feet and are grammatically neuter, just "things."[3] Perhaps Evans-Pritchard is a victim here of the obsession which also rules his *Nuer Religion*, according to which there must be a clean break between the uncontrollable Wholly Other that can only be worshipped in a symbolic personalistic medium of ritual and analogical language, and non-religious medicines that are literalistically and impersonally used for logical, pragmatic goals. Rudolf Otto is explicitly appealed to for support.[4] But as we know, Otto is no guide to African spirituality. Spirituality is deeply a part of pragmatic concerns, by the very nature of the spiritual. Medicines can be personal agencies.

Even if Evans-Pritchard were right about the medicines, there still remains the religious significance of the universe built up by witchcraft ideology. In this coherent, self-authenticating divine order, even the anti-cosmic thrust of witchcraft finally serves to confirm the existence of spiritual meaning. Truth responsive to human purpose is interwoven with the very fabric of the divine order. Structure triumphs over chaos.

But the medicines do have religious purpose and personhood. Evans-Pritchard admits that the word he translates as "spell" is the Zande word for "prayer" to the supreme being and spirits.[5] Prayers to the medicine spirits need not even be stereotyped; they need only be intelligible requests.[6] Most significantly of all, the *benge* poison used in the ordeal is explicitly said to mediate God's presence.[7] All power flows from God.

Since we have established even from the very classic that insists on the magical proto-scientific interpretation of witchcraft that it is actually religious, we must ask what exactly is the religious meaning of witchcraft and sorcery. After all, in such acts the primordial power of God is turned back on the universe he sustains, to destroy it. A closer look at the Fon may help us to answer this paradox.

The essence of sorcery among the Fon, Herskovits tells us, lies in the worker of evil obtaining control over a human spirit to do its bidding.[8] Witchery, for them, is a negative possession that diminishes or destroys the self.[9] The Fon tell many stories of how one individual or another who was thought to be dead was encountered in Togo or in Nigeria by a friend or acquaintance who had actually participated in the funeral. The individuals met so strangely, however, would not respond to their own name, nor did they recognize their old friends.

They were soulless beings, whose death was not real but resulted from the machinations of sorcerers who made them appear as dead, and then, when buried, removed them from their graves and sold them into servitude in some far-away land.[10]

Unlike the vodusi, these entranced beings were controlled not by divine spirits (who participated in the divine order), but by human beings. They were enslaved by wills that did not care for the cosmos or the victim, but only for themselves and their own engrandizement. Yet as we shall see, the zombie is the type not only of the witch's victim, but also of the witch himself.

The usual instruments of sorcery among the Fon are *gbo*, medicines, whose spirits or forces have sufficient consciousness to accomplish tasks set them. It is evident that the ghosts animating the medicines are the real power in them. These gbo are neutral in nature and can be used for good or evil.[11] But constant use for evil may end in their human master becoming their slave; he will not be able to wrench himself from evil. Such people are called the *azondato*, and are recognizable by their bloodshot eyes; two or three of them can be found at every market, it is whispered, and it will be noticed on close observation that they always do somewhat better business than merchants near them.[12] The *azondato* are organized into a guild that is reputed to meet deep in the bush at night to plan and perform their ghoulish deeds; they fly to their meeting in the form of bats, or transform themselves into other wild animals.[13] They are closely associated with the beasts of the wild, of whom they may be considered the human representatives, like a fifth column undermining society. Herskovits tells us, for example, that they are often held responsible for the devastating smallpox epidemics that occasionally ravage the population.[14] Their patron goddess is the Mistress of the Bush, Minona, who provides their gbo and rules them as she does all things of the uncultivated earth.[15] Minona is variously described as the mother of Mawu and Legba, as the sister of Legba, and as the mother of Fa. In a sense, she is Mother Earth itself, and "when Mawu went to live on high, Minona preferred to remain on Earth," according to one *bokono*.[16] She is the protecting deity of women, and every woman has a shrine to her in her hut where she is regularly honored. She is given the first fruits to be eaten before any humans may eat of the crops; this assures the fertility of the fields. Possessing all trees and herbs, she controls and dispenses the power in charms (gbo), and every Fon compound has many of her gbo prominently displayed as antiwitchcraft charms, fertility medicines and the like.[17] However, as mentioned above, witches and sorcerers are especially devoted to her. Not surprisingly, women are above all believed to be witches; they are generally the small traders in the marketplace, they serve Minona already, and as the more peripheral members of society they are easily assimilated to the bush.

These ideas of the Fon conform to a pattern that is pervasive throughout

Africa in regard to witchery.[18] In fact, the resemblances to witchery conceptions in non-African cultures are intriguing and disturbing; evidently there are powerful psychic uniformities in the conception of the demonic among very diverse cultures. European witches, too, are active at night, have witches' covens deep in the bush, fly about and have animal familiars and/or can assume animal shapes themselves (of which the bat is a favored type), thrive in marketplaces, and are generally women. Almost every one of these characteristics can also be found among the Navaho Indians of the southwestern United States.[19] They are indeed typical.

Variant and culturally specific social functions cannot be at the root of such conceptions, therefore, although many studies of African witchery have shown clearly the tendency of witchcraft accusations, and perhaps deeds, to follow the lines of social tension and conflict.[20] Some commentators, obedient to an extreme functionalism, have wished to argue that witchery beliefs are fundamentally useful and good for the societies in which they occur. They help to break up "dysfunctional" groups, for example, although it is likely we would not know the groups were so dysfunctional if it were not for the witchery accusations. More useful studies have pointed to the way in which accusations show the weak structural points in a society. Among the Pondo of Zambia, where family groups cluster together in their own territories and where therefore the incest taboo is daily tested, witches are thought to be incestuous and also to engage in intercourse with their animal familiars of the opposite sex. This shows their incest to be bestial and in every way antihuman. Among the Nyakyusa of Malawi, on the other hand, families dwell in much more diverse villages, so the incest taboo is not so onerous. But the sharing of food with other kinship groups is much more necessary and problematic; witches therefore are individuals who hoard their food and who are cannibalistic. They are so greedy for flesh that they feast mystically on their own relatives and neighbors.[21] In short, witches are individuals who refuse to submit to the ego-restraints and self-denials necessary for social intercourse. They insist on impulse gratification, even if it destroys the human cosmos and moral pattern of any kind. Incest and cannibalism are indeed the most typical activities of witches. Therefore we find that accused "witches" are often the people others have supposed to be filled with frustrated impulses. Among the Konkomba of Ghana, where the elder men rule everyone else, it is the younger men who are suspected of sorcery. The eldest brother is often suspicious of his younger brothers, who cannot by Konkomba custom share in the inheritance. A favored wife, or the eldest wife, often is ready to blame her resentful cowives for sudden runs of bad luck. And entire clans might suspect the baleful influence of the oppressed young wives who marry into the lineage from other clans.[22] The sorcerer and witch is the person who seeks to break out of the constricting circle of traditional morality and to achieve, despite the norms and structures of the universe, the satisfactions of wealth, power, and above all revenge.[23]

The resentment attributed to them makes witches lonely figures, and so does the violent exercise of forbidden impulses. The Konkomba witch is so solitary that, although he flies to gatherings of witches in the bush (sailing as a ball of fire through the night air), he only meets the others in order to disperse again to his missions of desolation and evil; there are here no wild dances or ghoulish feasts.[24]

We may see in these ideas the contorted workings of empathy. The oppressed person arouses in others a sense of his suffering, which in turn creates guilt and a negative attitude to the sufferer. To take a striking instance from outside of Africa, Leon Polikov has shown that it was only after Christians slaughtered whole cities of European Jews in the early Crusades that myths of Jewish well-poisoning, feasting on young Christian children, and international conspiracies began to circulate.[25] The victims of witch accusations are therefore generally the weak and exploited. But we do also find the successful accused, especially if they do not share with others; i.e., if they are solitary and therefore "misers," or if they are antisocial, or simply much too successful. Then one's own frustrations and resentments are expressed in accusing the other.

So in many ways resentment or attributed resentment (that is, suppressed impulse gratification) is expressed in dreams of witchery power and freedom of crude desires. Of course, these dreams can only be located in the bush, for they are not of society and even are against it. Witches enjoy the savage freedom of animals. They have animal helpers and can change into bestial form themselves; even their own bodies no longer constrict them. The Temne of Sierra Leone say that the witch's face turns into that of an animal at the very moment of bewitching, joining him utterly with the savage pact who aid him.[26]

Witches therefore systematically invert human values and are viciously antihuman. They participate in a realm all of whose characteristics are the opposite of decent, morally obedient, structured society. Among the Kaguru of Tanzania, for example,

> A witch's behaviour is inverted, physically, socially and morally. He works at night; he is ash-white, not dark; and he travels upside-down and without the impediments experienced by ordinary people. He treats kin like non-kin, for he has sexual intercourse with them. He treats all humans like non-humans, killing and eating people as though they were animals. He treats wild animals like humans, for they help him in his work and live near or in his house. . . . A witch enjoys badness, while most people enjoy doing what is good.[27]

Kaguru witches are sometimes organized into local societies, which meet

on unfrequented mountain tops or in the ruins of abandoned huts to share
their cannibalistic feasts.[28]

Yet the sources of their evil lie in the divine order they despise. They turn
the energies that flow through the universe against that universe, but the
powers themselves are neutral. A particularly poignant expression of this is
the Shilluk witch's prayer and lament, said prior to working his charms:

> You who are God (Jwok) give me this person to kill.
> Why was I created thus if it was not that I was to kill?[29]

The gbo medicines used by the Fon witches and sorcerers are neutral,
primordial and precultural forces. The Kaguru witches use *uhai* (charms,
spells, poisons, or simply inner force) to harm others or their possessions,
but uhai can also be used for antiwitchcraft and to increase fertility,
prosperity, and health. Only when it is too intense does it distort the inner
being of the user by taking him over. Any person who commits acts
especially horrifying to a Kaguru obtains uncontrollable amounts of
uhai.[30] It is as if the divine order has a power running through it that is
directed to good by the boundaries and norms of the structure; when these
are broken, however, especially at the most central points (where taboos
and norms cluster), the power is released to destroy the entire structure. In
any case, the power demands to be exercised, for that is the nature of
power. For the Kaguru, acts such as incest (which they simply call uhai,
witchcraft) destroy fundamental joints in the articulation of divine
structure: the guilty ones are irrevocably evil, "bad until they die."[31] The
same is true for cannibalism: these are the two definitively witchlike acts.
We can see that the Fon doctrine of gbo, the Kaguru concepts of uhai, and
the nearly universal association of cannibalism and incest with witchcraft
indicate a close homology between the forces the witch uses and his own
unrestrained and violent emotional nature. For like uhai, the desires are
good when moderately exercised. They only become antihuman and evil
when they are allowed to take over everything. Sexual desire, which is given
by the ancestors to generate descendents, is distorted when it dominates all
else, for then it breaks through all family and kinship boundaries (as incest
most graphically demonstrates) and becomes the enemy of the ancestors.

The witch may therefore be the "individualist,"[32] but he lacks real
personality. His enslavement to his resentments, hatreds, and rampant
desires reduces him to stereotyped emotive preconscious behavior. He is
the individualist without individuality. The denial of ego-consciousness is
evident in many ways: in the compulsive behavior, in the denial of the social
relationships that define the ego-self, and in the assault on the cosmology
that locates the self in a divine order. But, most interestingly, there is *the
peculiar distortion of the body image*, which provides much of the logic to
specific details in witchery symbols.

The very appearance of the witch is supposed to set him apart. His body is as distorted, twisted, and imperfect as his spirit. His gestures are peculiar, and there is something wrong about his gaze. But often the same cultures that insist on the witch's deformity will also point to extraordinarily beautiful people as witches.[33] Their bodies are not like other people's; their physical misfortune (with the empathetic response of "attributed resentment") or their great fortune (with the response of envy) sets them apart, and perhaps the visual impact and power to attract or repell also suggests witchery powers.

But the witch, as we know, can simply cast off his body and fly about as a bat, an owl, or even a fireball; he can become invisible or can change his shape into that of an animal. Unlike the rest of us, he will take salt when he is thirsty, or walk upside-down to his destination and rest hanging by his feet from a tree.[34] He clothes his body oddly, or not at all: many central and east African witches cast their spells by dancing naked in their enemies' compounds at night, working themselves up into a fury until they vomit poisons into holes in the ground, at thresholds or paths, which they cover. The victim will be affected when he steps over the poisons. So different is the witch's body that witch-finding ordeals are predicated on that complete otherness: the substance most people will vomit up the witch will not—or vice versa; the boiling oil that will sear the witch's arm will leave unharmed the innocent person's. In fact, the favorite foods of witches destroy normal human beings and are "poisons."

We can also see the definitive acts of incest and cannibalism as perverted meditations on the body: the normal body eats animals, and has sex with humans other than kin. But the witch's body relishes sex with animals and kin, and feasts on human flesh. The normal behavior builds up a harmonious physical universe; the abnormal destroys it. The effects of witchery often strike the victim's body in particular. He is impotent, or falls ill, or most decisively of all becomes a zombie, a complete physical slave without any control at all over the body.

The witch achieves his isolation by cutting himself off from the divine order. He also seeks to fill the entire world with the same compulsive solitude, a solitude that expresses hatred. The sight of any normal, positive interchange maddens him. The prosperous cycling of persons through the cosmic hierarchy, from child to adult, to ancestorhood and regeneration in descendents, the fruitful and happy interaction of marriage, and even the contentment of unrelated people at beer feasts triggers a deep antipathy that expresses itself in desperate attempts to destroy all generative transformations and interchanges. This is especially true since just at the point of liminal change the victim is momentarily outside the protection of normative structures and is most vulnerable. The threshold is always the most dangerous point.

So the witch attacks people in transition: pregnant women, the newly born and children, initiates, and even the newly dead. He also attacks people through those parts of them that are peripheral, which connect them with their environment and through which they interact with the cosmos: their children, wives, herds and crops. Or he directly afflicts the victims through the organs of the body that interrelate them to the world, causing impotency or venereal disease, diarrhea or constipation.

Above all the witch works to destroy the body image. Here we see again that what constitutes the witch is precisely what destroys the normal victim. The witch delights in human flesh, but slipping some bits of such flesh into the victim's food will destroy him. Menstrual blood, offal, or other excreta will do also. Cultures with strong taboos surrounding eating often are deeply frightened of witches.[35] As we have seen, Lugbara and Kaguru witches harm their victims by vomiting near their homes.

The love of exuviae (blood, sweat, hair, urine, vomit, etc.) well expresses the disintegrated body image of the witch. The leavings of the body, the result of the healthy organic interchange and participation in the larger divine order, are used to stop up the channels of ebb and flow. In and out are severed. Excrement is put into food, confusing the two so that what goes in and what goes out are no longer structurally differentiated. Nail parings are turned back on one in hostile charms. An individual will die if he cannot get rid of waste, for he lives only by constant mutuality and transformation.

The female sex most embodies the powers of generation and the role of mediator between nature and culture. For both reasons, it would seem, witches are most commonly stereotyped as women, often even when the actually accused witches are men.[36] Women, as we have seen throughout this study of African religions, are associated with the natural generativity of the bush and the wilderness. They are therefore suspect from the viewpoint of culture. The men can justify their own control of women on this account, and especially when the women get out of control it is a temptation to condemn them as witches. Precisely because women are considered to lack the extrinsic means of obtaining their desires that men have, their lack of cooperation, or their inability to bear children, or their strife as cowives, is thought to be expressed through intrinsic witchcraft. The same innate powers that create can also destroy; all the more so since these powers are outside of conscious control.

Not only the innate powers of femininity but also the intermediary role of women helps to further this demonic image. The witch is obsessed with transitions, as we have seen, precisely because he cannot make any transitions himself. Women, too, are deeply involved in transitions. In both matrilineal and patrilineal societies women provide the links between male centers of authority. They can often be suspected therefore of divided loyalties or of no loyalty at all. As mothers, they are also the link between generations in a way men can never be. When witches devour their own children they destroy this link. And binding together innately the natural and the cultural, the village and the wilderness as they do, women may insensibly slip over to the advocacy of the bestial. Their participation in so many opposed realms already makes them constantly "impure" (at menstruation and pregnancy).[37] It may cause them to dissolve forms altogether in demonic chaos.

In the stereotyping of women as witches we also see the unmistakable evidences of "bad conscience," the attributed resentment that was mentioned earlier. Women are accused of being witches precisely because they are weak. Mingled contempt of the weak and fear of their necessarily mysterious power to endure and assert their own independent existence is apparently one of the universal characteristics of humanity.

In the stereotyping of witches we also see the inner history of humanity's relation to the land and to nature. In witchery a violated cosmos works its revenge. Women, as we know, are generally associated with the land. The fecundity of both is one of the central concerns of African cultures and religions. In typing the wilderness as "evil" and bad women as therefore of the bush, man admits his alienation from both. Witchery is not at home in the subjugated, passively cultivated fields or the village; it is the outsider, ever anxious to turn structure and culture back into antistructure and wilderness. Hunting metaphors deeply shape witchery ideology. The Fon say that the gbo of witchery were first revealed to hunters, and witches are said to worship Minona, Mother of the Wild. The Cewa like many other peoples associate animalistic incest with witchery and also with good hunting.[38] So do the Ila.[39] Zande witches like so many others meet in clearings or mountain tops far away in the bush to devour their victims and plan their assaults upon their unknowing, decent neighbors. When they weave their evil net of death around their victims, however, they are really merely hunting human beings, turning the human pursuit of animals into an animal pursuit of humans, and taking the part of the ravaged wilderness against the farmers who violate it. Thus the Zande define *no* as "to bewitch," and also as "to shoot" a gun or bow and arrow.[40] The Barotsi are only one among several central and southern African peoples to borrow "projectile magic" from the Bushman hunting rituals for use as outright sorcery.[41] We recall the continuity between hunting ritual and sorcery among the Mbuti Pygmies, but what is still a unified religious realm for the hunters, the bush and divinity, is split for agriculturalists into many separate spheres in which sorcery and witchcraft come to occupy their own thoroughly evil sphere of existence. The good cultivated earth is set against the wilderness, the good fertile woman against the witch of death and sterility, controlled and cultivated normative purpose against rebellious, free expression of chaotic impulse.

Nature, women, evil and death are all "limit conditions" for males who have subordinated themselves to social norms. In confronting these realities, man loses control and is in danger of being completely overwhelmed by the "otherness" without and the primitive ascending symbolisms and feelings within. There is a tendency to collapse these realities into each other and in stigmatizing some women as "witches," to seek control over them all. The inner longings for wild freedom are harshly but incompletely subordinated to meaning and value, for inner violence is repressed by doing violence to its surrogate embodiment. The more desperate and half-hearted the longing for strict and clear hierarchies in the cosmos, the more threatening are witches. Witches represent the formlessness that might dissolve our universe and that eats at our hearts endlessly. Only the transcendental divine order can save us from them and their corrosive implication of us all in their nightmare freedom and chaos.

CONCLUDING REMARKS

In considering together the three manifestations of divination, possession, and witchcraft, we confront what is often condemned as "magic" or "superstition." But it is evident that these three conceptual responses to the *otherness of existence* involve profoundly religious and metaphysical problems. No matter how pragmatic the apparent goal, these actions and ritual beliefs express entire world views, and their frequent occurrence in a culture implies a great deal about that culture's underlying religious attitudes. Each of these ways of understanding the self and its relation to otherness is in fact an individual perspective on the universe; that these perspectives are so elaborately developed to their separate conclusions often within the same society suggests not only that the society is highly differentiated but also that it is no longer possible in such a complex environment to unify the total cosmos and community through community ritual action. The approach to the unity we found among the Mbuti, Lega, and Lele, and to a lesser degree among the Ila and related societies, is lost among the Fon; and even among the Mande cultures like the Bambara and Dogon it is broken up into distinct perspectives and esoteric grades of initiation. The need to have esoteric secrets that are only disclosed to some members of the society assumes the inability to unify the religious universe in the rituals accessible to all. In these societies, we see the community as a unified cultic body replaced with numerous separate cults, initiation societies, and individualistic paths like divination, possession trance cults, and witchcraft. As we have noted, the extraordinary refinements of wisdom divination in the Fon religion and other African religions are associated with centralized kingship or strongly centralized and politically powerful secret societies, for only such institutions assure the temporal continuity and instructional uniformity necessary to build up far-reaching, philosophically complex wisdom systems. We have also noted the tendency for possession cults to arise in such societies, for here the heteronomous assignment of ego-identity is most likely. Just in such societies, too, we find a tendency to conceive of the dispositional order and its cosmology as distinct from experienced social structures. This can be expressed cultically in the esoteric tendency of wisdom to push the cosmology of the universe back into ever deeper, more elemental levels of existence; or as the capitulation of the person in possession trance to personal powers that break through and displace his own social environment and ego-identity. Or again, by the increasing dualism of realms that even splits human society into "good" people and totally demonic witches, the latter of whom have succumbed to their banal, transitory desires and reject all norms.

As we have seen, witchcraft is like possession and divination a meditation on freedom, but in terms now of its evil and antihuman potentialities. The very powers that in archaic times aided hunting cultures' shamans in guiding and healing their people are now inverted. The parallels to shamanism help us to understand both the history and meaning of witchcraft. Shamans, too, among the South African Bushmen who were once spread throughout the unforested portions of Africa, and among the Siberian and American Indian peoples, the Australian Aborigines and others, could fly, change shape into animal form, live in fire, become invisible, seize souls, and talk to the animals who were their helpers. Often a shaman meets with other shamans far away from the hunting band, on mountain tops, and he is initiated by being himself "torn apart" and "eaten" as a living sacrifice to and by ancestral shaman spirits. Witches, throughout Africa, go through similar ordeals and gain similar powers, although most tellingly, their initiation involves not their own self-sacrifice for the sake of gaining benevolent powers to heal others but the inversion of this: close relatives or even children are offered up to be eaten together with other initiates. Others are sacrificed, to gain malevolent power.

What do these remarkably similar symbolisms signify? Speaking of the shaman, Mircea Eliade suggests that

> they all express a break with the universe of daily life. The twofold purpose of this break is obvious: it is the transcendence and the freedom that are obtained, for example, through ascent, flight, invisibility, incombustibility of the body. . . . The desire for absolute freedom—that is, the desire to break the

bonds that keep him tied to earth, and to free himself from his limitations—is one of man's essential nostalgias. And the break from plane to plane effected by flight or ascent similarly signifies an act of transcendence; flight proves that one has transcended the human condition, has risen above it, by transmuting it through an excess of spirituality.[42]

As was said before, witchery accusations express the desperate longing for order. The claim of the ascending symbolisms for freedom is rejected as an expression of the demonic, and so represents itself through the image of the hated witch. The witch, for his part, presumably secretly enjoys all the hated freedoms that one lacks. In short, witchery both for the witch himself and the accusor is a meditation on the demonic and negative aspect of the nostalgia for absolute freedom.

The witch is the victim of powers and structures; he implies a universe so rigid and hostile to individual desire that the only recourse is a maddened rejection. The witch-accuser, of course, has not rejected those hierarchies and powers, but clearly there is a danger of it, which the witch has succumbed to. We note how often the witch is a person already on the periphery of society, an outcast; only a step further will carry him into complete inversion of values.

Yet there is an irony here, for the obsessive desire for freedom that the witch so hideously and pathetically embodies can only express itself through compulsive attention to the most banal and repulsive details of everyday life. The witch is not only a rebel exulting in perverse freedom, but he is also a prisoner of everyday life and the very structures he flees. He must abort all transformations, attack the entire divine order whenever it presents itself, for him to achieve self-definition as a free rebel. Since there is *no* other divine order, he only survives by continual engagements with the one he denies. Like a malevolent evangelist, he must try to communicate to others the isolation he himself "enjoys." In this is his entire character—that is, he has no true self, for his ego is identified with his passions. The finite desires are directed to the unrelenting, impossible, and therefore doomed compulsion to make themselves infinite. All "otherness" is evil to him, but the Other can never be avoided.

Sacrificial structures control all of these religious options. We need only mention the sacrificial core of divination, both possession and wisdom types; sacrifice usually ends and even begins consultations. The trickster is an image of sacrificial transformation, and often is the patron of divination (Legba for the Fon, Eshu for the Yoruba, Yurugu-Ogo for the Dogon, Telike for the Bambara, Ananse for the Ashanti, and so on). Possession cults likewise center on sacrifice, even of the self, while negative possession, i.e., witchcraft, characteristically inverts sacrifice in offering up hecatombs of victims to the hated divine order, in the futile hope one can escape from it. The multitude of the forms of otherness is humbling, but each provides the center in relation to which entire lives have lived and continue to live out their days.

NOTES TO CHAPTER 12

1. (Oxford: Clarendon Press, 1937).

2. Several essays in Robin Horton and Ruth Finnegan, eds., *Modes of Thought*, (London: Faber & Faber, 1973), refer to it, as do a number of the contributors to *Rationality*, ed. Bryan R. Wilson (New York: Harper and Row, 1970).

3. Evans-Pritchard, *Oracles*, pp. xviii and xxi.

4. E.E. Evans-Pritchard, *Nuer Religion* (Oxford: Clarendon Press, 1956), pp. 8, 100ff., 315; also see pp. 133, 139ff.

5. Evans-Pritchard, *Oracles*, pp. 10, 450ff., 465; see the trenchant critique of H. Philsooph, "Primitive Magic and Mana," *Man* n.s. 6, no. 2 (June 1971): 182-203, to whom I am indebted for some of the points in this paragraph.

6. Evans-Pritchard, *Oracles*, pp. 450-53.

7. Ibid., pp. 441f.; Evans-Pritchard seeks to underplay this derivation of *benge* and all medicines from Mbori, the supreme being, by saying that it is only "vague" and "mythological." These are very peculiar objections, which could no doubt serve to dismiss the major affirmations of any religion. The Zande demonstrate the mythic importance of *benge* by surrounding the search for it with elaborate rituals; the medicine itself is said to grow only where Mbori himself dwells, far off in dark, damp regions filled with caverns and streams. The pilgrimage to it must pass through alien territory, dangerous both for evil spirits and hostile human inhabitants. See ibid., pp. 215-19. The references recall the pilgrimage mystique surrounding the search for peyote among the Huichol Indians; see Barbara G. Myerhoff, *Peyote Hunt; The Sacred Journey of the Huichol Indians* (Ithaca: Cornell University Press, 1974). More to the point, the medicines are clearly symbolically homologous to the Lele pangolin, the Mbuti rainbow serpent-trumpet, and the Ila Itoshi serpents who all also dwell in similar regions and even effect many of the same reconciliations.

8. Melville J. Herskovits, *Dahomey: An Ancient West African Kingdom*, Vol. II, p. 243.

9. "Witchery" is meant to refer both to "sorcery" and to "witchcraft." These two were distinguished first by Evans-Pritchard, *Oracles*, and enthusiastically extended to all African instances by his disciples, but are now admitted to be often indistinguishable. See, e.g., Victor W. Turner, *The Forest of Symbols* (Ithaca: Cornell University Press, 1967), pp. 118-24.

10. Herskovits, *Dahomey*.

11. Ibid., pp. 262ff.

12. Ibid., p. 287.

13. Ibid.

14. Ibid.

15. Ibid., p. 287; also pp. 260ff.

16. Ibid., p. 260.

17. Ibid., pp. 261-87, 297-304. Herskovits holds that the gbo cultus is a separate stratum entirely of Fon religion, the least organized but the most pervasive; ibid., p. 297.

18. For general recent discussions of African witchery, see Geoffrey Parrinder, *Witchcraft: European and African* (Harmondsworth: Penguin, 1963); Lucy Mair, *Witchcraft* (New York: McGraw-Hill Book Co., 1969), and my study, "On the Nature of the Demonic: African Witchery," *Numen* 18, no. 3 (December 1971): 210-39.

19.   Cf. Clyde Kluckholm, *Navaho Witchcraft* (Boston: Beacon Press, 1967, 1944).

20.   In addition to the discussions in the works mentioned in the previous two notes, see Mary Douglas, ed., *Witchcraft: Accusations and Confessions* (London: Tavistock Publications, 1971); Max G. Marwick, *Sorcery in Its Social Setting* (Manchester: Manchester University Press, 1965), and *idem*, ed., *Witchcraft and Sorcery* (Baltimore: Penguin Books, 1970); John Middleton, ed., *Magic, Witchcraft and Curing*; American Museum Sourcebooks (Garden City, N.Y.: Natural History Press, 1967) and *idem* and E. H. Winter, eds., *Witchcraft and Sorcery in East Africa* (London: Routledge and Kegan Paul, 1963). All of these works provide further bibliographies.

21.   Monica Wilson, "Witch Beliefs and Social Structure," *American Journal of Sociology* 56 (1951): 307-13.

22.   David Tait, "Konkomba Sorcery," in *Magic, Witchcraft and Curing*, ed. John Middleton, p. 170.

23.   Ibid.

24.   Ibid., p. 156, 167.

25.   Leon Poliakov, *History of Anti-Semitism* (Madison: University of Wisconsin Press, 1969), Vol. I, pp. 102-105.

26.   James Littlejohn, "The Temne House," in *Myth and Cosmos: Readings in Mythology and Symbolism*, ed. John Middleton (Garden City, N.Y.: Natural History Press, 1967), p. 338.

27.   T.O. Beidelman, "Sorcery in Ukaguru," in *Witchcraft and Sorcery in East Africa*, eds. Middleton and Winter, p. 67.

28.   Ibid., p. 64.

29.   D.S. Oyler, "The Shilluk's Belief in the Evil Eye—The Evil Medicine Man," *Sudan Notes and Records* 2, no. 2 (April 1919): 131.

30.   Beidelman, "Sorcery in Ukaguru," pp. 61-62.

31.   Ibid., p. 62.

32.   R.G. Lienhardt; "Some Notions of Witchcraft among the Dinka," *Africa* 21, no. 4 (1951): 317-18, as quoted by Mary Douglas in her Introduction to *Witchcraft: Confessions and Accusations*, p. xxxv.

33.   For the Kaguru, see Beidelman, "Sorcery in Ukaguru," p. 68, and also note in the same volume Jean Buxton, "Mandari Witchcraft," p. 105.

34.   Cf. John Middleton, "Witchcraft and Sorcery in Lugbara," in ibid., pp. 271ff.; E.H. Winter, "The Enemy Within: Amba Witchcraft," in ibid., pp. 292ff.

35.   See Robert F. Gray, "Some Structural Aspects of Mbugwe Witchcraft," in ibid., p. 163, for a striking instance.

36.   Among the Cewa, for example, the "typical" witch is supposedly female, but the actually accused witches turn out to be 58 percent male, according to a survey taken by Marwick, *Sorcery in Its Social Setting*, pp. 96-103. Social stresses do however modify the sex image of witches in some societies: see S.F. Nadel, "Witchcraft in Four African Societies," *American Anthropologist* 51 (1952): 18-29, but also see the reservations expressed in my article "On the Nature of the Demonic: African Witchery," p. 215 n. 8.

37.   See Sherry Ortner, "Is Female to Male as Nature is to Culture?" in *Woman, Culture and Society*, eds. Michelle Z. Rosaldo and Louise Lamphere (Stanford: Stanford University Press, 1974), and other essays in this collection for some interesting developments of these ideas; also see Harriet Ngubane, "Some Notions of 'Purity' and 'Impurity' among the Zulu," *Africa* 46, no. 3 (1976): 274-84.

38.   An unprincipled hunter will put the bullets in his gun into his sister's bed, for her to sleep with close to her private parts; these bullets will certainly kill. See Marwick, *Sorcery in Its Social Setting*, pp. 70, 80. The Nso call incest "witchcraft of the sun," likening it to a kind of cannibalism: "It is like 'witchcraft of the night' because it is as though the culprits were eating one another and they would, unless action were taken, not only die or go mad but in some

cases bring death to their children and other members of the compound involved. It is described not merely as bad . . . or dreadful. . . , but as revolting or disgusting (*ko'oi*, a term also applied to a corpse found in a decayed state, to excrement, suicide, and leprosy)." Phyllis M. Kaberry, "Witchcraft of the Sun," in *Man in Africa*, ed. Kaberry and Mary Douglas (London: Tavistock Publications, 1969), p. 179. Here we see an extension of the common usage of "to eat" as "to have sexual intercourse" to incest, fusing together the acts of incest and cannibalism as really one single act, the basic impulse behind witchcraft.

39. Edwin W. Smith and A.M. Dale, *The Ila-Speaking Peoples of Northern Rhodesia* (London: Macmillan & Co., 1920), Vol. II, p. 135; I, p. 261.

40. Evans-Pritchard, *Oracles*, p. 37.

41. Cf. Barrie Reynolds, *Magic, Divination and Witchcraft among the Barotse of Northern Rhodesia* (Berkeley: University of California Press, 1963), pp. 39-41, 59, 79, 83; and Isaac Schapera, *The Khoisan Peoples of South Africa*, (London: George Routledge and Sons, 1930), pp. 195-201.

42. Mircea Eliade, *Rites and Symbols of Initiation: Birth and Rebirth* (New York: Harper & Row, 1958), p. 101; see the full discussion in Eliade, *Shamanism: Archaic Techniques of Ecstasy* (New York: Pantheon Books, 1964), although the connection to witchcraft ideology is not made.

Chapter 13

The Sanctification of Life through Ritual

There is a central irony that we have been skirting throughout the entire discussion of various African religions. We have found amazing depths of spiritual insight in one after another of the ritual structures of African religions, yet most of these religions do not insist on intellectual elaborations or justifications for their actions. Those that have developed complex esoteric systems, as we have seen, are in a way announcing the religious insufficiency of their world, not its spiritual fullness. Ritual, that is to say, is spiritually more profound than any theology; it accomplishes more for those who participate in it than any number of rarified mystical treatises for jaded antiritualistic modern connoisseurs of the "occult." Yet ritual is not immediately universalistic or profound. It deals with very specific realities that are not transportable into our living room for our casual inspection.

Yet the very concreteness of ritual is its profundity, while (to take up the other side of the same paradox), the very universality of our favorite theology is its superficiality. It may be dismaying to say so, but we must conclude that if the Lega, Mbuti, Lele, Ila, Ndembu, and others we have considered made less use of concrete ritual and proverbial symbolism, and more use of abstract metaphysics, their cults might seem more immediately comprehensible and "profound" to us, but their efficacy and self-authenticating reality to participants would be much less.

The deepest form of knowing is through doing. Being is less adequate a religious good than Becoming. In the final analysis, it is only when we act out concretely our deepest convictions that they become our real convictions, that we truly experience their truth—or discover their falsity. As human beings, we are in constant flight from our own concrete existence; we take refuge in idealities such as myth and theology, we long for primordial being, and we thirst for ultimate states that will remove us from our own insufficiencies and mortality. Pascal put it very well in his *Pensées* when he described man as caught between two infinities, the infinity of the immense vastness of the universe and what lies beyond, and the infinity of the nothingness that dwells within every atom of our being. Because of that, Pascal declared, man flees from himself; he cannot endure to contemplate himself; he develops philosophies, states, machines, anything to forget himself for just a moment, to avoid recognizing his mere mortality. Science, too, serves this function, to help man pretend he is more than just a body doomed to disease, old age, and death.

Perhaps that is why we do not appreciate ritual. Ritual immerses us in process and Becoming, forces us back into the concrete, and makes us recognize our body. We wish to deny this two-eyed, ten-fingered, two-legged aspect of ourselves; ritual does not let us. It is too humbling, especially now when Western man's hubris, and the risks that pride entails, are so much greater. Ritual and the scientific attitude are poles apart. The one urges and even forces us into an acceptance of our "built-in" limitations, the other receives all its inspiration from our desire to destroy those limitations. At least intellectually, we hope to encompass the entire universe and master it. But even the most "magical" ritual, as we have seen, is as much appeal and supplication as it is mechanical anticipation. The greatest truth in the world of magic is mystery.

What we must realize about ritual, perhaps, is not only that it announces our limits and humbles us by showing us our bodies, but also that it indicates that our limits and bodies are sanctified participants in a larger marvelous whole, a divine order. Just because ritual does this to us on the bodily level, it can be nothing else than concrete and specific, engaging our particular sensory world, our family and neighbors, our house and plowing instruments. This is the saving grace of ritual, in every sense. The remarkable thing is that this grace is directly experienced. It is not theoretical.

It *is* in fact possible for us to understand the miraculous power of ritual intellectually (though not as such to experience it). A great deal of our discussion so far has been really on this theme, especially the discussion of the way ritual unifies the ascending sensory symbolisms of the body and its world and the descending systematic symbolisms developed in clear thought. In an early discussion of ritual symbolism, Susanne Langer already mused on the interesting fact that so much ritual surrounds the most common and banal bodily functions, such as eating and sexuality.[1] Just the pervasiveness of these two themes has permitted entire theories of ritual, one type arguing that all ritual centers on increasing the food supply (through magical acts, of course)—we think of Sir James Frazer, for example, and the entire myth-and-ritual school—the other arguing that all ritual expresses sexual Oedipal complexes. But we can now suggest a more profound reason for this striking fact. Not only in the areas of sexuality and eating (two of the most rudimentary and powerful of bodily experiences) but also elsewhere ritual makes use of activities that are deeply familiar and intimate, which when engaged in involve the body very strongly and emotionally, or which have perhaps been done so often that they have taken on a habitual and automatic nature. These actions have thus become part of the deepest and most certain underlying reality of the experiential world. They are deeply "known." The very depth with which they are known makes them largely preconscious. They involve too much of the self to be directly cognized in clear thought; only symbols can begin to reach to all the levels of experience involved. Especially since these experiences are *actions*, even cognitive symbols do not directly touch them. Only actional symbols, i.e., rituals, can involve these deep layers of reality. But rituals "raise" these experiences into an explicitly divine order and conform them to divine imperatives. From the roots of his being man is brought into contact with transcendental norms. Ascending symbols and descending symbolisms are united in the moment of action. And since these most common actions involve the widest area of each person's experience, their associations branching out and touching almost everything, the ritualization of them affects the individual in all areas of his being.

In a more philosophical sense, we may use the categories suggested by Edmund Husserl in his analysis of consciousness as such. He finds two basic realms interacting in all experience. There is the For Itself of consciousness, which can never escape itself and its own relative perspectives on everything, and the In Itself of "things-in-themselves," which always lies isolated and self-sufficient outside of any direct knowledge we may obtain of objects.[2] When we perceive a rock, what we perceive are really our *own perceptions*; the rock remains forever beyond our ken in its own inwardness. Consciousness, therefore, is trapped in itself. This is why Descartes tried to break through the solipsistic trap by asserting that at least insofar as I can think about, and doubt, everything, I am sure of being real in myself. It is a pathetic ruse and not really convincing.

Rather, the location of consciousness in a body is its sole guarantee that there exists a bridge into an objective world. The body is both a thing and a generative medium of consciousness. It unites in a most wondrous fashion the In Itself and the For Itself. It sets flexible but decisive limits to the awareness it sustains. We always run the danger that in seeking to escape it we abandon ourselves to unreality and madness. Thus the body is the actualizer in every sense of consciousness and gives consciousness a shape. Could an awareness that was not anchored somewhere in time or space have any structure at all? Would it not disappear entirely?—Metaphysical questions, like how many angels can dance on the head of a pin. In fact, the specific body of the author, and of the reader, make possible any relation at all between them, or any thoughts at all. However, ritual, the way the body articulates *true, enduring, and ideal structures* in its world, is the highest mode the body has for melding together consciousness and physicality. Ritual is the highest form, it therefore follows, of the unity between the In Itself of awareness, and the For Itself of the world. It is the heart of religion. No intellectual exegesis can replace it.

These everyday miracles of ritual cannot be admired enough, and they are worthy of all our contemplative efforts. The core impulse of ritual, as we have seen in so many ways in the previous pages, is the integration of all experiential realities (material, sensory-motor or "orectic," personal, social, and ideal) in transcendental "otherness." That is why no explanation of it that focuses on only one of these realities or levels of experience can finally do justice to ritual or religion. The functionalist will argue that ritual is basically social and will instruct us on the constant social referents of religious behavior, but the Freudian will scorn the seemingly tight reasoning of his colleague and insist that instead all religion is shaped by the irresistible logic of the passions and the libido. The consistency of a Geza Roheim (to name one prominent anthropologist-psychoanalyst) is indeed admirable, but it does not convince the structuralists, whose logic is even more rigid and scholastic. Religion, they say, is really merely the working out of absolute cognitive laws that govern the universal Mind: each culture and religion is really the essentially meaningless cybernetic experiment of thought with itself.[3] Or they will eschew such extreme idealism and instead point to the social concomitants of all thought, thus building up a dialectical calculus of social stimulus and cognitive response. Many of the results of such endeavors are indeed enlightening (though some especially relating to Judaism and Christianity, are distorted dismayingly by quite unstructuralistic bias and passion, not to say prejudice),[4] but in the final analysis ritual and religion itself escapes their net. In fact, the more they close the circle of their logic upon themselves, the more scholastic and irrelevant the demonstrations become.

This cul-de-sac is inevitable for any reductionistic theory of religion. Yet each theory does in truth connect together a great number of important facts. It can be understood that this is possible, when we remember the multivalent, multidimensional property of ritual symbols so often pointed out in our discussions. Thus the Mbuti rituals made use of material items like whistles or trumpets and invoked sexual analogies in the process of distinguishing social roles and space, relating the band to the moon and forest, and cognitively combining serpent, elephant, and leopard. However all this got its focus by being united in the forest-deity. We could start from any level of Mbuti experience, cognitive, sexual, social, mythic, or what have you, and involve all the realities that they recognized. Symbols bind together many things, and thus they are constituted as symbols.[5] But none of these approaches can explain the religiosity of ritual, simply because they are internal to the symbol. The symbol exists as such only because it refers to something it is not. Religiously, it refers to the transcendental center of all reality, of which all things social, sexual, cognitive, and so on pivot. This center is both primordial and normative; it undergirds the Pygmy universe, and therefore is not identical with anything in it. The explanation of ritual symbols, therefore, must recognize that only a totalistic approach, based on the transcendental intentionality of symbols, can even begin to be adequate to them.

Thus the Ila home, village and universe utter forth the mysterious structures of eternity; the new year's festival among them, the Ashanti and others is the repetition of primordial creation; the Shilluk divine king's "disappearance and resurrection" manifests again the first deeds constituting reality; and even the Ndembu girl's initiation repeats the first woman's entry into true femininity. In the appropriation of the symbolic structures of reality, the Nyakyusa mourner transcends his or her own physical limitations, passions, and social station—so that he or she can truly accept them again as part of a divine order. Ritual saves from madness, including the madness of partial explanations of life that are bound finally to fail before the mute fullness of a simple ritual gesture, or even the perceptual actuality of a stone.

Ritual, that is to say, may be rooted in the body, but it achieves expression only in otherness. The transcendental center of symbolic action is the real heart of ritual. Ritual mediates between real and ideal, flesh and mind, material and spiritual, giving each a shape which is that of the other. "Centeredness," as we called it earlier, is the real action of ritual, through which Being is translated into Becoming.

Thus, through such other-centeredness, the whole of life can be sanctified. "The means by which its sanctification is brought about are various, but the result is always the same: life is lived on a twofold plane; it takes its course as human existence and, at the same time, shares in a transhuman life, that of the cosmos or the gods."[6] African spirituality, above and beyond the specific focus of particular ritual actions, is always a piety directed toward the sanctity of the universe as a whole. Every action on its deepest level seeks to sustain the divine order and its continual self-regeneration; in this sense every ritual enactment, however superficially oriented to utilitarian goals, is utterly selfless. The African who unself-consciously and humbly bends, sweating in the brilliant sunlight, over some "medicines" and dirt mounds at the edge of his field to invoke the ancestors and God, is not just praying for the maintenance of his family and fields. In the deepest level of himself, he is praying for the preservation of the entire astonishing fruit-bearing reality he moves in and knows so well, from the celestial spirits to the textures of the wild grasses in his fingers.

NOTES TO CHAPTER 13

1. Susanne Langer, *Philosophy in a New Key* (New York: Penguin Books, 1948), pp. 130-31.

2. Edmund Husserl, *Ideas: General Introduction to Pure Phenomenology*, trans. W.R. Boyce Gibson (New York: Collier Books, 1962), pp. 120ff., 134, 139, etc. In a way, what the For Itself of consciousness means is that thought is innately without any form at all; the relativity of perspectives is infinite, and infinitely contradictory. It is really the horror of this chaos, perhaps, that Pascal expressed in his meditations on the "two infinities"; all human action is an attempt to anchor possible realities in the surely real, producing the flight from the self into things or ideas or even ecstatic states. Man seeks to know the In Itself beyond the body, forgetting that the body is the only path to contact with otherness, and is actually already a thing "in itself."

3. See Claude Lévi-Strauss, *Mythologiques* (Paris: Plon, 1964), 4 vols., and the considerations of his method in Ino Rossi, ed., *The Unconsciousness in Culture; The Structuralism of Claude Lévi-Strauss in Perspective* (New York: E.P. Dutton, 1974). A disciple of Lévi-Strauss who has followed the implications of the meaninglessness of mythic and all other forms of thought to their final conclusion is Dan Sperber, *Rethinking Symbolism*, trans. Alice Morton (New York: Cambridge University Press, 1975).

4. Edmund Leach, for example, permits his desire to discredit biblical and later Judaism on behalf of Christianity confuse completely his supposedly structuralist analysis of *Genesis as Myth, and Other Essays* (London: Jonathan Cape, 1970): the Eden story is dealt with on the level of unconscious but "universal" motifs (life, death, incest, marriage), but Solomon's genealogy is discussed on the level of unconscious but nonuniversal exclusivism, while the Virgin Birth passages of the New Testament are read on a phenomenological, conscious and nonuniversal level. Leach's treatment of the Solomon question is criticized in a devastating essay by Margaret Pamment, "The Succession of Solomon: A Reply to Edmund Leach's Essay 'The Legitimacy of Solomon'," *Man* n.s. 7, no. 4 (December 1972): 635-43; also see Maurice Bloch, review of *Genesis as Myth*, *Man* n.s. 5, no. 3 (September 1970): 530-31 and Bertel Nathhorst, *Formal or Structural Studies of Traditional Tales;* Stockholm Studies in Comparative Religion, 9 (Stockholm: Almqvist & Wiksell, 1969). The confusion evident here about what level of consciousness structuralism applies to and how is not in fact unusual in structuralist circles. Lévi-Strauss himself argued for the conscious coherency and "tightness" of Australian totemism and similar forms of classificatory thought, in *The Savage Mind* (Chicago: University of Chicago Press, 1966) and in *Totemism*, trans. Rodney Needham (Boston: Beacon Press, 1963), while most of his other writings, and especially *Mythologiques*, assume the looseness and incoherency of any particular conscious cultural system: only unconscious processes working themselves out in regional, continental, and even world-wide patterns can explain the structures of local conscious thought.

5. See Heinz Werner and Bernard Kaplan, *Symbol Formation* (New York: John Wiley & Sons, 1963), or Jean Piaget, *Play, Dreams, and Imitation in Childhood*, trans. C. Gattegno and F.M. Hodgson (New York: W.W. Norton and Co., 1962).

6. Mircea Eliade, *The Sacred and the Profane*, trans. Willard R. Trask (New York: Harcourt, Brace and Co., 1959), p. 167.

Selected Bibliography

(Articles in symposia and anthologies are not listed separately)

Adler, Alfred and Andras Zemplani. *Le Bâton de l'aveugle: Divination, maladie et pouvoir chez les Moundang du Tchad.* Paris: Hermann, 1972.

Bascom, William R. "The Sociological Role of the Yoruba Cult Group." *American Anthropologist* 44 (1944).

_____. *Ifa Divination: Communication between Gods and Men in West Africa.* Bloomington, London: Indiana University Press, 1969.

Baumann, Hermann. *Schöpfung und Urzeit des Menschen im Mythus der afrikanischen Völker.* Berlin: Dietrich Reimer, 1936.

_____. *Das Doppelte Geschlecht.* Berlin: Dietrich Reimer, 1955.

_____, and Dietrich Westerman. *Les Peuples et les civilisations de l'Afrique.* Translated by L. Homburger. Paris: Payot, 1957.

Beattie, John. "Aspects of Bunyoro Symbolism." *Africa* 38:4 (October 1968): 413-32.

_____, and John Middleton, eds. *Spirit Mediumship and Society in Africa.* London: Routledge, Kegan & Paul, 1970.

Beidelman, T.O. "The Ox and Nuer Sacrifice." *Man* 1 (1966): 453-67.

_____. "Swazi Royal Ritual." *Africa* 36:4 (October 1966): 373-405.

_____, ed. *The Translation of Culture.* London: Tavistock Publications, 1971.

Biebuyck, Daniel. *Lega Culture: Art, Initiation and Moral Philosophy among a Central African People.* Berkeley: University of California Press, 1973.

Bourguignon, Erika. *Possession.* San Francisco: Chandler & Sharp, 1976.

_____, ed. *Religion, Altered States of Consciousness and Social Change.* Columbus: Ohio State University Press, 1973.

Calame-Griaule, Geneviève. *Ethnologie et langage: La parole chez les Dogon.* Paris: Gallimard, 1966.

Chodorow, Nancy. "Being and Doing: A Cross-Cultural Examination of the Socialization of Males and Females." In *Woman in Sexist Society,* edited by Vivian Gornick and Barbara K. Moran. New York, London: Basic Books, 1971.

Cunnison, Ian. "Headmanship and the Ritual of Luapula Villages." *Africa* 26:1 (January 1956): 2-16.

de Heusch, Luc. *Le roi ivre, out l'origine de l'état; mythes et rites Bantous.* Paris: Gallimard, 1972.

Deren, Maya. *Divine Horsemen: Voodoo Gods of Haiti.* New York: Chelsea House, 1970.

Dieterlen, Germaine. *Essai sur la religion Bambara.* Paris: Presses Universitaires de France, 1951.

————, and Meyer Fortes, eds. *African Systems of Thought.* London: Oxford University Press, 1965.

Douglas, Mary. *The Lele of the Kasai.* London: Oxford University Press, 1963.

————. "Animals in Lele Religious Thought." *Africa* 27: 1 (January 1957): 46-58.

————. *Purity and Danger: An Analysis of Concepts of Pollution and Taboo.* New York: Frederick A. Praeger, 1966.

————. *Natural Symbols: Explorations in Cosmology.* New York: Pantheon Press, 1970.

————, ed. *Witchcraft: Accusations and Confessions.* London: Tavistock Publications, 1971.

Durkheim, Emile. *The Elementary Forms of the Religious Life.* Translated by Joseph W. Swain. New York: Collier Books, 1961.

————, and Marcel Mauss. *Primitive Classification.* Translated by Rodney Needham. Chicago: University of Chicago Press, 1963.

Eliade, Mircea. *Cosmos and History: The Myth of the Eternal Return.* Translated by W. R. Trask. New York: Harper & Brothers, 1959.

————. *Patterns of Comparative Religion.* Translated by Rosemary Sheed. Cleveland: World Publishing Co., 1963.

Evans-Pritchard, E.E. *Witchcraft, Oracles and Magic among the Azande.* Oxford: Clarendon Press, 1937.

————. *Nuer Religion.* Oxford: Clarendon Press, 1956.

————. *Social Anthropology and Other Essays.* New York: Free Press, 1962.

Field, Margaret Joyce. *Religion and Medicine of the Ga People.* London: Oxford University Press, 1937.

Forde, Daryll, ed. *African Worlds: Studies in the Cosmological and Social Values of African Peoples.* London: Oxford University Press, 1954.

Fortes, Meyer, and E.E. Evans-Pritchard, eds. *African Political Systems.* London: Oxford University Press, 1940.

Gelfand, Michael. *Shona Religion*. Cape Town: Juta & Co., 1962.

Gluckman, Max. "The Lozi of Barotseland in North-Western Rhodesia." In *Seven Tribes of British Central Africa*, edited by Elizabeth Colson and Max Gluckman. London: Oxford University Press, 1951.

_____. *Politics, Law and Ritual in Tribal Society*. New York: New American Library, 1965.

Goody, Jack and Joan Buckley, "Inheritance and Women's Labour in Africa." *Africa* 43: 2 (April 1973): 109-21.

Griaule, Marcel. *Conversations with Ogotemmêli*. London: Oxford University Press, 1965.

_____, and Germaine Dieterlen, *Le Renard pâle*. Travaux et Mémoires, 72. Paris: Institut d'Ethnologie, 1965.

Herskovits, Melville J. *Dahomey: An Ancient West African Kingdom*. 2 vols. New York: Augustin, 1938.

_____, and Francis S. Herskovits. *An Outline of Dahomean Religious Belief*. Memoire, 41. New York: American Anthropological Association, 1933.

Hofmayr, Wilhelm. *Die Schilluk: Geschichte, Religion und Leben eines Niloten-Stammes*. Anthropos Bibliothek, II, 5. St. Gabriel, Modling bei Wien: Anthropos Verlag, 1925.

Horton, Robin. "Ritual Man in Africa." *Africa* 34: 2 (April 1964): 85-103.

_____. "African Traditional Thought and Western Science." *Africa*, 37: 1 & 2 (January and April 1967): 50-71, 155-87.

_____, and Ruth Finnegan, eds. *Modes of Thought: Essays on Thinking in Western and Non-Western Societies*. London: Faber & Faber, 1973.

Hubert, H., and M. Mauss. *Mélanges d'Histoire des Religions*. Paris: Alcan, 1909.

Husserl, Edmund. *Cartesian Meditations*. Translated by Dorion Cairns. The Hague: Martinus Nijhoff, 1973.

La Fontaine, Jean, ed. *The Interpretation of Ritual*. London: Tavistock Publications, 1972.

Leach, Edmund. "Ritualization in Man." *Philosophical Transactions of the Royal Society*, Series B, Col. 251 (1966), 403-408.

Lebeuf, Jean-Paul. *L'Habitation des Fali, montagnards du Cameroun septentrional*. Paris: Hachette, 1961.

Lessa, William A. and Evon Z. Vogt. eds. *Reader in Comparative Religion: An Anthropological Approach*. 3d ed. N.Y.: Harper & Row, 1972.

Lévi-Strauss, Claude. *The Savage Mind*. Chicago: University of Chicago Press, 1966.

Lewis, I.M. *Ecstatic Religion: An Anthropological Study of Spirit Possession and Shamanism.* Baltimore: Penguin Books, 1971.

Little, Kenneth. "The Role of the Secret Society in Cultural Specialization." *American Anthropologist* 51 (1949): 199-212.

Long, Charles H. "The West African High God: History and Religious Experience." *History of Religions* 3: 2 (1964): 328-42.

McCall, Daniel F. "Wolf Courts Girl: The Equivalence of Hunting and Mating in Bushman Thought." *Papers in International Studies,* Africa Series, 7. Athens, Ohio: Ohio University Center for International Studies, 1970.

Maupoil, Bernard. *La Géomancie à l'ancienne Côte des Esclaves.* Travaux et Mémoires, 42. Paris: Institut d'Ethnologie, 1943.

Mbiti, John. *African Religions and Philosophy.* New York: Praeger Publishers, 1969.

Marwick, Max G. *Sorcery in Its Social Setting: A Study of the Northern Rhodesian Cewa.* Manchester: Manchester University Press, 1965.

————, "How Real is the Charmed Circle in African and Western Thought?" *Africa* 43:1 (January 1973) :59-71.

Merleau-Ponty, Maurice. *The Phenomenology of Perception.* Translated by Colin Smith. New York: Humanities Press, 1962.

Middleton, John. *Lugbara Religion: Ritual and Authority among an East African People.* London: Oxford University Press, 1960.

————, and E. H. Winter, eds. *Witchcraft and Sorcery in East Africa.* London: Routledge & Kegan Paul, 1963.

Murdock, George Peter. *Africa: Its Peoples and Their Culture-History.* New York: McGraw-Hill Book Co., 1959.

Needham, Rodney, ed. *Right and Left: Essays on Dual Symbolic Classification.* Chicago, London: University of Chicago Press, 1973.

Pettersson, Olof. *Chiefs and Gods: Religious and Social Elements in the South Eastern Bantu Kingship.* Dissertation, Lunds Universitet, 1953. Lund: CWK Gleerup, 1953.

Piaget, Jean. *Play, Dreams, and Imitation in Childhood.* Translated by C. Gattegno and F.M. Hodgson. New York: W.W. Norton & Co., 1962.

Radcliffe-Brown, A.R. and Daryll Forde, eds. *African Systems of Kinship and Marriage.* London: Oxford University Press, 1950.

Ray, Benjamin C. *African Religions: Symbol, Ritual and Community.* Prentice-Hall Studies in Religion. Englewood Cliffs, New Jersey: Prentice-Hall, 1976.

Reynolds, Barrie. *Magic, Divination and Witchcraft among the Barotse of*

Northern Rhodesia. Robin Series III. Berkeley: University of California Press, 1963.

Richards, Audrey I. *Chisungu.* London: Faber & Faber, 1956.

Rosaldo, Michelle Zimbalist and Louise Lamphere, eds. *Woman, Culture and Society.* Stanford: Stanford University Press, 1974.

Rosaldo, Michelle Zimbalist and Jane Monnig Atkinson. "Man the Hunter and Woman: Metaphors for the Sexes in Ilongot Magical Spells." In *The Interpretation of Symbolisms*, edited by Roy Willis. ASA Studies, 3. New York: John Wiley & Co., 1975.

Schärer, Hans. *Ngaju Religion: The Concept of God Among a South Borneo People.* Translated by Rodney Needham. The Hague: Martinus Nijhoff, 1963.

Schebesta, Paul. *Die Bambuti-Pygmäen vom Ituri.* Bd. I-II. Mémoires, Institut Royal Colonial Belge, Section des Sciences Morales et Politiques, Coll.-in-4°, IV. Brussels: Georges van Campenhout, 1938-50.

______. *Les Pygmées du Congo Belge.* Mémoires, Institut Royal Colonial Belge, Section des Sciences Morales et Politiques, Coll.-in-8^0, XXVI, 2. Brussels: Duculot, 1952.

Seligman, C.G. "Cult of Nyakang and the Divine Kings of the Shilluk." *Wellcome Tropical Research Laboratories, Fourth Report.* Vol. B: General Science. Khartoum: Published for the Department of Education, Sudan Government, 1911.

Smith, Edwin W., ed. *African Ideas of God: A Symposium.* 2nd Ed. London: Edinburgh House Press, 1961.

______, and A.M. Dale. *The Ila-Speaking Peoples of Northern Rhodesia.* 2 Vols. London: Macmillan & Co., 1920.

Stanner, W.E.H. *On Aboriginal Religion.* Oceania Monograph, 11, Sydney: University of Sydney, 1966.

Thomas, Elizabeth Marshall. *The Harmless People.* New York: Vintage Books, 1958.

Turnbull, Colin. *The Forest People: A Study of the Pygmies of the Congo.* Garden City, N.Y.: Doubleday and Co., in cooperation with the American Museum of Natural History, 1962.

______. *Wayward Servants.* Garden City, N.Y.: Natural History Press, 1965.

Turner, Victor W. *The Forest of Symbols: Aspects of Ndembu Ritual.* Ithaca: Cornell University Press, 1967.

______. *The Drums of Affliction: A Study of Religious Processes among the Ndembu of Zambia.* Oxford: Clarendon Press, 1968.

————.*The Ritual Process: Structure and Anti-Structure.* Chicago: Aldine, 1969.

————. *Revelation and Divination in Ndembu Ritual.* Ithaca: Cornell University Press, 1975.

van Gennep, Arnold. *The Rites of Passage.* Translated by Monika B. Vizedom and Gabrielle L. Caffe. Chicago: University of Chicago Press, 1960.

Werner, Heinz, and Bernard Kaplan. *Symbol Formation.* New York: John Wiley & Sons, 1963.

Willis, Roy. *Man and Beast.* New York: Basic Books, 1974.

Wilson, Monica. *Rituals of Kinship among the Nyakyusa.* London: Oxford University Press, 1957.

————. *Communal Rituals of the Nyakyusa.* London: Oxford University Press, 1959.

————. "Nyakyusa Rituals and Symbolism." In *Myth and Cosmos: Readings in Myth and Symbolism,* edited by John Middleton. Garden City, N.Y.: Natural History Press, 1967.

Young, Michael W. "The Divine Kingship of the Jukun: A Reevaluation of Some Theories." *Africa* 36: 2 (April 1966): 135-52.

Zahan, Dominique. *Société d'initiation Bambara.* Paris: Mouton, 1960.

————. *La Dialectique du verbe chez les Bambara.* The Hague: Mouton, 1963.

Zuesse, Evan M. "Meditation on Ritual." *Journal of the American Academy of Religion* 43: 3 (September 1975): 517-30.

————"Action as the Way of Transcendence: the Religious Significance of the Bwami Cult of the Lega." *Journal of Religion in Africa* 9:1 (1978): 62-72.

Zwernemann, Jürgen. *Die Erde in Vorstellungswelt und Kultpraktiken der sudanischen Völker.* Berlin: Dietrich Reimer, 1968.

Index

Abnormality, 3-4, 7, 67, 120, 122, 124, 128. *See also* Liminality; Monsters; Rituals, "Obscenities" in; Rituals, of reversal; Witchery.

Action, as the deepest mode of transcendence, 238-42. *Also see* Body image; Centering.

African peoples, ethnic history of, 17, 36 n.1.

Agriculture, and religious symbolisms, 26, 63-71, 158, 160, 161, 187, 231-32; economic forms of, and women's status, 79. *Also see* Conquests and settling land; Earth; Matrilineality; Priests of the Earth; Women; Witchery.

Alienation, 20, 176, 186, 191, 226-32. *Also see* Evil and the Demonic.

Alur (Uganda-Zaire), 184, 200-01.

Ancestor cult, 81, 82, 86, 112, 116, 156, 192, 207.

Ancestors, 19, 37 n.8, 86, 93, 107 n.99, 108, 114, 124, 125, 127, 158, 219, 228.

Androgeneity, 51, 57 n.10, 81, 159, 161, 207.

Anthropological study of religion, ix, 4. *Also see* Culture-historical anthropology; French school of anthropology; Functionalist anthropology; Marxist anthropology; Myth and Ritual school; Structuralist anthropology.

Anti-structure, 122, 130 n.42, 227-28, 231. *Also see* Abnormality; Evil and the Demonic.

Arabs, 131 n.52, 164 n.7. *Also see* Islam.

"Ascending" and "Descending" symbolisms, *see* Symbolism.

Asceticism, 31-32, 39 n.40. *Also see* Taboos, sexual.

Ashanti (Ghana), 116, 217, 221 n.33, 234.

Astrology, 211, 220 n.25, 221 n.38.

Architextural symbolism, 79-86, 158-59, 160, 161. *Also see* Women, and domestic space.

Bambara (Mali), 152-56, 232, 234.

Bantu cultures, 5, 23, 34, 41-42, 56, 58 n.10, 124, 151. *Also see* Central Bantu.

Barotsi, *see* Lozi.

Baumann, Hermann, 26, 38 n.27, 58 n.10 & 19, 104 n.2, 165 n.16.

Beidelman, T.O., 130 n.37; 236 n.30.

Biebuyck, Daniel, 5.

Birth rites, 20, 29, 82-83, 88. *See also* Rites of passage; Rituals.

Blood brotherhood, 30, 39 n.32.

Body image, 45, 131 n.48, 143-49, 158-61, 186, 228-30, 239-41. *Also see* Social aspects of ritual and symbolism.

Booth, Newell S., 129 n.7.

Bourguignon, Erica, 187-88, 203 n.4-6, etc.

Brainwashing, 148-49.

Buber, Martin, 122.

Bushmen (South Africa), 17, 30, 36 n.1, 40 n.46, 55, 60-63, 231, 233.

Cannibalism, 226-30, 236 n.38.

Cassirer, Ernst, 26, 53, 58 n.24.

Centering, as the essential religious process, 126-28, 145-49, 178, 183, 242. *Also see* Repentance; Rituals, and space.

Central Bantu, 38 n.30, 39 n.32, 124; as culture-province, 78-79, 96, 104 n.1-2; chieftainship amongst the, 94; myths of, 131 n.48-49; smithing, 96; women's initiations amongst the, 83, 136.

"Central" symbolism, 77.

Cewa (Zambia), 231, 236 n.36 & 38.

Chameleon, 21, 45, 58 n.10.

Chieftainship, religious aspects of, 63, 78, 87-95, 110, 115, 117-25, 129 n.33, 157, 183. *Also see* Conquest and settling land; Culture-heroes; Kingship, divine; Priests of the Earth; Rainmakers; Women, and chieftainship; Witchery, and chiefs.

Chinese and East Asian religions, 19, 46, 165 n.17, 191, 220 n.25, 221 n.35.

Chokwe (Angola), 96, 193.

Christianity, ix, 3, 7, 21, 32, 39 n.40, 46, 57 n.3, 109, 129 n.4, 131 n.53, 165 n.17, 170, 174 n.5 & 11, 199, 204 n.25, 227, 241, 243 n.4.

"Closed" religious universes, 128, 131 n.53, 183.

Conquest and settling land, 41, 87, 92, 94, 119-20, 157. *Also see* Culture-heroes; Earth.

Consciousness, modes or levels of, 6, 43-44, 124-28, 128 n.1, 135, 167, 173, 176-79, 192, 194, 198-99, 202, 211-12, 240-42, 243 n.2 & 4. *Also see* Action; Body image; Centering; Dispositional awareness; Preconscious awareness; Symbolism.

251

Index

Otto, Rudolf, 3-5, 7.
Ovimbundu (Angola), 194.

Paleolithic culture and ritual, 17-18, 26, 38 n.28, 46, 62, 72 n.12.
Pangolin or scaly anteater, 11, 69, 103, 235 n.7. *See also* Monster; Pools and rivers; Serpent.
"Paradigmatic" aspect of ritual, 29. *See also* Mythic archetypes; Ritual; Symbolism.
Pascal, 238-39, 243 n.2.
Pedi (South Africa), 222 n.22.
"Performative" aspect of ritual, 52, 58 n.22. *See also* Action; Ritual.
Pettersson, Olof, 56.
Phenomenological approach, defined, ix, 4, 8-9, 12, 141. *See also* Eliade; Husserl; Merleau-Ponty; Schütz; van der Leeuw.
Piaget, Jean, 145, 149 n.1-2, 243 n.5.
Plato, 219 n.19.
Pondo (Zambia), 226.
Pools and rivers, 23-24, 35, 67-68, 94, 102-03, 107 n.82 & 99, 156-57. *See also* Serpent.
Possession, ideology and trance, 46, 104 n.2, 113, 119, 166, 171, 183-205, 206-09, 211-12, 224-25.
Prayer, 7, 24, 35, 43-44, 99, 100-101, 102, 111, 112, 113, 124, 126-28, 171, 224, 242.
Preconscious awareness, 35, 63, 65, 66, 68, 135, 137, 141-49, 176-79, 240. *Also see* Consciousness; Dispositional Awareness; Symbolism.
Prejudice, religious-theological, 3-5, 10, 41-43, 57 n.1 & 3, 58 n.11, 129 n.4, 131 n.53, 174 n.5, 203 n.6, 227, 231, 241.
Priests of the Earth, 5, 78, 93-94, 157. *See also* Earth; Kingship; Rainmakers.
Prophets, 101-02, 110, 164, 165 n.17, 186, 217, 221 n.34. *See also* Supreme being.
Proverbs, 5-7, 9-11, 153, 210.
Pygmies, 17-60, 63, 64, 65, 77, 104 n.1, 188, 231, 232, 235 n.7. *See also* Negritoes of South-east Asia.

Radcliffe-Brown, A.R., 141.
Rainmakers, 78, 183. *Also see* Chieftainship; Kingship; Priests of the Earth; Prophets.
Rāmānuja, 36. *Also see* Indian religions.
Religion, characterization of, 4, 11-12, 177, 238-42; and the two transcendental intentionalities, 4, 12, 170-71, 177, 211-12; and "centering," 126-28, 145-49, 178, 183, 242; two types of, as "religions of structure" and "religions of salvation," 7-8, 177; not

an opposite to "magic," 26-27, etc. (*see also* "Magic"). *Also see* Action; "Closed" religious universes; Consciousness; Liminality; Morality and norms; Myths; Ritual; Sacrifice; Shame; Social aspects of ritual; Symbolism; Taboos.
Religious Studies field, ix, 3.
Repentance, 38 n.30, 63, 111, 116, 122. *See also* Centering.
Right and left as symbolic directions, 82, 135, 138. *See also* Ritual, and space.
Rites of passage, 108, 136. *See also* Birth rites; Funeral rituals; Initiation; Liminality; Marriage rites; Maturation; Ritual.
Ritual, and "ascending" symbolisms, 135, 136-49, 161-62, 166-67, 173, 176, 191-200, 207, 234; and the body, 142-49, 186, 228-30, 239-41; and "communitas," 122, 164 n.6, 168; and conflict, 53, 64, 94, 113-14, 116, 117-27, 138, 166-68; culture-heroes and archetypes as models for, 50, 86, 110, 112-13, 137, 143, 144, 160-62, 210; and "freedom," 167-68, 208, 232, 233-34; hermeneutics of, 9, 135-36, 138-42; and historical change, 8, 41, 162-64, 165 n.17, 166, 194, 232-33; "obscenities" in, 33, 113-17, 121, 123; and power, 191-93, 199-200, 208, 211, 213, 233-34; of "rebellion," 121-28; of "reversal," 113-28, 139, 166, 167; and self-image, 145-49; and sexuality in general, 142, 239; and sickness, 7, 19-20, 29, 34, 39 n.32, 43, 64, 84, 127-28, 183, 192-94, 199, 201, 206-07, 210-11, 215; and space, 8, 9-10, 18-26, 35, 84, 85, 108, 121-23, 140, 142, 144, 173; symbolic nature of, 7, 8, 95, 119-24; and time (including calendrical rites), 11, 107 n.99, 109-28. *Also see* Religion; Sacrifice; Social aspects of ritual and symbolism; Symbolism; Taboos.
Ritualization of life, 6ff. 18, 52, 56-57, 238-42.
Rotse, *see* Lozi.
Ruanda (Ruanda-Burundi), 221 n.33.

Sacrifice, 7, 158-59, 160; as the unifier of time and space, 125-28; divine king a sacrificial victim, 119-21; and divination, 206, 209, 211, 212, 215, 218, 234; in funerals, harvest festivals and new year's, 89, 112, 116, 124; amongst hunting peoples, 25-26, 57 n.9; occurs at thresholds, 81-82, 124; pivotal dynamic of, in religion, 69, 100, 125-28, 234; subdues sacred power, 192, 200-01, 218; and taboo, 123, 169. *Also see* Centering.